Get in the Game!

CAREERS IN THE GAME INDUSTRY

Marc Mencher

New Riders

201 West 103rd Street, Indianapolis, Indiana 46290

An Imprint of Pearson Education

Boston • Indianapolis • London • Munich • New York • San Francisco

Publisher
David Dwyer

Associate Publisher
Stephanie Wall

Editor in Chief
Chris Nelson

Production Manager
Gina Kanouse

Managing Editor
Kristy Knoop

Acquisitions Editor
Jody Kennen

**Senior Marketing
Manager**
Tammy Detrich

Publicity Manager
Susan Nixon

**Senior Development
Editor**
Jennifer Eberhardt

Copy Editor
Kelli Brooks

Senior Indexer
Cheryl Lenser

Composition
Jeff Bredenstiener

**Manufacturing
Coordinator**
Jim Conway

Book Designer
Aren Howell

Cover Designer
*Beverly Cambron
Aren Howell*

GET IN THE GAME: CAREERS IN THE GAME INDUSTRY

International Standard Book Number: 0-7357-1307-3

Library of Congress Catalog Card Number: 2002103198

Printed in the United States of America

First edition: October 2002

06 05 04 03 02   7 6 5 4 3 2 1

Interpretation of the printing code: The rightmost double-digit number is the year of the book's printing; the rightmost single-digit number is the number of the book's printing. For example, the printing code 02-1 shows that the first printing of the book occurred in 2002.

Trademarks

Warning and Disclaimer

CONTENTS AT A GLANCE

TABLE OF CONTENTS

ABOUT THE AUTHOR

Marc Mencher—Game Recruiter Gone Wild!

 Marc Mencher worked for game companies such as Spectrum Holobyte, Microprose, and 3DO before starting GameRecruiter.com (www.GameRecruiter.com), a game industry-recruiting firm. Marc served as President, and later as an advising board member, of the International Game Developers Network. He has spoken and held roundtables at several Game Developers Conferences and is a regular speaker at International Game Developers Association (IGDA) events around the country. In addition to representing the game industry's hottest talent, Marc also volunteers his time as a career coach for graduates from Full Sail Real World Education, helping them land their first game industry jobs. His articles have been featured in *GIGnews.com*, *Gamasutra*, and *GameWEEK*.

Currently, Marc is working with the IGDA (www.IGDA.com) on chapter development and with Games-Florida (www.gamesflorida.com), a non-profit organization formed with the intent of nurturing and expanding the interactive multi-media industry in the state of Florida. He is also Technical Advisor and Executive Producer for the recently released PC Adventure Game *Watchmaker*. Marc is working on the release of the PC Adventure Game *Tony Tough and The Night of the Roasted Months* (PC) and an Action Shooter *Tsunami 2265* (PC and PS2), all published by Got Game Entertainment (www.GotGameEntertainment.com). Prior to joining the game industry, Marc was the Producer/Project Lead on an $11M joint AI research project funded by the United States Air Force in conjunction with Carnegie Mellon University's Robotics Institute, General Electric, and Pratt Whitney Aircraft Engine Group.

This book is dedicated to Howard, my life partner and best friend.

And to my little bro Kenney, who always has my back—www.Kenney-Mencher.com.

And to my mom, Helen—from Charlotte's Web *till now…who knew?*

And to Al and Elaine, in your presence I feel reborn.

ACKNOWLEDGMENTS

Beverly Cambron of Rocco Media (www.RoccoMedia.com), thanks for keeping me sane!

Howard Horowitz and Got Game Entertainment (www.GotGameEntertainment.com), for use of assets from PC Adventure Game *Watchmaker*, PC Adventure Game *Tony Tough and The Night of the Roasted Months*, and an Action Shooter *Tsunami 2265* (PC and PS2).

My heartfelt thanks to everyone who had a part in the creation of this book: Dustin Clingman, Matt Scibilia, Will Wright, Sanjay Balakrishnan, William Anderson, Troy Dunniway, Evan Birkby, Perry Rodgers, Andrew Paquette, Rick Reynolds, Melanie Cambron, Murray Taylor, Bran Kelly, David Perry, Randy Beverly, Ray Boylan, Brett Close, Paul LeFevre, Paul Steed, William Wetherill, Jason Spangler, Eric Yiskis, Eni Oken and her students Gunilla Elam, Madeleine Wettstein, Kim Oravecz, Molly Barr, and Mary Degnan, Jennifer Eberhardt, Jody Kennen, Stephanie Wall, Kristy Knoop, and the team at Full Sail Real World Education (www.FullSail.com).

TELL US WHAT YOU THINK

As the reader of this book, you are the most important critic and commentator. We value your opinion and want to know what we're doing right, what we could do better, what areas you'd like to see us publish in, and any other words of wisdom you're willing to pass our way.

As the Associate Publisher for New Riders Publishing, I welcome your comments. You can fax, email, or write me directly to let me know what you did or didn't like about this book—as well as what we can do to make our books stronger. When you write, please be sure to include this book's title, ISBN, and author, as well as your name and phone or fax number. I will carefully review your comments and share them with the author and editors who worked on the book.

Please note that I cannot help you with technical problems related to the topic of this book, and that due to the high volume of email I receive, I might not be able to reply to every message.

Fax: 317-581-4663

Email: stephanie.wall@newriders.com

Mail: Stephanie Wall
Associate Publisher
New Riders Publishing
201 West 103rd Street
Indianapolis, IN 46290 USA

Preface

When I first got into the game industry, a formal education was essentially frowned upon. Quite frankly, it was feared that any creative juices would be all but sucked out of you by the time you earned your "establishment" degree. Many industry pioneers equated having formal training with being "assimilated by the Borg." In those days, gamers were the unruly ones, people who did not quite fit the norm. Hands-on game development experience, or an ability to demonstrate your creativity, was the only qualifying factor for getting a job. Today, these are still very important qualities, but as games have grown more complex, and as game development budgets have ballooned to the multimillion-dollar range, game professionals are more formally trained and, certainly, better respected. In short, the unruly ones have grown up.

AUTHOR NOTE

"We're not just geeks in dark basements wearing weird clothes anymore. We're geeks in dark basements wearing weird clothes and making money doing it!"

- Marc

The inspiration for this book came from the thousands of emails I receive asking the same daunting question: "How do I get a gig in the game industry?" I wish I possessed a single simple, and magical, answer; alas, I do not. However, based on my years of developing the careers of some of the industry's brightest stars, what I do possess are proven job-getting techniques. If you take these techniques seriously, and apply them appropriately, you will not only land that game job, but you will also be placed firmly on a career development track that will take you to the height of your aspirations.

Through my recruiting firm, GameRecruiter.com, I have placed thousands of people in game industry jobs. I have witnessed the astonishing growth of this industry as it has grown, in both size and stature. I've also witnessed the increasing number of people wanting to work in it. If you are one of those people—or maybe you're an industry veteran in need of a career "refresher"—this is the book for you.

In this book, you'll learn the various types of game jobs available in the industry, what the game companies are looking for, and how you can get the job you want. It is my sincere hope that when you finish this book, and if you apply the principles found in it, you should be well on your way to a successful career.

Throughout your job search, try to remember that YOUR thoughts about YOUR career and life direction will create YOUR destiny, so be careful about what you think. In short, stay focused and positive! And, remember, my virtual door at marc@GameRecruiter.com is always open should you need additional advice or direction.

Good Luck and *Get in the Game!*
Marc Mencher

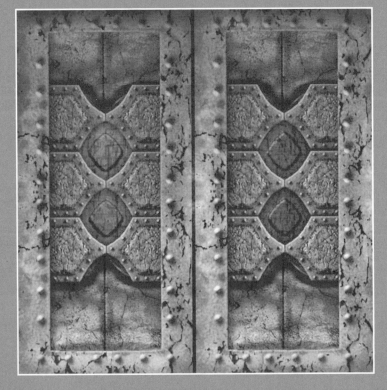

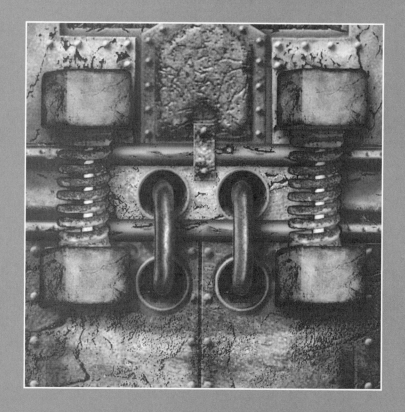

Part I

Industry
Backgorund

**Images courtesy
of Molly Barr**

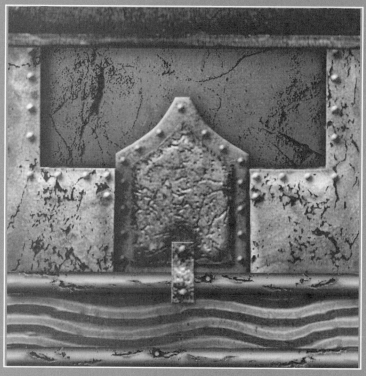

Chapter 1

Introduction to the Gaming Industry

Knowing some history of the game industry will help greatly in your quest to become a professional in this business. To be taken seriously by other gamers, you will need a basic knowledge of the industry's evolution. This chapter provides a brief (very brief) history of the industry, beginning with the birth of SEGA and noting, in particular, milestones in hardware development. This chapter also includes an overview of the various game genres, the key businesses within the industry, and the development process.

IN THE BEGINNING—A BRIEF HISTORY LESSON

Originally an American company providing coin-operated, or arcade, games primarily for military bases, SEGA began life as Services Games. After purchasing a Japan-based machine company in the early 1960s, the company transformed itself into SEGA. During this same time, an industry founding father, Nolan Bushnell, designed an arcade version of *Asteroids* to play on his newly developed dedicated game machine. Thus was born the first cartridge-based game system, introduced to the market as VCS, and later known as the Atari 2600. During this era, other companies created other game systems, including Coleco (Colecovision), Milton Bradley Electronics (Microvision, Vectrex), Mattel Electronics (Intellivision), and Commodore Computer (Commodore 64), all of whom had impact, but eventually left the scene.

Although not a dominating force until the mid–1980s when it caught the attention of the American gaming community with the introduction of the Nintendo Entertainment System (NES), Nintendo was actually founded in 1889 and is, historically speaking, the oldest game company. Atari and SEGA competed head to head with Nintendo, but the company proved a worthy opponent with the release of Game Boy and the smashing success of the Super Nintendo (SNES). Over the next few years, the unfolding battle witnessed SEGA's release of Sega Master System to compete against NES, and Atari's release of the 7800. Commodore Computer also entered the fray with the CDTV. Although the TurboGrafx-16, SEGA Genesis, and Atari Lynx machines tried to compete, Nintendo ultimately stole the bulk of the market share. Thanks to its portability and associated free games *Tetris* and *Super Mario*, Game Boy sales were significant.

www.atari.com

www.nintendo.com

When Sony entered the scene, the 32-bit console wars began. Initially, Sony and Nintendo collaborated on the development of a CD player to work with the SNES. Although this development project failed, it gave Sony an idea. The company chose to develop a 32-bit game machine known as PlayStation (PSX) to compete directly with Nintendo. Among other notable competitors who jumped on the 32-bit bandwagon was The 3DO Company, started by Electronic Arts (EA) founder Trip Hawkins, who announced his new 32-bit gaming console in association with Panasonic. However, Panasonic eventually acquired the 3DO technology for use in other devices.

Trying to reclaim lost market share, Atari then introduced its doomed 64-bit system called Jaguar. By the late 90s, the market was totally confused as evidenced by alarmingly sluggish sales. SEGA 32X and Saturn came and went, and Nintendo bombed with a few platform releases as well. Eventually, Atari was forced out of the hardware business.

Currently, the industry's popular development platforms are the Personal Computer (PC), Sony's PlayStation 2, Microsoft's XBox, and Nintendo's GameCube and Game Boy Advanced (GBA). The market for PDAs and mobile phones is also gaining momentum and promises to be the next growth focus. These products will also have online multiplayer capabilities.

Today, we have Sony, Nintendo, and Microsoft competing for market share. SEGA is still creating games but has chosen to halt production of hardware. Atari chose this same path years ago when they stopped making hardware. Does SEGA face the same fate Atari did?

Will you contribute to the continuation of this story?

www.scea.com

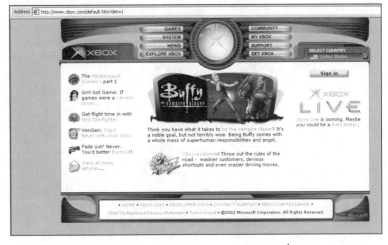

www.xbox.com

Time Line

Year	Significant Games Developed That Year	Platforms Introduced or Further Developed That Year (Games developed that year were not necessarily played on these platforms.)
1961	*Spacewar* developed by MIT student on mainframe computer.	
1972	Atari's *Pong* (arcade version).	Magnavox Odyssey.
1974	Atari's *Pong* (home version).	
1977		Atari VCS/2600.
1978	*Taito* (Japan). *Midway* (America). *Space Invaders* (Arcade).	Bally Professional Arcade and Magnavox Odyssey2.
1979	Namco's *Galaxian*, which gave way in 1981 to its sequel, *Galaga*. Capcom's 1984 release of *1942* used the same pattern as *Galaxian*.	Mattel Intellivision and Milton Bradley Microvision.
1980	*Pac-Man* (arcade). Infocom's *Zork*. Berkeley students' *Rogue* (BSD UNIX).	
1981	*Galaxian* gives way to its sequel, *Galaga*.	Emerson Arcadia 2001.
1982	Namco's *Pole Position* (arcade) (point of view), which inspired Midway's *Rush* and Namco's *Ridge Racer* series.	ColecoVision Atari 5200 and Milton Bradley Vectrex.
1984	Namco's *1942*.	Atari 7800.
1985	Super Mario Bros. (NES), which inspired *Donkey Kong*. Capcom's *Commando* (arcade), which inspired *Ikari, Warriors, Mercs, Time Soldiers, Heavy Barrel, Guerrila War, Jackal, Gun Smoke, Irem's, Kung Fu Master,* and *Renegade*.	Nintendo Entertainment System (NES) and Sega Master System.
1987	Technos Japan Corp.'s *Double Dragon* (arcade), which inspired Capcom's *Final Fight*, as well as 1993's *Dungeons and Dragons: Tower of Doom* and 1994's *Aliens vs. Predators*. Nintendo's *The Legend of Zelda* and *Tetris* developed by Alexey Pajitnov. Copyright mistakes allowed several	Nintendo Entertainment System (NES) and Sega Master System.

companies—Nintendo,
Atari, and Spectrum
Holobyte—to publish
versions of the game and
resulted in legal battles.

Year		
1988-1989	*Tetris* released as the flagship title for Nintendo's handheld video game console, the Game Boy which spawns the later releases of Atari's *Klax* and Capcom's *Super Puzzle Fighter II*. *Dragon Warrior* (NES), which spawned *Final Fantasy* and other Role Playing Games (RPGs).	Atari Lynx (Portable), Nintendo Game Boy (Portable), NEC TurboGraphix-16, and Sega Genesis.
1991-1992	Capcom's *Street Fighter II* (arcade). Sega's *Virtua Racing* (arcade). *Doom* *SimCity*	Super Nintendo Entertainment System, Sega CD (System add-on for Genesis), NEC TurboDuo, and Philips CD-I.
1993-1994	*Dungeons and Dragons: Tower of Doom* (scroll and punch). *Aliens vs. Predator.* Namco's *Ridge Racer.* *Myst.*	Panasonic 3DO and Atari Jaguar.
1995	Infogrames' *Alone in the Dark* (PC). Namco's *Tekken.*	Sega Saturn, Sony PlayStation, and Nintendo VirtualBoy (Portable).
1996-1997	Capcom's *Resident Evil* (PlayStation). Sony's *Super Mario 64* (Nintendo 64). Sony's *Final Fantasy VII* (PlayStation).	Nintendo 64.
1998	*Legend of Zelda: Ocarina of Time.*	
1999	Sony's Gran Turismo 2. Activision's *Tony Hawk's Pro Skater.*	Dreamcast.
2000	Sony's *Gran Turismo 3* (PS2).	PlayStation 2.
2001	Konami's *Metal Gear Solid 2* (PS2).	Xbox. GameCube. Game Boy Advance. Dreamcast production is ceased.
2002	Rock Star Games' *Grand Theft Auto III* (PC).	

Sources: The History of Videogames, Gamespot (www.gamespot.com); A Brief History of Home Videogames, Samuel Nils Hart (www.geekcomix.com); The Videogame Timeline, Net4TV (www.net4tv.com).

DID YOU KNOW?

Did you know that Namco created *Pac-Man*, which became the most popular arcade game of all time?

Did you know Midway, not Namco, created *Ms. Pac-Man*, also a huge hit?

Did you know Gumpei Yokoi was the inventor of three game platforms: Game Boy, Virtual Boy, and WonderSwan?

Did you know that the Toshiba/Sony 250MHz microprocessor, dubbed the Emotion Engine, is the brains behind the PlayStation 2?

Did you know that the XBox is equipped with an Intel 733MHz Pentium III CPU, an Nvidia NV2a 250MHz graphics processor, 64MB of unified RAM, and an 8GB hard drive?

Did you know Nintendo almost used the name Dolphin, then Starcube, before settling on GameCube?

Did you know that Capcom's *Street Fighter* brought new life to the arcade business?

Did you know that Atari's *Battlezone* was the first video game to be used for military training?

Did you know that *Defender* was a pinball manufacturer's first video game and that the game designer was Eugene Jarvis?

Did you know that Nintendo Artist Shigeru Miyamoto created *Donkey Kong*?

Did you know that *Mario* by Nintendo was originally named *Jumpman*?

FROM THE EXPERT

"Not all games fit neatly into one genre or another, even though they seem like they do on first glance. A game like Giants: Citizen Kabuto, was predominately a third person shooter, but also had elements of a real-time strategy game. The elements seemed to have been included to make a more interesting experience for people who play shooters, versus trying to make a hybrid game that appealed also to strategy game players. This is in contrast to a game like Battlezone, which was specifically designed as an Action / Strategy hybrid. This game specifically tries to maintain enough aspects of both to be appealing to both audiences."

– Troy Dunniway, Head of Game Design for Microsoft

GAME GENRES

How and why a game is made is always different. Some games start as one person's idea. Other games come about because the owner of a license or intellectual property wants a game created. Some games are sequels, expansions, or improvements on a previously successful game. Take a stroll through your local store and, needless to say, there are a wide variety of games on the market. Some work better on a PC; whereas, others execute best on a console.

Action

Equally popular on PCs as well as consoles, action games such as *Tsunami 2265* (Got Game Entertainment) and *Max Payne* (Gathering of Developers) are generally fast paced and require skill and reaction time to win.

Strategy

This type of game dominates the PC world and is not popular on consoles. Most of these games come from classic board games. Examples of strategy games include *Age of Empires* (Microsoft) and *Civilization* (Microprose).

Role Playing Games (RPGs)

These are considered the most difficult type of game to design due to the number of characters required, the depth of plot, and necessary the art assets. These games have their roots in classic paper games like *Dungeons and Dragons*. RPGs are usually games about character building, exploration, and adventure. The hottest trend right now with RPGs is online games that allow thousands of people to play simultaneously.

www.microprose.com

Adventure

This type of game dominates the PC world and is not popular on consoles. Typically, these games require a player to navigate through a world, interact with people, explore, and solve puzzles. Adventure games are slow paced and depend heavily on the skill level of the player for advancement or success. Examples include *The Watchmaker* (Got Game Entertainment) and Escape from *Monkey Island* (LucasArts).

Puzzles

This type of game dominates the PC, PDA, and mobile phone worlds and is not popular on consoles. Most are short, simple games like *Tetris*.

Sports

This type of game—such as football, basketball, soccer, and so on—dominate the console platforms. There is a wide variety of sports games on the market, in fact, almost any sport you can imagine. It is interesting to note that although sports games are easier to design, they are more complex to develop.

www.tetris.com

11

Simulations

There are two main kinds of simulation games: flight or driving simulators and *SimCity*-type games. The former are games that allow the players to feel like they are flying or driving; and the latter, *SimCity*-type games, allow players to create an environment and see how it behaves.

Kids, Family, and Edutainment

These types of games dominate the PC market. These are broad appeal mass-market games like *You Don't Know Jack* or simple adventure games geared towards children like *Tony Tough*.

Hybrids

These types of games dominate console platforms, but are also available on PC. These can include action/adventure, action/strategy, and action/RPGs. If you've played *Outcast* (Infogrames), you've played a hybrid.

INDUSTRY STRUCTURE

Within the game industry, you find three different kinds of key businesses: publishers, developers, and hardware manufacturers. These days, most publishers have their own in-house development teams, however the majority of companies developing games are still small, independent studios. Let's look a little closer at these key businesses.

Publishers

Publishers are responsible for bringing games to the distribution channels by funding development of an original, licensed, or conversion title, then overseeing that development. They also handle marketing, sales, duplication, and packaging of the game. Publishers usually pay the development studios an advance against future royalties, based on achieved milestones to cover development costs. As the game is sold and the publisher recoups its investment, the development studio begins to receive additional royalty payments.

Developers

Development studios create original content, licensed content, or conversions, also known as ports. An original game is based on an original concept. Most original games are created by independent developers who then seek funding and/or distribution by a publisher. Although publisher-owned development studios do create original games, most publishers prefer that original products, which are considered riskier because there is no built-in fan base, be developed by independent developers, also known as external third-party developers. A licensed product is a game based on an intellectual property like a major movie, cartoon, toy, book, TV show, and so on. A conversion or ported game is a game that has been created on one format and then is ported or copied to another. To sell as many games as possible, most games are ported to as many platforms as possible. Development studios can be small or large, and they may create products for a variety of publishers on a variety of platforms. Third-party developers may also specialize in specific genres or on a particular product line.

Hardware Manufacturers

Hardware manufacturers are the companies that build and sell the game machines also known as consoles or platforms. Currently, the PC enjoys a deep market share, but it presents some issues with compatibility and configuration because PCs are "open" systems. That is, an owner of a PC can, and often does, alter the standard manufacturer's configuration settings. You alter these settings by simply installing new software, printer, graphics, or sound cards. This compounds the challenge of ensuring the game will work correctly when loaded.

Console systems offer a solution to this problem but have their own pros and cons. Nevertheless, on the pro-side, closed systems use proprietary technology, with strict definitions. This means that the owner of the machine cannot do much to alter the system and, therefore, less compatibility and configuration issues arise for the developer. Unlike other industries, hardware manufacturers in the game industry take a very active role in software development and even the publishing process.

GAME DEVELOPMENT PROCESS

Before getting into the details of the game development process, let's look at a 30,000 ft. view:

A game begins its life as an idea or concept, which is then expanded into a full-fledged story by the Game Designer. The Designer creates a detailed design document that describes all the games features. The document not only covers a description of the game play, but also the visual and audio style, including examples.

In some companies, the Game Designer also acts as Producer; whereas in other companies, the Game Designer is focused solely on fleshing out new treatments or concepts. The Project Manager or Producer is assigned to the project to produce a task list and schedule for the development of the game. This person manages budgets and ensures the creative intent of the game is maintained throughout the development process.

After a design is complete, the development team usually prototypes the game before jumping immediately into full development. The aim is to develop a working prototype of the game that shows that the design concepts are sound. This is also done so the development studio has a demonstration, or demo, of its game idea to show publishers when seeking funding. If the idea is a flop, there is no need to spend additional time and money.

After the game concept gets purchased or funded, the writing of the game's programming code and creation of the game's assets, such as art and sound effects,

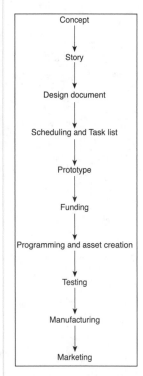

Overview of a game's life cycle.

gets serious. This process takes several months to complete. During these months, the various departments work on their portion of the game, which are ultimately combined or linked together to create the finished game.

Generally speaking, the Producer oversees and manages this entire process. This person has a tough job making sure all the highly creative Artists, Programmers, Game Designers, and other team members play nicely in the sandbox, while keeping the creative vision of the product consistent. Additionally, the Producer communicates to the development studio's management and the publisher the progress and problems during the development cycle.

After all of the game's assets have been linked together, the game is tested for errors, or bugs. The game's playability is also reviewed and tweaked as needed to ensure the end-user has a smooth experience when playing the game. This is known as the testing and tuning of the game.

If the game is intended for one of the game consoles, the hardware manufacturer gets involved in the testing and approval of the game. The manufacturer knows its own closed proprietary operating systems and wants to ensure the game performs flawlessly and consistently on the platform. This approval process takes place before being sent to the duplicator for manufacturing. Products developed for the PC do not need this type of approval as these computers are not proprietary.

After the game is manufactured, the hardware manufacturer begins the marketing process to build awareness of the product so consumers are interested in purchase. Independent development studios may choose to only use a publisher for product distribution. In fact, many development studios can and do fund and market their own games. Obviously, in these kinds of agreements, the third-party developer gets a much higher cut of the profits because it takes on more of the risk.

Months prior to the game's street release, the sales and marketing folks employed by the publisher, the development studio, or an independent sales/marketing company, focus on "selling" the retail community on the game. Sell sheets, screen shots, and product description information are created to highlight elements in the game and excite the retailer and consumer. When the game hits the market and is available for sale, you want a presence for it. It's hard to generalize this process because there are several options available for getting the game on the store shelves. Basically, it costs a lot of money to have an internal marketing and sales staff, but, at some point, a company grows large enough that it makes financial sense for them to bring these functions in-house. Typically, smaller development studios prefer to utilize the hardware manufacturer's distribution strength or the strength of an independent sales and marketing organization. It's hard for a single, small company to get the attention of the major retailers such as Wal-Mart, CompUSA, and Electronics Boutique. After the game is out on the shelves, of course, the players take over. And, hopefully, all the hard work and talent that went into the game pays off.

Chapter 2

Common Tools of the Trade

Having working knowledge of the following frequently required programs will ensure success in your game industry career. This chapter describes the most common software used by the games industry.

BUSINESS APPLICATIONS SOFTWARE

Having basic working knowledge of Microsoft Word and Microsoft Excel is not going to cut it in the game industry. Work yourself through the tutorials of these products and learn them cold. Knowing Word and Excel is important for any game industry career. Will Wright, Legendary Game Designer, Co-Founder of EA/Maxis, and man behind SimCity and The Sims Series, actually uses Excel for prototyping simulations. He can change economic conditions in his Sims world and watch the economy react. If you just think Excel is limited for use by accountants as a spreadsheet, you don't know Excel well enough. The same is true for Microsoft Word. Sure it's a word processor, but it has much more functionality than just being used as a old fashioned typewriter. Learn these products well!

It is also a great idea to learn Microsoft Project. Project allows you to create a database of easily sorted information for a group undertaking. You can group, sort, and filter your data based on the specific needs of your development project. As for database software, having working knowledge of FileMaker Pro is a great idea.

PROGRAMMING LANGUAGES

Even if your career goal has nothing to do with programming, if you work for a game company, you will have to interface with the programming staff. Obviously, if you're a Programmer, you must know C and C++, but this will also help you in any game industry career.

It is a given that you should know how to code in C, C++, Visual Basic, and Java. These are by no means the only languages that exist, simply the more common ones.

C

C is the lowest level of the *high-level* languages. Being a more structured language makes it easier in which to program, but it is still fairly fast and well-suited to programming on the gaming consoles. It's the primary language used to program Sony PlayStation and other games. C is considered a high-level language because it makes a layer between the Assembly level instructions and the syntax of the C language. This sort of abstraction allows for more work to be done in a smaller amount of code and, quite frankly, less code is best for everyone. C is an important language to at least be familiar with, as it has been used for almost 30 years. There are a considerable number of coding tools that have been written in C.

Here's an example of C code:

```
Printf("("Hello World" " \n);
```

C++

An extension of the original C language, C++ uses a different structure and is known as an *object-oriented* programming language. Used to program application software, C++ is an improvement on C because it allows for better organization of an application's design. At one time, developers believed C++ was too slow for video game applications; however, with the advent of better hardware and cheaper RAM, the benefits gained by utilizing C++ rather than C are exponential. That is, C++ allows the Programmer better control access to the data in a program, which makes it a lot easier to control as well as debug. Today, C++ is considered by many to be the most important language to know for game development.

Here's an example of C++ code:

```
Ship.GetX(*ship);
Cout>> ""The stuff we want is over here";";
```

Visual Basic

A programming language created by Microsoft, Visual Basic is also a high-level language, typically used in web and database application development. As the name suggests, Visual Basic is mostly done within a visual medium. Objects like checkboxes and windows can be made in a relatively quick way. This tends to speed up the overall time it takes to develop a game.

Here's an example of Visual Basic code:

```
Public Sub Main()
    Send CGI_CONTENT_TYPE_TEXT_HTML
    Send vbCrLf
    Send "Hello World!"
End Sub
```

Java

A programming language invented by Sun Microsystems, Java is an object-oriented language very similar to C++. Java is most widely known for its platform independence, which means that a program written on a PC can run on a Mac or anywhere Java is designed to run. This saves the Programmer time porting or transferring a program from one platform to another.

Here's an example of Java code:

```
System.out.println("("Why is this Java code");");
```

Assembly

Assembly is a "fast language" used in many of the gaming systems including Nintendo Entertainment System (NES), Super Nintendo Entertainment System (SNES), Game Boy, SEGA's Saturn and Genesis, even Pocket PCs and N64 utilize Assembly techniques. Assembly is great for solving specific problems that are speed critical. It's the faster way to do things because other languages act as buffer layers to the Assembly instructions. Because Assembly talks directly to the instructions for the processor, it's called a *low-level language*. Assembly is still used in newer generation consoles and embedded devices because of its speed. There are several different variations of the assembly language:

80x86 or i86	Intel-based Assembly
68000	Apple computer-based Assembly (Macintosh and so on)
Z80	Used to program Nintendo Game Boy games
SH-2	Used in SEGA Saturn. Utilizes a dual processor configuration
ASM	Used for Game Boy Advanced
MIPS	Used for Pocket PC games

17

Here's an example of Assembly code:

```
.model small
.stack
.data
message   db ""Hello world, This sure can be ugly code."
." "$".code
main    proc
    mov   ax,seg message
    mov   ds,ax
    mov   ah,09
    lea   dx,message
    int   21h
    mov   ax,4c00h
    int   21h
main    endp
end main
```

3D: ANIMATION AND MODELING SOFTWARE

Getting an art job in the game industry also requires experience with at least one software program such as 3D Studio MAX, a 3D animation and modeling software package by Discreet. Other frequently required programs include Alias|Wavefront Maya, NewTek LightWave, Bones Pro (a skeletal deformation plug-in), Caligari trueSpace, Character Studio, and Avid SoftImage. Although less well known, many industry pros also highly recommend Mirai.

In short, all of these toolsets are worthy of every Artists' attention as they each have brought many wonderful new methods for generating characters, worlds, and effects for the game development industry. However, with the new game consoles and enhanced PCs bringing greater graphics capabilities and performance to our industry, Maya's enhanced character animation capabilities and new world-building features may well serve future product cycles with a higher production value and quality aesthetic.

Ultimately, the choice of art tools relies on the comfort and productivity of the Artist , the cost of setup and training on the package, and the goals of the particular development house. If an Artist has decided on a company, or particular title/genre, that he wants to work on, he should research the software being utilized in the development of that project and by that team, and decide on which to pursue and master. By scanning job boards and employment ads in the game industry, the aspiring Artists will be able to judge best which packages are most prevalent in the industry, and thereby, decide on which to pursue and master.

3D Studio Max by Discreet

The large installed base of 3D Studio Max places this package in the unique market position to remain as the *de facto* standard for many game production groups. 3DSMax continues to add many features, which enhance the Game Artists' toolset and productivity, including many world-building utilities and character modeling and animation enhancements. Many consider this tool a premier 3D content creation tool for the next generation game consoles such as XBox and PS2. For more information, visit `http://www.discreet.com/products/3dsmax` and find your local 3DSMax User Group.

Maya by Alias|Wavefront

Maya has come on strong in recent versions, with character animation tools that have surpassed all others in many professionals' opinions. Maya gives the Artist state-of-the-art controls and a flexibility to adapt its environment for many differing animation and modeling projects.

For more information, visit `http://www.aliaswavefront.com/`.

SoftImage by Avid

SoftImage has been the standard toolset for top quality character animation for years and has included many game specific enhancements to its system. The installed base is not as prevalent as 3DSMax, but many developers have worked with, and continue to work with, this package. For more information, visit `www.softimage.com`.

LightWave by NewTek

NewTek's LightWave includes two models: the Modeler and Layout modules provide the 3D Artist with one of the more powerful off-the-shelf solutions for animation and modeling. Many recent television and motion picture productions have used LightWave for visual effects (*Babylon5*, *Titanic*, and others) and, in an increasing trend, the entire content has been created within the package (*Jimmy Neutron: Boy Genius*). Many Modelers and game Developers swear by LightWave as the best available polygon modeler. LightWave 3D includes many of the tools that other packages require to be purchased separately, such as soft-body dynamics, particles, hair, fur, and unlimited render nodes. For more information, visit `www.newtek.com`.

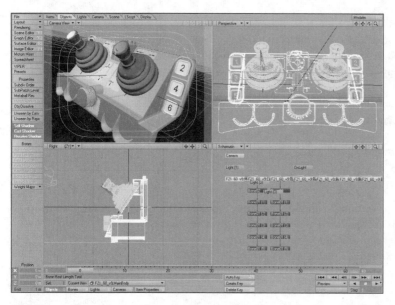

Based on the old Symbolics code and for various reasons, Mirai has gone through several incarnations at different companies. It's been known as Symbolics, ArkGeometry, TripleI, Del Rey Graphics, Nichimen, Mirai, and possibly, Winged Edge. Now under IZWare, Mirai comes with a deep tool set and also allows you to work on multiple objects in multiple windows simultaneously, switching back and forth at will and having your changes updated instantly. For more information, visit www.izware.com/mirai.

LightWave is just one example of the great 3D programs on the market.

2D: BITMAP AND VECTOR-BASED GRAPHICS SOFTWARE

There are several packages an aspiring Game Artist should learn to work with as each has a separate purpose in the art production pipeline; and dependent on the project's goals, each is necessary for the successful completion of asset development. Artists need to be comfortable working with both vector-based and bitmap graphics programs.

Adobe Photoshop and Others

Certainly, every Game Artist should be comfortable with Adobe Photoshop, the standard 2D art tool for the majority of development groups.

Dependent upon the style of the production aesthetic, Painter may be used to generate assets with a more traditional art method presentation.

Right Hemisphere's Deep Paint/Deep Paint 3D with Texture Weapons also expands on traditional art styles, with a strong focus on texturing.

Adobe After Effects and Adobe Premiere are more appropriate for pre-rendered asset creation and editing. And Debabilizer Pro is utilized for batching art asset edits, format, and/or palette adjustments.

Adobe Illustrator

Illustrator is also considered by many industry insiders to be an invaluable tool and something of an industry secret weapon. This software can be utilized to create custom spline shapes, which then can be imported into the 3D software packages noted previously and serve as modeling splines.

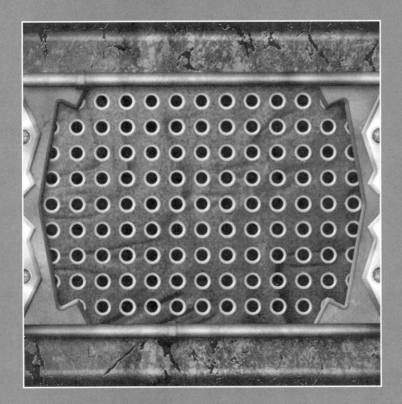

Part II
Careers in Gaming

**Images courtesy
of Mary Degnan**

Chapter 3

Playability Testing & Quality Assurance (QA)

Do you love computer games passionately? Do you live for them? Like nothing better in the world than playing and talking about them? Then here is the job for you!

In this chapter, we cover the various careers available in game testing and Quality Assurance (QA), along with the tools of the trade. We also cover how to get into the position you want.

FROM THE EXPERT

"The Testing and QA department usually contains the
highest ratio of 'gamers' in a
game company. They are the
ones who sit and test games
all day—many go home and
play games all night."

– Ray Boylan, Worldwide
Director QA, Mattel

FROM THE EXPERT

"When I review a stack of
resumes for hiring temporary
in-house staff, I look for who is
highlighting their gaming
skills either by listing the
games they play or by going
the extra mile by participating
in Beta Testing."

– Evan Birkby, Manager of
Quality Assurance,
Electronic Arts

TESTING VERSUS QA

One of the best ways to establish a game industry career is by starting as a Playability Tester or Quality Assurance Technician. Testing and QA are often confused; a good start is understanding the differences and the types, which we cover in the following sections.

Beta Tester

To do a playability test, you usually send out Beta copies of the game and elicit feedback via the Internet or bring in temporary playability testers and observe them while they use the product. Beta testing is a volunteer job that can be done on your own time, at home or work—wherever you have Internet access. This is the easiest way to gain game industry experience. Beta Testers are typically people who are not paid by the company to test the game but, rather, do it just for the pure fun of it.

Although Beta testing has become more popular, the industry still favors in-house testers. The ability to observe tester reactions—verbally, physically, and emotionally—to the game play experience provides invaluable information, not only for the marketing folks, but also for the Producer, the Game Designer, and the Artists. Playability Testers also provide immeasurably valuable feedback to Customer Service in the form of FAQ files and workarounds.

Playability Testing

See Mom, I told you I wasn't wasting time!

Playability Testers are people who get paid to sit around all day long and test games with the goal of uncovering and researching the cause of as many defects as possible so they can be corrected. Playability testing is a very important function. A game is designed to provide the player with an "experience," and playability testing ensures the game is put into the hands of actual game players for feedback. Is the game fun? How does it compare to similar games created in the past? What features might you improve, add, or delete? The "fun factor" is what game design and development is built around, and there are no better judges of this aspect of game development than the testers.

This is why game companies choose to hire the bulk of their play tester staff on temporary assignment. Typically, the playability testing department posts openings for temporary testers on their company web-site, local Internet gaming sites, with temporary employment agencies, or on college job boards.

A playability testing department usually consists of one to four full-time, paid employees running a staff of one to thirty temporary testers. The size of the temporary team depends on where the game is in its development cycle and how complex the game is to play. In larger environments, there is more than one project, in which case, scheduling the amount of testers on each project based on where the projects are individually in the test cycle is critical.

On a regular basis, you will find every department manager and every executive level person within a game company casually walking around the testing lab. You will even find the president of the company hanging around. These people spend serious time in the testing lab and they listen. They listen to the testers to derive and implement new features. They seek ideas on how to improve game play. They want opinions like, "I think the game is boring because..." Playability testing is an important function and provides much more information than just what bugs or defects can be found.

Ready for an industry secret? A playability testing job provides a strong platform from which to grow your career. Just think, all those department heads with the power to hire visiting your corner of the company every day! Show your competence when performing as a temporary tester. Take advantage of the situation when a hiring manager walks by your testing station. Devise a way to demonstrate good verbal, written, or creative skills. If you're testing a new game and the Art Director wants to explore your reaction to the art's quality, take the opportunity to show your own artwork. Create images specifically suitable for the game you are testing. Show a new level design to the Game Designer.

This is how you get positive attention and eventually hired when a position opens. It's easy to walk yourself right into any game industry career, but as reiterated throughout this book, you must have a focused plan of action in place. The playability testing department provides you with face-to-face contact with game industry people with whom you can develop a mentoring relationship, or use to network yourself into a new job. (QA is to the gaming industry what the mailroom was to corporate America: access.)

From the testing department, you can get into QA, Artist, Programmer, Game Designer, Marketing, or any game industry profession. Like an internship in the film industry, however, you are *earning* your way into a career, and the work functions you perform in the beginning are less than glamorous. But, as you gain respect and experience and as you develop an expertise, your career will blossom! Just keep in mind that there will be a period of low pay as you work yourself from an hourly playability tester into a full-time salaried employee.

Black Box Testing Versus White Box Testing

Black Box testing, essentially, is as the term implies. You don't see what is inside the box. You're reviewing a final product and paying attention to what does work or doesn't work from a user/player standpoint. Often, in Black Box testing, a tester has no idea what is wrong with the game, other than something doesn't work. For example, a tester could be working with a new first-person shooter. During testing, it is discovered that when you select the third weapon, the gun fires incorrectly. Or the airplane does not bank the way it's supposed to. Or the story doesn't progress to the next mission and it crashes. Good testers are adept at tracing the steps necessary to recreate the bug, thereby providing invaluable insight into a possible fix.

White Box testing, on the other hand, is akin to pulling the lid off the box. You can look inside and see what contents are there. White Box testing is often referred to as QA Engineering. A QA Engineer is someone who reads the code and says, "I see some bugs here in the code." A QA engineer runs the game with the debugger turned on and finds code errors. The QA Engineer often has access to the programmer or mission scripter who wrote the code and can show the appropriate individual where there is a code error. On occasion, the QA Engineer may fix problems directly, as well. A QA Engineer also utilizes a scripting language to create a script to test a game. For example, a QA Engineer looks at the programming logic and sees if it's correct. Often, the White Box person is the back end of Black Box testing—the flow of information is critical to making it all work.

Quality Assurance

Establishing standards and procedures for the development of a game is critical, as this provides the framework from which the software evolves. The QA function is one of process monitoring, product evaluation, and auditing. For example, QA is concerned with documentation and design standards, which specify the form and content of the game. They provide rules and methods for translating the software requirements into the software design. QA is also concerned with code standards, which specify the language in which the code is to be written and define any restrictions on use of language features (define legal language structures, style conventions, rules for data structures and interfaces, and so on). QA is about final analysis. You're looking at the final product and saying, "Does this pass the requirements we have in the company?" Most often, both a publisher and a third-party development studio have their own respective QA and testing departments. The actual testing that is done at both facilities is often identical. However, from a developer standpoint, you have people testing at a lower level, actually looking at code and repairing it. The main focus here is rooting out as many bugs or software defects as possible.

Because the publisher must give the final stamp of approval, it evaluates a product from the standpoint that it wants to ensure the game meets expectations. The focus here is whether the development team met its contractual agreement to deliver this milestone. The publisher tests the game to determine if the portion of the game it is reviewing meets the requirements of the development contract. If the answer is yes, the developer is awarded more funds to go to the next development phase of the project. Again, QA tries to test to a standard. That is, by saying, "to achieve an Alpha status or to achieve a Beta status or to achieve a Gold master status, you must have these various areas working." So, the publisher tests to see if you've met the respective goal.

Actually, both test teams test to see if you've met the respective goal. The publisher QA is different in two significant ways:

- It is a final pass organization as opposed to an on-going test, so they only spend a specified time period with each product during each milestone as opposed to continuously testing the product.

- The QA group is often given approval authority, which means the product will pass or fail a milestone based on the QA report.

Often, a large publisher has separate test teams to cover both the continual test process and the QA process. The publisher assigns one team to the developer's product for the bulk of testing and an additional specific QA group just for milestone acceptance tests. QA teams often are further broken down into QA that focuses on system standards, compatibility, and playability, or fun factor.

A system standards group is concerned with general requirements for all products for a specific system, such as how the controller buttons are defined, how the memory cards will be addressed, or that copyright and company logos are properly displayed.

Compatibility testing focuses on the hardware issues and is primarily concerned with PC products. These testers check memory configurations, video cards, sound cards, and joystick or controller support.

The playability group often is in charge of running focus groups or taking care of large scale Beta tests.

Alpha Cycles

The following list describes the Alpha criteria:

- At least one path is playable from the beginning to end of the game and QA can navigate that path to the finish.

- All the major features exist and can be tested. Some may still be in modules for QA purposes.

- Primary language text is final.

- Basic interface is complete and preliminary documentation for QA is available.

- Game is compatible with most specified hardware and software configurations.

- Game will run on minimum system requirements.

- Game logic is implemented.

- Most controllers work.

- The game runs on target media and is available on the distribution media.

- Final or placeholder art is in for all areas of the game.

- Placeholder audio is in the game.

- Multi-player functionality can be tested.

- Installer is specified and a preliminary version can be tested.

- A draft of the manual is available.

The following list describes the Alpha objectives:

- By the end of Alpha, test all modules in the product, at least once.

- Create a bug database and test plan.

- Record bugs and performance results.

Beta Cycles

The following list describes the Beta criteria:

- All features and options are implemented.

- All language version text is implemented and ready for simultaneous release.

- QA can navigate entire game on all paths. All bugs that close areas of game to testing are gone.

- Entire user interface is final.

- Game is compatible with all specified hardware and software configurations.

- Game will run on minimum system requirements.

- Game logic is final.

- All controllers work.

- The game runs on target media and is available on the distribution media.

- Final artwork for screen shots, including credits, animation, and movies are in. Game copyrights and trademarks are in the software.

- Final audio is in the game.

- Installer is integrated, and any needed drivers are automatically installed.

- A complete manual is available.

Note that release-level performance on the minimum machine is not required at Beta entry but must be achieved by the end of Beta.

The following list describes the Beta objectives:

- Isolate all significant bugs and performance problems.

- Complete testing, bug fixing, and performance tuning.

- Complete install testing.

- Test on the full range of supported platforms.

Release (Gold) Cycles

The following list describes the release (Gold) criteria:

- Senior management has reviewed the product and bugbase and agrees that it is ready for final test.

- Install is complete and ready for release.

- All activities, functions, and content are complete and ready for release including graphics, sound, and video.

- Performance is appropriate for release.

- Online user documentation is complete, accurate, and ready for release.

- All known Severity 1 bugs (crashes, hangs, major function failures) are fixed.

- 95 percent of all known Severity 2 bugs fixed, 90 percent of all known Severity 3 bugs fixed (can be circumvented by a consensus of senior management).

- Open Severity 2 bugs have a work-around, described in the Readme file.

- Product is ready for release on all supported platforms.

Traditional Software QA Versus Games QA

All QA, game software or otherwise, is similar in the sense that the focus is to try to find problems. The idea is that you're trying to find errors in the code. For every hundred lines of code, there's usually something wrong with it somewhere, and any type of bug can potentially affect the consumer.

Given this, a tester must really do two things at the same time:

- Represent the consumer by addressing if-I-were-a-consumer-what-would-I-look-for type of issues, which sets the standard for trying to make the game meet the requirements of the user.

- Help the developers find the bugs so they don't have to spend the time doing it themselves. After all, the development team is a customer of the QA department.

Of primary importance is communication between the QA team and development team. Each must be in agreement as to the design document and features that make up the game. Each must also be aware as to what version or build of the game is in test. Both teams have to be on the same page.

With regard to game testing versus testing in a non-game environment, the big difference is that with a game you're concerned with sound, graphics, and game logic issues, not to mention the subject matter itself of the game; whereas, non-game testing tends to be just make sure the tables are correct. It is very test- and data- oriented, making sure that the data has integrity. There are some other issues that also make game testing more of a challenge.

31

Non-game testing usually lets you access the entire product. In other words, you can look at any aspect of the product and test any aspect of the product as needed. With a database program, for example, nothing keeps you from a particular area of the database. With a game, on the other hand, you cannot get to certain areas of the product until you complete a level or until you reach a certain score. Therefore, certain aspects of the game cannot be easily tested until a certain goal is achieved. You must work your way through the software, because you don't have immediate access to the entire product. For example, in an adventure game, you must expect some *pathing*. There is a lot of pathing in computer games, which means "if I do this, then I can do this, and then I can do this." You must ensure all of those paths or links work.

The biggest difference in game versus business application testing is that the business application has strict parameters and right and wrong results. Game testing has expected results but there are many paths and approaches to them.

Automated Testing for Games

Unlike traditional software products, game products don't usually behave in the same manner twice. Traditionally, business software like databases, word processors, and spreadsheets, are designed and coded in a linear fashion. Simply defined, this means the user has only a few logical paths or options to perform functions. Because traditional business software is fairly predictable in how it will behave, it is possible to automate a majority of the testing functions. A game, however, is not designed this way. The software is actually designed to challenge the user. Access to other portions of the software is granted depending on the user's choices or actions. This is not very linear as there are so many options a player can choose. This is why, to date, use of automated testing techniques utilized for traditional software development has not been very effective.

Automated testing is also not as feasible for games due to the short development cycle of games. The average game takes 18 months to develop versus traditional software, which averages a 30-month development cycle. The amount of time it takes to develop the automated test often doesn't justify the benefit from it. Automated testing is more financially attractive the longer the product development cycle. Another reason automated testing has not caught on in the gaming industry is that it is very hard to automate something when you have limited access to the entire product, as previously explained. It is very hard to get a sequence of events that will yield a successful result every single time, especially when any aspect of the game might change. Also, just to keep things interesting, games tend to have quite a bit of randomness going on. Without a predictable sequence of events, it's very hard to have an automated script do anything for you.

One solution to this problem has been the use of *cheat codes*. These codes are placed into the game so programmers and testers have access to areas of the game that require skill or time playing to actually get there. A game usually has some form of cheat code; otherwise, if you have a 20-level game and it takes five days to get to the 20th level, every time a new build is tested, it will take at least five days to get to the end of the game and test it. Lately, it has become more and more popular to actually leave these cheat codes within the final shipped product so that the marketing folks can hype them when advertising.

Still, as game budgets increase, so will the time it takes to develop the product, and automated testing may become an affordable option in the future.

FAQ

How do I find out what temp agency has this kind of contract with my fantasy game company?

You can contact the HR department at the company you are interested in and ask if they do any work with temp agencies.

Are there particular times of the year that are really good to try to get these contract work temp jobs?

It's hard to say. About four or six months before Christmas is when most companies start to hiring a lot of temps because they've got Christmas releases and they're trying to get their product out at the last minute. Also, any time prior to a big release schedule is a good time, but sometimes companies miss their schedule. It's probably a really dry time right after Christmas, but it usually picks up again a couple of months after that.

TYPICAL JOB TITLES AND FOCUS

In this section, we tackle the job titles available in both playability testing and Quality Assurance groups.

Temporary Playability Tester

In this capacity, you're playing a copy of a game that hasn't been released to market yet. You may not even have the whole game, just a portion. For example, there may be thirty missions planned, but only five have been written so far. Initially, you play those first five missions and, eventually, you play the entire game. Not only are you asked what is fun about the product, but you're also expected to find out what elements have not been completed yet and whether the completed levels are working properly. How well is the story being laid out for you? Do links between episodes function properly? Are proper objectives being scored? For a game that deals with any type of environment, you may be given a map of what the world is supposed to look like, and you are to compare the map of the plan to what is actually in the product. You must be very patient with the game. It breaks (a lot) and you document it. A temporary Playability Tester tends to do an awful lot of learning on the job.

In this position, you can generally expect to earn $7.00 to $12.00 per hour. Work is typically contract or hourly and usually lasts four to six months.

Compatibility Tester

Compatibility testing deals more with hardware compatibility than game functionality. This corresponds to the following questions: "Do the joysticks work?", "Does the mouse control work?", "Does the controller work?", and "Are we meeting the standards of the operating system?" In this job, you learn about different hardware and various video or sound cards. You're an expert who knows what's on the market, along with the pros and cons of each product. Having the ability to use the hottest selling sound card or mouse or console add-on device can directly affect sales of a product!

For example, prior to the release of *Stellar 7*, it was the compatibility tester who had the wisdom to present a case to the development team. This new company had just released a sound card known as Sound Blaster. The tester researched the new hardware that used a new digital chip, but there was no support for this in any game. He convinced them to go ahead and put in digital support. *Stellar 7* was the first game to actually use digital support for a Sound Blaster card, and this critical decision contributed heavily to the product's sales. Obviously, this guy was promoted!

In this position, you can generally expect to earn $12.00 to $20.00 per hour.

Lead Tester or Game Analyst

Playability Testers who are hired as full-time salaried employees are usually given the title of Lead Tester. As a Lead Tester, or Lead, you are specifically assigned to a particular project. In this job, you look for 3D geometry or modeling errors. You make sure that the models look correct, are to proper scale, and that the textures are properly applied. You look at the art of the game and make sure it is aesthetically pleasing and properly put together. You're checking game logic. You test all kinds of different aspects. There are a huge variety of things within a game with which to concern yourself.

The Lead's most important function is to manage the data entry process of the Playability Testers who are reporting bugs. The information gets centralized and classified into the database. The Lead is responsible to ensure the Playability Testers are looking for bugs in the right sections of the product. The Lead is also responsible for determining if the bug discovered is important enough to be repaired or just noted. As a Lead, you must be able to summarize the status of your project at any time in both written and verbal form.

In this position, you can generally expect to earn $14.00 to $20.00 per hour.

GAME TESTER OR ANALYST

DESCRIPTION

The primary function is to document, track, test, bug hunt, and research for the production team.

RESPONSIBILITIES

- Assist the producer in day-to-day maintenance, organization, and management of the project (for example, help maintain the task and bug databases and so on).

- Maintain daily builds; ensure that Artists have good builds with which to test assets.

- Burn CDs as needed.

- Do deliveries to and from the client, as needed.

- Take meeting notes and distribute them within one day of meetings.

- Assist with setting up and tracking equipment for the project.

- Product testing.

    Perform, supervise, and document the testing and analysis of the game—including verification of all testables in commits and otherwise.

    Write test plans, including milestone acceptances, play tests, and focus tests.

- Research

    Research and analyze competitive products, input findings in the appropriate database, and keep the team informed of key discoveries.

    Assist in locating and organizing reference materials for the team.

SKILLS

- Ability to maintain project-related documents, schedules, lists, and so on, using commercial software (for example, Microsoft Office and FileMaker Pro).

- Organization and communication.

- Detail-oriented.

REQUIREMENTS

Interest in and general knowledge of video games.

RELATIONSHIPS

Reports to: Producer

Supervises: Temporary Playability Testers

Supervised by: Operations Director, Executive Producer, Lead Game Designer

Supervisor/Manager

Some companies have a large enough playability group to also have a Supervisor/Manager. In this role, you are responsible for multiple projects. Most likely, you have several Lead Testers reporting to you. You manage a budget and interface with upper management to ensure products are developed in a timely manner. If the company has other development studios located in different areas, the Supervisor/Manager interfaces with these groups as well.

QA Engineer

The primary function of this position is to find, accurately report, and verify fixes of bugs in software code. Your mission will be to proactively find and reproduce software flaws and design issues from Alpha through Final development stages of software. You will exercise your ability to document software flaws and design issues in a clear, detailed and objective manner. Your proactive attitude will prompt you to communicate pertinent information to other test team members. Verify that test plan and various checklists are accurate against the software. Expect to use your writing skills to produce instructional documents (walkthroughs) on an as-needed basis. You will perform hardware and compatibility testing along with other tasks as assigned.

Here's an example of a potential job listing:

Successful candidate will have proven to execute the following: the ability to work effectively under severe time constraints, the ability to maintain focus in a distracting environment, the ability to maintain positive attitude throughout test project especially during "crunch" time, and the ability to work off-site at various development and production sites. The ideal candidate will have excellent strength in deductive and analytical skills, as well as strong interpersonal, written, and verbal skills.

Must have at least one-year prior experience in a game-testing environment, with familiarity with bug databases essential.

Responsibilities

- Responsible for root cause analysis and implementing corrective action.

- Perform records and oversight for review of completed work packages to ensure flow down of customer requirements.

- Interface with customers to resolve quality issues and with outside vendors to ensure quality compliance.

Requirements

- Related engineering degree.

- Minimum two years experience in driving quality initiatives.

- Outgoing, personable individual with innovative problem solving skills.

- Expertise should include in-depth understanding of quality systems.

QA Supervisor/Manager or Director

Although the titles depend on the size of the QA department, the primary objective is staffing each project with the right mix of play testing talent. Secondarily, the QA Manager needs to ensure that the information flow remains constant—and pertinent—to the goals of the project. Often, the QA Manager's biggest obstacle is losing the best Playability Testers to the production department.

QA Supervisor/Manager or Director—Years Experience: 6-15

The primary function of the Quality Assurance Manager is to supervise, coordinate, and monitor all required Quality Assurance duties and responsibilities to ensure compliance with all company policies, customer specifications, and regulatory requirements, if they exist. This person is also responsible for supervising, training, scheduling, and monitoring the duties and activities of Quality Assurance personnel.

TOOLS OF THE TRADE

There are a number of ways to get into a test department. Some people are lucky enough to qualify for a project just because they have a skill that specifically applies to the game being developed. For example, you might be a football player, so you could test a football game. You may know zilch about computer games, but you sure know football backwards and forwards. Or, perhaps you are a pilot who happens to also have F16 experience that would instantly qualify you to test flight simulation games like *Falcon*. The ability to speak Kanji or another foreign language can also instantly qualify. You could test the translations for all the characters in the game.

College Knowledge

If you are in college now and working on obtaining your Bachelor's degree, one great way to gain a little industry experience is to do playability testing. Ability to code, utilize the common art tools, or knowledge of 3D modeling instantly qualifies you for the job. All types of skills apply. If you are trying to transition into the industry, Beta testing or playability testing jobs are a great way to start.

Know the Genre

Prior to working in a game company, you need to simply understand games. You need to understand how games generally behave and what might be considered acceptable or unacceptable. Usually, companies develop similar projects; so if you are targeting a specific game company, get experience playing older products developed by the same company. You also want exposure to as many similar types of games as possible. If you know a lot about computers and how the computer memory works or how video cards work, you might be hired as a Compatibility Tester. Having in-depth knowledge of a subject gives you an edge over other applicants competing for the same job.

Strong Grammar and Writing Skills

Being able to communicate clearly and concisely through the written word will help you in any career but, in the testing department, these skills can be utilized for proofreading the new manuals and making sure that they are written properly. You can even review the text within the game itself ensuring the use of proper grammar, spelling, and punctuation.

Database Software

The number one tool of any test organization is the database, so you should be comfortable with data entry into a database. Deep knowledge of any database product—FileMaker Pro, Act, Access, Outlook, Lotus Notes, or Goldmine—is good. Just find a database product you feel comfortable using and learn it cold. Read the manuals and do the tutorials. Although you can get by with only the basic skills and knowledge with most software, don't do this with your database software. It is really the most important tool for your life, both personally and professionally. Used correctly, a database is like having a full-time personal assistant who reminds you of appointments, things to do, telephone calls to make, reports to write, or birthday gifts. Getting intimate with any database software will be the single best investment you can make for your career!

Professional database software—Tracer, Alien Brain, and Dev Track—are specifically designed for testing, but you can create a testing database yourself. Obtaining a playability testing job will afford you access to one or two different QA databases that are used. Get very comfortable in data entry and using a bug database. For testing and QA, the database is a central repository for all the bugs. In your life, use a database as a central repository for all your personal and professional activities.

Know How to Create a Test Plan

The second tool that is required is to understand the function of test plans. Any QA book lays out the basics of a test plan. You want to know how to construct test cases and lay out a descriptive test plan. With a test case, you create, essentially, a checklist for testing a portion of the game, itemizing each aspect or area that needs to be looked at. Then, you mark down the areas getting checked, classifying the status of the product by how much of it has been tested and how much it is working. A descriptive test plan is a method for documenting the procedures describing how you're going to test the game and access its various components. You need to be familiar with tables and charting so that you can show graphic results, or at least numerical results to the tests. You also want to track the *find rate*, which is how many bugs are being found versus how many bugs are being fixed, and, of course, the total number of bugs. For bugs you have yet to fix, keep track of how many are being found and how many are being fixed so you can predict when the actual bug count will get down to zero.

Microsoft Excel

Having an Excel background is almost essential to testing, because Excel is used often to build test plans. If it is not used for test plans, at least some element of tables or charts or some elements of testing is often done with Excel. It is also important to know Microsoft Project and Microsoft Word.

Scripting Languages

Python, Visual Basic, and JavaScript are the most popular scripting languages currently being used in the industry. Knowledge of any type of scripting language is useful. Some testers are given an opportunity to look at the scripting language in the product, which allows bugs to be identified more quickly and gives the a sort of White Box entry into the testing environment. The ability to read, repair, and use a scripting language is also part of the function for mission building and scenario development. This ability can also walk you into a game design or game art career.

Programming Languages

Knowing how to code in C and/or C++ is a basic requirement of all game programmers. If this is your career goal, having coding experience will help you transition here. Of course, you can initially use your coding skills in QA. Having the ability to read and then repair game code is very valuable.

Compatibility Testing

This is a job for which you can immediately start training. Make a list of all the sound and video cards on the market. Research joy sticks, controllers, and any and all hardware devices that could be used for games.

WRAP-UP

Generally speaking, the testing department can be used to transition into any game industry career.

Use the time you have wisely. Do your testing job, but work extra hours. Focus on developing whatever skills you are weak in that pertain to your dream game job. Don't know scripting or modeling packages? Learn them! Often the computers used in the testing department are very high speed with plenty of memory. Because the game being tested does not consume that much of the resources you have, a good idea is to take advantage of the situation and learn the tools people in your area of career interest need to know to be successful. Take the initiative yourself! A rewarding and high paying career is not an accident. When you interview successful people, they all laid out a plan to gain the experience they needed to leverage themselves into another job. You can do the same!

FROM THE EXPERT

"My best advice is to learn whatever you can about coding. In QA, you have to interface with Programmers. If you understand what Coders have to deal with, that's helpful. If you don't want to be a Programmer, at least get familiar with terminology and the methodology behind programming."

– Ray Boylan, Worldwide Director QA, Mattel

FROM THE EXPERT

"G-force cards are pretty much the dominant cards now so it would make sense to be familiar with this product line. Visit the company web site to begin research, review articles written about its performance against others. Start using a database to organize this information."

– Evan Birkby, Manager of Quality Assurance, Electronic Arts

Chapter 4

Designers

See the ball. Be the ball. See the game. Be the Game Designer.

Many people dream of becoming a Game Designer like the legendary Sid Meier, Will Wright, or Yu Suzuki. Game Designers seem to have the fantasy industry job. They formulate cool ideas, then devise their accomplishment. Unfortunately, the chances of a person coming up with a new idea, writing a game design, and selling it to a publisher is, say, one in a million. Further, very few people are hired just as Game Designers. Rather, most earn their way into this position through another game industry job like QA/Testing, Producer, or Programmer.

Not to burst your bubble, but there probably is no completely unique thought in this world. Ideas are a dime a dozen, and no matter how cool you think your game idea, game companies already employ a bunch of creative people, all with their own really cool ideas.

A successful Game Designer should also be exposed to the major art, literature, philosophy, and history movements. How can you create a game like *Civilization* without knowing anything about history? Even the study of psychology bears relevance on game design. Games are made to be played by people. Studying the mind and how people react or interact provides valuable insight for good game design. Some games are small enough to only need a single designer, whereas others need several designers. For example, role playing games (RPGs) tend to need larger design teams.

FROM THE EXPERT

"The most sought-after skill in a Game Designer is the ability to visualize and construct a cohesive design. In other words, not only having an ability for idea creation, but also an ability for idea execution. To execute thoughts into reality is the Game Designer's function and it requires highly developed English, writing and verbal communication skills to accomplish the task."

– Will Wright, Legendary Game Designer, Co-Founder of EA/Maxis, and man behind SimCity and The Sims Series

To be a likely success, a Game Designer must be an avid game player. Playing games spawns ideas and inspiration. In good games, bad games, old games, and new games, you will often discover that the answer to a design problem has been dealt with before. It makes more sense to tackle a design issue knowing how others tried to handle the same or similar issue rather than re-walk the same path.

Not all game treatments can be executed due to current limits in technology, the goals of the game company, and the amount of time you have to accomplish those goals. Assessing the proper tradeoffs is a significant part of a Game Designer's job.

TYPICAL JOB TITLES AND FOCUS

Game Designers are the modern Dantes. With their words and vision, they create the levels of today's *Divine Comedy*—the video game. They take an intangible concept and translate it to the tangible.

There are several levels (so to speak) of Game Design careers. Peruse the game job boards and you will see openings for very specific design positions, such as Lead Designer/World Builder, Lead Designer-Racing, Senior Designer (Flight Sim), Principal Game Designer, Lead Designer (Sports), and Assistant Designer—just to name a very few.

More generally speaking, however, what is the function of Game Designer? An overheard explanation at an industry party went like this:

A couple of guys have an idea for a game: The Googly-Goos want to capture the evil empire of the Fiddly-Foos. The guys go to the Game Designer with the premise of the game. The Game Designer then writes the equivalent of a novel that describes the action that will take place and the various scenarios that may occur. For example, at the moat to the fortress of the Fiddly-Foos, the Game Designer decides if a Googly-Goo soldier steps on a certain rock, the gate will open. But if the Googly-Goo steps on another rock, he will be catapulted over the wall.

Easy enough. But, if you're interested in actually becoming a Game Designer, you need to know a few more basics. As indicated by the above list of job opening titles, game design jobs can be very specific. Game Designers are frequently categorized by the types of games they create such as RPG, Action, Adventure, Flight Simulation, or Sports.

A great way to familiarize yourself with current requirements is to look over job listings covered in the following sections.

Interface Designer

The primary function of the Interface Designer is to design and implement user interfaces that integrate the required visual style, functionality, and usability.

INTERFACE DESIGNER

RESPONSIBILITIES

–Design

- Set the visual design and content for the user interface (UI) during pre-production; ensure that its style and content set the right mood for the game, support the anticipated functionality, and satisfy the idiosyncratic requirements of clients and other key parties.

- Oversee the development of the UI, within the requirements and constraints of the game design, game engine, parameters of target platforms, TV display, and usability.

- Communicate the visual design, development, and functionality of the UI to the team and client through verbal discussions and visual aids (for example, still screens, animated video presentation, and so on).

–Art Production

- Create and maintain art assets for the UI (for example, fonts, screen layout, transitions, movies, animations, special effects, and so on).

- Process UI assets delivered by the client for inclusion in the UI.

- Proactively seek feedback from the Art Director in style and mood.

–Testing and Collaborations

- Coordinate with QA (Quality Assurance) to test the usability of the UI, and enhance the design and implementation of the UI accordingly.

- Lobby for needed resources to produce the UI.

- Collaborate with the Lead Game Designer (functionality), Art and Creative Directors (style and mood), Technical Writer (flow and usability), and Programmer (technical implementation) regarding the UI.

SKILLS

- Creation of 2D art and animation assets using Photoshop, Illustrator, and Flash.

- Creation of 3D art assets using Maya.

- Creation of videos using AfterEffects and Premier.

- Selecting, manipulating, and animating type.

- Visual special effects.

- Understand the differences between designing for monitors and regular televisions.

- Photography and videotaping.

- Ability to visually develop diverse concepts.

- Verbal and visual communication of ideas through sketches and other illustrations.

- Willing and able to work closely with Game Designers and Programmers.

- Organized.

- Detail oriented.

- Creative and innovative.

REQUIREMENTS

- Minimum of 2 years experience in motion graphics design, preferably for TV broadcasting, DVD menus, and/or game UIs for TV display.

- Background in fine art (for example, drawing, painting, and so on) and computer graphics.

- Bachelor's degree in Graphic Design a plus.

- Formal training in Interface Design or Cognitive Science a plus.

- Background in film a plus.

- Willing to learn proprietary art tools.

- Game experience preferred.

RELATIONSHIPS

Reports to: Producer

Managed by: Lead Artist or Game Designer

Supervised by: Art Director, Game Designer

Level Designer/World Builders

Level designers/world builders work on designs, models, textures, and lights architectural environments—places and scripts entities/objects in environment. Each works with the Lead Designer to define and refine game play mechanics, details game play mechanics, story lines, character biographies, and asset inventories in design documentation. The primary function of the Level Designer is to integrate gameplay and art ideas into fun 3D.

LEVEL DESIGNERS/WORLD BUILDERS

RESPONSIBILITIES

–Game play Development

- Design detailed levels for the game, including the attributes and relative locations of terrain, rooms, and objects therein.

- Design levels that fulfill the requirements of the project's game design and visual design as documented by specifications, style guides, and appropriate reference material.

- Assist with implementing the level design (for example, building terrain/rooms), as needed.

–Game Design and Testing

- Give input on game design issues and propose game play ideas.

- Test levels for bugs, playability, and fun. Fix any problems.

- Collaborate closely with the Game Designer on testing levels interactively.

–Tracking, Research, and Collaboration

- Use appropriate tracking and management tools.

- Understand the requirements and constraints of game design, engine, and platform.

- Stay current on trends in games.

- Research relevant games in depth.

- Understand the target audience of your game.

- Work closely with the Lead Game Designer, Art Director, Lead Artist, and team Artists through all phases of designing and implementing game levels.

SKILLS

- Understanding of 3D spatial relationships.

- Verbal and visual communication of ideas through sketches and other illustrations.

- Familiarity with the iterative process (for example, design, implement, and review. Repeat.)

- Game play—including playability, pacing, and fun.

- Ability to use 3D modeling software, such as Maya or 3D Studio Max.

- Ability to use 2D art software, including Photoshop and Illustrator.

- Willing to work closely with Game Designers and Programmers.

- Ability to take direction.

- Creativity and innovation.

- Problem solving.

REQUIREMENTS

Experience designing and refining levels.

RELATIONSHIPS

Reports to: Producer

Managed by: Lead Artist

Supervised by: Lead Game Designer (game design elements and game play), Art Director (visual design)

Lead Level Designer

Guides Level Designers to ensure that all the environments in the game are completed properly and timely. Acts as a liaison between Level Designers and Programmers.

Game Designer

Designs and develops story lines, game play, rules systems, play balance, interface design, game structure, and "mechanics." Writes proposals, treatments, storyboards, and flow charts for upcoming projects.

GAME DESIGNER

RESPONSIBILITIES

- Give input on game design issues and propose game play ideas.

- Build missions/races in the appropriate editor and test them for bugs, Artificial Intelligence (AI) performance, playability, and fun.

- Modify AI parameters in source files, using appropriate scripting languages and tools, under the direction of the Lead Game Designer.

- Tune intermediate player entities (for example, characters, vehicles, and so on) based on reference

- Help test, balance, and tune all other game play parameters.

- Tune the UI for usability, in collaboration with the Interface Designer and Technical Writer.

- Help create scenarios, scripts, and character descriptions for the game.

- Transcribe all verbal communications between the Lead Game Designer and the team and help update game design documentation accordingly.

- Take direction from the Lead Game Designer and Technical Writer on all issues relating to documentation.

- Test level geometry—terrain, rooms, towns, jungles, themed areas, tracks, shortcuts, physical puzzles, props, and so on—for bugs, playability, and fun.

- Use the appropriate 3D software to fix any problems.
- Take direction from the Lead Game Designer and Level Designer on all issues relating to level design.
- Stay current on trends in games.
- Research relevant games in depth.
- Understand the target audience of your game.

SKILLS

- Familiarity with geometry.
- Familiarity with programming or scripting languages.
- Ability to use 3D software.
- Ability to maintain project-related documents, schedules, lists, and so on, using commercial software (for example, Microsoft Office and FileMaker Pro).
- Willing and able to work closely with Programmers and Artists.
- Communication and interpersonal interaction with varied audiences.
- Creativity and innovation.
- Problem solving.

REQUIREMENTS

- Experience with designing, tuning, and balancing levels for games.
- Console experience preferred.

RELATIONSHIPS

Reports to: Producer

Supervised by: Lead Game Designer, Game Design Director

Lead Game Designer

Acts as the creative guide and overall creative vision keeper for the game. This critical role is a third of the team leadership consisting of a Lead Programmer, Lead Artist, and Lead Game Designer. The Lead Game Designer works with the Producer and team to develop game concepts, design documentation, game play mechanics, story elements, script/dialog, implementation plans, and strategic planning documentation for the game. In addition, this person works with the Sound Designer and writer to create and record dialog, as well as with the writer and game team to develop ideas, characters, and storyline. Provides direction to design team members, leads to execute development plans, executes design, and works through design revisions as needed.

47

LEAD GAME DESIGNER

RESPONSIBILITIES

–Game play Development

- Define the game play of the prototype and actual game.
- Propose game play ideas and specifications and iteratively test their implementation.
- Encourage input from team members, but make final decisions on game play.
- Design and/or approve the functionality of the front end, user interface, and audio.
- Test, balance, and tune all aspects of game play.
- Define missions, AI parameters, and control of player entities (characters, vehicles, and so on).
- Attend all game-related meetings.

–Documentation

- Create and update the content of the game's Concept Proposal, Game Design Document for the client, and Functional Specification for the development team.
- Help create scenarios, scripts, and character descriptions for the game.
- Collaborate with the Technical Writer on all issues relating to documentation.

–Level Design

- Supervise the related-related design of detailed game levels.
- Critique the related-related functionality of levels-in-progress.
- Place objects critical to related (for example, characters, vehicles, and so on) in levels.
- Collaborate with the Level Designer on issues relating to level design.
- Stay current on trends in games.
- Research relevant games in depth.
- Understand the target audience of the assigned game.

SKILLS

- Familiarity with game engines and concepts/terminology for computer graphics.
- Familiarity with programming/scripting languages.
- Ability to use 3D software.
- Ability to maintain project-related documents, schedules, lists, and so on, using commercial software (for example, Microsoft Office and FileMaker Pro).
- Willing and able to work closely with Programmers and Artists.

- Communication and interpersonal interaction with varied audiences.
- Creativity and innovation.
- Problem solving.

REQUIREMENTS

- Minimum of 1 year of experience designing games, including the completion of 1+ full cycle of game production.
- Experience with designing, tuning, and balancing levels for games.
- Console experience preferred.

RELATIONSHIPS

Reports to: Producer

Supervises: Project's Game Designer, Interface Designer, Game Tester

Supervised by: Game Design Director

Director of Game Design

The primary function of the Game Design Director is to lead and mentor the members of the Game Design Department.

DIRECTOR OF GAME DESIGN

RESPONSIBILITIES

–Proposals, Clients, and Prototypes

- Oversee the development of new game concepts.
- Analyze concept proposals, in close collaboration with the CEO and other departments.
- Help evaluate schedules, risks, allocations, and task assignments for proposed and current projects.
- Understand how the target audiences of all proposed and current projects affect them.

–Game Design Management

- Take ultimate responsibility for the creation and successful development of related for all.
- Periodically review the game design of all current projects, with emphasis on the development of innovative and immersive related.
- Coordinate the efforts of the Game Design staff to eliminate redundancy, best utilize the specific skills of each individual, and maximize productivity.

- Respond to concerns and suggestions of the Game Designers.
- Insist on a developmental environment (hardware, software, and so on) that best supports the needs of team members.
- Support efforts to tune, balance, and test related.

–Staff Support

- Set up and maintain guidelines and quality standards for the Game Design department.
- Collaborate in the recruitment and dismissal of Game Designers.
- Train and orient new Game Designers.
- Support the continuing education and professional development of Game Designers.
- Collaborate with the Technical Writer to ensure that game design documentation meets departmental standards.
- Do periodic performance reviews.
- Actively study, analyze, and refine the developmental process used by the studio.
- Research tools for prototyping, producing, and tuning related.
- Stay current on trends in the game industry.
- Research relevant games in depth.
- Recommend research & development (R&D) to help the studio achieve and maintain a competitive edge.

SKILLS

- Manage multiple people.
- Deep understanding of the game industry.
- Familiarity with programming/scripting languages.
- Ability to use 3D software (for example, Maya).
- Ability to use software for project-related documents, schedules, and so on (for example, Microsoft Office and FileMaker Pro).
- Willing and able to work closely with Programmers and Artists.
- Creativity and innovation.
- Communication and interpersonal interaction with varied audiences.
- Problem solving.

REQUIREMENTS

- Minimum of 5 years designing games, including the completion of 5+ full cycles of game production.

- Experience working with different clients.

- Experience designing, tuning, and balancing levels for different types of games.

- Console experience.

RELATIONSHIPS

Reports to: CCO

Supervises: Lead Game Designers (directly), Game Designers (indirectly)

TOOLS OF THE TRADE

The following is required of a Senior Game Designer at a California game company:

"Must be able to create high quality game designs from 1 page high concepts to a more fleshed out 10-30 page concept outline to complete 200 page design documents. Must be able to lead Designers to completion of certain game tasks."

As a Game Designer, all of those tedious high school and college English assignments may finally pay off. Virtually every job listing for a Game Designer requires "strong technical and creative writing skills." Necessary skills also include a "vivid imagination," "creative problem solving," and "organizational skills."

More tangible tools required include a working knowledge of writing software, such as Word, and a project management software, such as Microsoft Project. Some companies also require that the Designer be familiar with software design programs such as 3D Studio Max for world building. Designers also need a grasp of programming to understand the technical obstacles Game Programmers face. If you have not already done so, read the chapters in this book on Game Programmers and Game Artists to better understand who and what you will be working with and designing for.

AUTHOR NOTE

"As in virtually every industry, it is always helpful to have a role-model—someone to emulate. If you're looking to work in the game industry, chances are you enjoy playing games. What are your favorite games? You can probably find Designer diaries posted somewhere on the web. Also, check out developer websites for team bios. Learn the histories of your favorite Game Designers."

– Marc

THE TOOLS AND SKILLS YOU'LL NEED

The following sections describe the basic software tools and skills you'll need as a designer.

Microsoft Software

Microsoft Project allows you to create a database of easily sorted information for a group undertaking. You can group, sort, and filter your data based on the specific needs of your development project. It's also essential that you be able to work with Word and Excel.

Good Grammar and Excellent Writing Skills

With the advent of email, many people who were already on the bubble when it comes to writing skills, just completely fell apart. Read that job description again: "Must be able to create high quality game designs from 1 page high concepts to a more fleshed out 10-30 page concept outline to complete 200 page design documents."

This is a job that requires serious writing skills! So, start working on them today. The following is from an actual email inquiry from an aspiring Game Designer:

> "I have been around games since the first nintendo came out. I have had long term experience in lots of games up till the plastation 2 x-box and game cube. If you reading this and say just another person who wants a job that is true but not many others have my imagination and no 2 people have the same ideas so if your interested in a lot of great ideas and threes a job spot opened Id be you man."

What's wrong in that email? Plenty. But don't laugh, because you may be making many of the same mistakes. If you're still in school, start paying attention in your English classes! If you're already out of school, and you don't know the difference between "your" and "you're" or "its" and "it's," you should consider taking a continuing education class. Good writing skills are *absolutely fundamental* to being a successful Game Designer.

You must be able to create a massively detailed document detailing every part of the game imaginable. This requires the ability to visualize the game you're designing. Can you imagine exactly how the player object will move, react to control input, react to things in the environment, and so on? It's not enough to write: "pressing the jump button makes the player jump." You must be able to effectively describe to the Programmer, via the document, *how* the player will jump. How fast? How high? Can the player perform actions during a jump? What happens in condition X? What happens in condition Y? A? B? C?

Art and Programming Skills

Next, so you don't have unrealistic expectations of visuals, a Game Designer must possess a total understanding of the graphics side of development. A total understanding of programming is also essential, especially in order to write custom scripts for character/unit behaviors and level scenarios—depending on the game genre—and to tweak controls. An understanding of user interface design, game player psychology, and other intuitive subtleties come in handy as well. And, to construct game levels, it certainly doesn't hurt to be experienced with 3D modeling software either.

Phew!

In short, the ideal Game Designer needs strong skills from both sides of the fence: artistic and programming. But if you're headed to college, Computer Sciences (CS) may serve you better in the long run rather than Graphic Arts. With a CS degree, when you get out of school, you can use your programming skills to start creating your game design ideas. If you're lacking in art, you can get help easily. But even without good art, you can prototype your game ideas.

THE DESIGN DOCUMENT

If you want to be a Game Designer, you need to understand the fundamentals of the design document. Just as a blueprint aids the construction of a house, a design document shows where every element of a game fits in the larger picture. Because there are just as many ways to produce a design document as there are ways to write a book, for the purposes of this chapter, a relatively basic and familiar format will be used. Don't panic at the detail in the following; this is just to familiarize you with what you'll tackle in your professional life.

Creating a Design Document

First, before you even sit down to draft a design document, you ask yourself, "Who will be reading this?" If this is a document to sell your idea to a marketing staff, or to get funding, you might focus on shorter explanations of technical subjects and move the meat and potatoes to the beginning of the document.

Also, before the actual design document drafting begins, you need to have had creative meetings and a pooling of all the best ideas, design notes, and diagrams that will make up the game play and look of the product. Don't worry if everything is not nailed down in minute detail, that will work itself out once you reach the assignment stage. Just get all of the key elements down, including your "Killer Apps" or applications. Also known as "that which will make this product stand out in game play, looks, and feel," Killer Aps are critical to the overall success of your product, and where you will spend most of your production time.

FROM THE EXPERT

"Having basic knowledge and understanding of programming helps the game designer foresee mechanisms for implementation and communicating game design issues more fully to the development team. Understanding how to code also helps a designer understand rule structures and behaviors. Even sub fields of Computer Science like understanding chaos theory, system dynamics, and adaptive systems is useful to game design. There is just a heck of a lot of things you need to be exposed to in order to become an effective Game Designer."

– Will Wright, Legendary Game Designer, Co-Founder of EA/Maxis, and man behind SimCity and The Sims Series

FROM THE EXPERT

"Try writing game pitches and design documents. You'll eventually start putting game systems and worlds together in your head."

– Troy Dunniway, Head of Game Design for Microsoft

KEEP YOUR DESIGN DOCUMENT READABLE!

Avoid using strange and unreadable fonts and sizes. Although it may look cool and give some personality to your work, in the long run, people will just get annoyed by it and might skip vital information. In sections where you really need to make the information clear, simply use **bold face**.

FROM THE EXPERT

"Without these visual aids, you will probably need to keep reminding them, and some-times yourself, what the end game will be. Believe me, it can get very hard to stay focused when a project goes over the 12-month mark."

– William Anderson, Founder of Eagle Claw and Game Design of Maximo

FROM THE EXPERT

"Some companies have sev-eral different types of game design documents. While no one standard game design document exists […], a design document will at least give you the basics."

– Will Wright, Legendary Game Designer, Co-Founder of EA/Maxis, and man behind SimCity and The Sims series

Your pre-drafting compilation should also include any conceptual art. If you don't have any, you should definitely consider having some made. One of the key responsibilities a Designer, Producer, or Manager has on a project is keep-ing the team focused on the vision of the game. Because the art staff on a proj-ect tends to make up almost two thirds of the production team, visual aids such as conceptual art and storyboards, are critical to getting the art staff excited and motivated.

In the following section, you will find a breakdown of the different subjects used to outline a typical design document. Please keep in mind that you may want to add or remove subjects that are not applicable to your particular concept design. For example, if you are making a Puzzle game, the idea of a Player or Monster character may not fit into the design; however, for purposes of this arti-cle, we are assuming these elements are part of the design.

Title Page and Copyrights

A title page for a design document is very important. It will be seen often, so avoid a title name or font format you are unhappy with. Regardless of whether you like it, it will grow on people until it is assumed approved for the final prod-uct, at which time it becomes more difficult to change. Certain copyright and trademark information must also be presented for you and/or your company's legal protection. The following is a list of elements that should always be on a title page for a design document:

- **The title of your project in a clean font.** Although your marketing group or legal team may ask for changes, you should always put your ideas up front.

- **The contact names for this document.** This should be the Designer, Producer, or any other managers responsible for producing the document. Questions will arise, and this contact information will give the reader a convenient way to reach the right people.

- **Document version number and date.** As your project moves deeper into production, vague ideas will be increasingly fleshed out until you have a final design. At this point, the design document will need some revisions. Adding the version number and date to your design document will elimi-nate confusion as to the most current document.

- **Copyright, trademark, and legal information.** If this is your property then a simple "Copyright © 2002 by Acme Game Design" may be suffi-cient. But if you are working for a development house or under the fund-ing of a publisher, you may need to learn what particular copyright information it wants included on the document. It also important to include this copyright line at the bottom of every page of the design docu-ment in the event pages are removed from the core document.

- **Document filename.** This is up to you, but some Designers like to add the filename of the document. Because so many documents may be written during production, keeping track of each document's filename is, quite frankly, a pain.

Table of Contents

The table of contents is basically designed to give the reader an overview of what is contained within the design document, including page numbers. From the Designer's standpoint, it becomes very useful in helping him see how all of the subjects in the design flow into the overall structure of the product design. This information should be kept simple, to the point, and very easy to read.

Production Mission Statement

A mission statement is a relatively concise, often one-page description of what you want this product to accomplish for the company. It should include target market, age group, and target system.

Here are some key points that may be used:

- **Theme of the product.** This is something like Action/Adventure, Puzzle Game, or RPG.

- **Style of product.** Is it, for example, a 3D Adventure game or a 2D Top-Down Shooter product?

- **Style of game play.** What does this game play like? *Tomb Raider, Zelda,* or *3D Racer*?

- **Character art style.** Are the player and monster characters cartoony, gothic realistic, or other?

- **Background art style**. Will it be Dark Fantasy, Science Fiction, or other?

- **Story sequence.** Will it be done in Real Time 3D shorts or other?

- **Target age group**. What age group are you targeting with this product?

- **Target rating.** What is the Entertainment Software Rating Board (ESRB) rating for the product? To find out more information about this rating system and guidelines, visit the official ESRB web site at http://www.ESRB.com.

- **Target platform**. For what system are you planning this production (Sony PlayStation, PC, or other)?

- **Special hardware**. Will this game require any special hardware not normally included with the sale of the target platform? For example, a light gun or special plug-in device such as a modem.

- **Hardware requirements.** What are the minimum hardware requirements? If this product is for PCs, what operation system will it run under? Video card and memory requirements are important.

- **Estimated production team size.** This will vary greatly from concept to concept and you may want to wait on adding this information until after the design is fleshed out and the production schedule is closer to final.

- **Scheduled completion date.** Depending on tools, training, and pre-existing technology, on average, 12-18 months is not unrealistic for an Action/Adventure product. When do you intend to have this game done and ready for market? Always buffer in tuning time before committing to a completion date.

- **Competitive products.** Put together a short list (no more than three) of competitive products on the market. Make certain you explain your edge over these titles point by point because a clone of another product makes a poor sales pitch.

- **Reference products.** List some reference products you might have used in coming up with this concept. And if you only note items like art or mechanics in a reference product, be sure to note it here or you risk the reader judging the wrong thing. For example, if you don't tell the reader you like the art of a product but hate the game play, you risk conveying the wrong idea.

Team Mission Statement

Each production is a learning and growing experience for the team as much as it is for the company. Therefore, it is of the utmost importance to establish a number of goals the team ultimately hopes to accomplish. Depending on the team and the project, these points can vary widely. Think about where you want to be as a team at the end of the project and, as a reminder, write it down in this section.

The Game Concept Overview

In this section, you break down all of the key points that will make your concept great—almost like a sell sheet the sales and marketing department would use to promote the game. If you had only one page of text to get across all of the things that make this concept great and sellable, what would be on that one page? Don't get overly technical at this point. This is the section that most marketing and sales people will review, and you don't want to scare them off with techno-babble. Also, don't omit how you came up with the idea and why you have picked it as your production goal. You want to bring the skeptics around to your way of thinking.

The Game Back-Story

Although the back-story for a product is often fluff, it helps to bring your team into the world you envision.

The Product Flowchart

A product flowchart is a handy device to demonstrate how all of the big elements fit together to make the product. In this section, you simply walk the reader through each stage of the start-up interface, all the way down into the game, and back out to all possible endings, making sure to show how each section branches off to the different options. Don't worry about the level-by-level and bonus section stuff just yet, that will come in the next section.

The Game Play Flowchart

In this flowchart, you walk the reader through each playable stage of the game, including all possible branches and sub endings. Make sure to list all the levels out by name or number. This helps avoid confusion during production.

The Game Interface

The typical video game interface has several primary functions:

- Introduce the publisher and/or developer.
- Inform the public about the copyright and trademark status of the product.
- Present a pre-rendered, pre-animated, or static story that leads the player into the game.
- Give the player the lead-in options for the game, such as Start, Options, or Difficulty.
- Display an ongoing status of the game while you play.
- Present the player with special rewards for goals achieved.
- Explain the punishment for failing goals.

The complexity of these sections really depends on the performance level of the system for which you are developing. For example, because of the memory limitations of the Game Boy, you would not want to create a lengthy introduction interface. Also, if your target audience is expecting an Action game, a lengthy lead-in interface can become very frustrating for the player. Key things to keep in mind when designing these interface systems are:

- Production time required
- Cost to produce
- Need for the feature
- Viability for the target audience and style of product
- User friendliness

Listed in order, the following are some of the key elements that make up your standard video game interface. Please note that these elements do not go into game play interface, victory, or defeat systems because they totally depend on your concept, and a blanket design would not work. The best advice on these areas is to review other products that are similar to yours, making sure to note the five points listed in the preceding. Here are the elements to include:

- **System start-up screen**. System start-up screens are only required by console systems like the Sony PlayStation and Dreamcast. They are not required on PCs.

- **Company/publisher introduction.** This information is often provided by your publisher and/or licensor. No matter what type of game, this information is needed.

- **Legal/copyright screen.** Some system manufacturers require this information to be on the screen for a specified number of seconds, so make sure to do your homework.

- **Game title screen.** The game title screen can be, and often is, contained within a playing CG story and, when done, will default to the main start-up/option screen. (Note that the standard with these types of sequences is that the player can exit at any time by pressing any key on the controller or keyboard.)

- **Main start-up/option screen.** This can be just about anything you want, but there are some established norms for defaults, such as the cursor always starts on [Start] when the game boots up and some system manufacturers require the game to self demo if there is no interaction within x number of seconds.

It is always good to review the interface requirements of a commercial system before laying out your designs for the interface.

Game Play Overview

Here is where you explain all of the elements that make up the core game play for this product. Or, more simply, this is where you walk the player through the product's play experience. For example, here you would list out Level 1-2-3 and so on, making sure to explain where the level is in the game and what elements make up the game play for that world. Also, don't forget to add notes on what the level might look like; this will give the Art team a starting point.

After the design document is done, you would use these notes as your starting point for designing out each level in the game, but that's another book!

The Player Character

Here is where you explain all of the things that make up your player character, including looks, abilities, and limitations:

- **Description.** Ideally, in this section, you find the conceptual art for the player character along with a description of moves that may range from a simple walk to a back flip, as long as they are part of the basic movement command set of the player.

- **Special Acquired Abilities.** A player character can pick up special abilities from any number of sources during the game. However, if they are not placed and tuned properly, they could badly offset the balance of the game.

- **Combat and Defense Abilities**. If this is a combat-style game concept, you will need to outline the player character's abilities. If the player has combat abilities that don't require a pickup item, what might they be? You might want to list type, range, and damage potential.

Name and role	Personality	Look
Tony Tough main character	Main characteristics of Tony can be summed up by the following adjectives: **Insecure:** pay attention to his continuous: "Ehm…but…actually" **Sciolistic:** His knowledge is based on superficial factual knowledge. Tony will free himself from him insecurity just when he decides to make some sarcastic comments, when he wants to plead for his own creeds (i.e. good, justice, wigs which Tony is really obsessed with, human rights and so on) and right when he wants to show his useless encyclopedic knowledge off. **Fussy:** Tony always complains about dirt, stench, deterioration with some strange noise: "puah…bleagh." **Innocent:** Tony is naive and he is particularly care with children. This character represents a typical grind, crazy for TV serials, chess and scientific subjects. Armed with his raincoat he fights with great obstinacy for the strange ideals of a private investigation agency. He does not realize what is happening around and when he is not able to face up reality he uses set phrases, proverbs and expedients like: "Mommy used to say…" Tony looks like Woody Allen, perhaps and he is often ironic about himself. His typical exclamation is: "For all the flying saucers!"	

Main character description from the game Tony Tough Guy.

What types of defensive abilities does the player have? Does the player have a shield or special move that can help him avoid damage and, if so, how much protection does it give to the player? Include notes on any limitations and examples of how those defenses might be used.

What types of weapons can the player use in the game? Here, you show what the weapons might look like, including detailed information. Are there any pickup items in the game that will increase the player's current weapon attack range, damage, or effect? If so, do they time out or affect the game in other special ways? Obviously, there are many different questions that spawn from this, so just chart it out to track the best balance of items in the game.

Will the player take damage from fire, sharp objects, or other items in the game? If so, what would the damage be and does the player character have any reaction? An example might be if the player character falls into fire, he burns up! This type of information is really necessary for building your final character animation list and schedule.

Name and role	Personality	Look
Butch, detective, Tony's collegue.	Butch and his colleague, Dudley, are the first characters in the game who meet Toney. He is a detective at Wallen & Wallen just like Tony. But Butch is very clever. He is full of himself and likes to go hunting in his spare time. Butch is always on the lookout of teasing his neighbor especially if his name is Tony Tough.	
Dudley, detective, Tony's collegue.	Dudley is another diamond point at W&W, and he is always ready to ridicule Tony. He is a typical tough guy's stooge.	
Timothy and The Convict, They are the first visitors who meet Tony at the Park.	The Convict is Tim's father and he only just escaped from prison (note his hindered foot). First off he takes his son to the amusement park. He got very tired because of that heavy ball. Whereas Timothy would like to go around all the amusements, The Prisoner stays sitting. He acts very badly and sarcastically to Tony and he is very irascible too. He has got a deep and hoarse voice.	

Description of minor characters from Tony Tough Guy.

What might the player character reaction be from being hit by monster? Does she get knocked back or stand and take it like a super hero?

- **Game Controls.** In this section, you might provide a drawing of the game controller or keyboard and show what features can be invoked by pressing which buttons. Also, note if the controls might be changed by the player prior to or during game play.

- **Game Characters.** This is where it gets really fun, where you get to create all of the great monsters and other characters for your game. Think in terms of the real-level fighting with the player and all of the unknowns that might be called into play.

- **Game Pickup Items.** Game pickup items are any items in the game that the player might encounter and can collect.

The Game World Design

Here in the next two sections is where all of the prior information feeds down into what will make up the heart of the game. It's a great idea at this stage to sit down with some of the Programmers and work out what they need to know about all of the elements that will make up the game. A successful design document must be usable by Designers, Programmers, and Artists alike.

The following, listed in level-by-level style, are all of the topics that make up each stage of the game. You simply can repeat the following list for all of the levels in your design:

- Description of any lead-in CG cinematic to the level section.

- General description of the level section.

- Art description of the level section.

- Description of ground-based game play.

- Notes on any land-based or sky-based level animations required.

- Description of platform or special mechanic game play.

- Art notes on the sky-box or backdrop to the level.

- What story characters are located in each level?

- What pickup items are in each section—treasures, power-ups, and weapons?

- Are there any background danger items and how do they work?

- What monster, sub-boss, or boss characters are in this section?

- And anything else you can think of…

Game World Mechanics

In this section, you outline all of the mechanics needed for all of your game levels:

- **Game Play Placement Guide.** A great tool for weeding out thin spots in the game play experience.

- **Splash Screen Art Requirements.** Splash screen and opening interfaces are normally one of the last things anyone starts to focus on in a product, which is why it is near the end of the design document. In this section, you provide drawings and outlines for how each interface screen would work, including a list of what art and animations might be required.

- **Environment Art Requirements.** Here you place a breakdown of all of the art needed for the game in a point-by-point format. Because this is just for scheduling out the entire art task, descriptions are not needed. As before, you would list in production order depending on what needs to be up and running first, such as the player characters animations and level 1 art.

- **Cinematic Storyboards.** To control cost, companies often farm-out the CG story sequences to Hollywood-type production history boards, if possible.

- **Music and Sound Effects List.** A music and sound effects list has a number of important uses, including costing the work out. Also, it is important to list in order of need so the music and sound contractors know what to deliver first.

Engine Overview

This section includes information from your programming staff on what the game system and engine can and can't do. If needed, prototype to learn the limits, and set realistic guidelines for your project. Some of the information might be:

- Number of character you can have on the screen at once.

- How many animations per character?

- Camera and game view restrictions.

- How many polygons per level and character?

- Number of colors per texture map.

- And more… All of this information will guide the Designers and Artists in the direction of the final design. It is critical to know as much as possible. After this document is in hand, you can move on to producing the real production schedule for the game.

Setting the Production Schedule

There are two types of schedules: a projection schedule that is based on your experience of what it will take to get a game done like this and a projection schedule that is based on the outline in the design document.

Without a design document that outlines all of the items in this article, a production schedule will not hold and, in the end, the game and/or the budget will suffer.

Software Knowledge

Getting a game design job also requires experience with at least one of the following Art-oriented software programs: Discreet 3D Studio Max, Alias|Wavefront Maya, Adobe Photoshop, and Adobe Illustrator. (See Chapter 6, "Artists," for more detailed descriptions of these products.) Partially disabled versions of many of these products are available on the web. Teach yourself how to use them!

It has become common practice for PC games to release the developer tools with the game. This encourages the MOD community to create new levels and additions to the game. It is also a great way to learn the tools that your target game company utilizes. How impressed do you think the hiring manager at Smokin Games is going to be if you can demonstrate the ability to use the company's own development tools? Very Impressed!

EXPERIMENT WITH AS MANY DIFFERENT GENRES AS YOU CAN

Blizzard Entertainment and Westwood Studios are known for releasing their games with great editing tools. You can even swap out the art and other game resources replacing them with your own stuff. Experiment! If you are into real time strategy games, *Warcraft3* has a nice editor. If you are a role playing game fan, *Neverwinter Nights* has an editor you can utilize to show off your skill in creating a story and building related around it. For you action adventure types, *Dungeon Siege* has some nice tools.

You can see why most people have to earn their way into being a Game Designer. There is a heck of a lot to know. It is important to know basic coding utilizing Visual Source Safe and/or Visual Studio, C, and C++. Most game engines have their own proprietary scripting languages or use languages like Unreal Script, Java, Python, and MEL. Learn at least one of these scripting languages. Some popular editors are Worldcraft for Quake and QE Radiant. Popular engines are Quake3, Unreal Engine (UnrealED, a C style language), Unreal Tournament Engine, Unreal Warfare (akin to Tribes 2 style of multiplayer game), and Unreal2 (focused on solo play experience). Both engines heavily rely on 3D Studio Max and Maya for creating detailed geometry and environments.

So, do you still want to be a Game Designer? It is much more than simply coming up with cool game ideas. It's about excellent writing, communicating, organizing, art, and programming.

Chapter 5

Programmers

A couple years ago, there was a car commercial featuring a few twenty somethings enthusiastic about how they looked forward to cruising down the open road in their shiny new car after days and nights of creating code. Even Madison Avenue, it seems, has recognized the indisputable fact that Programmers are "in." The geeks of yesterday are the hipsters of today. So, what does it take to be a Programmer?

Game Artists create wondrous landscapes and bizarre characters. Game Designers write the documents that plot how the game will play, and what the bizarre characters will do to thwart the player. Without programming code, however, all you would have are pretty pictures and a bunch of words. Game Programmers, also known as Software Engineers, create the code that makes a game work. They make a game interactive and "alive." Without Programmers, the good guys and the bad guys couldn't do much more than sit around eating crumpets and sipping tea.

Of all the programming disciplines, coding for games may be one of the most difficult and challenging. Incorporated under just one title, Game Programmer, are many different programming disciplines and skills, such as graphics, animation, collision detection, networking, physics, database, GUI (Graphical User Interface), audio, input, and more. As if that weren't enough, the aforementioned skills must be done in real time. However, before you start feeling intimidated by the number of skills required, just remember that you won't be asked to know all these at once. Frequently, people choose "pockets" of specialization, dipping into other areas only as needed.

As indicated, programming careers in the game industry can be very specialized. Generally speaking, in terms of experience, there are several levels in the food chain: Associate or Junior Programmer, Senior Programmer, Mid-Level Programmer, Lead Programmer, and Tech Director or Director/VP of Engineering. More specifically, programming jobs also depend upon the type of programming language used for the respective game platform.

Just about anyone with a little bit of programming skill can write a *Tetris* or *Pong* clone. At its most basic level, a Programmer's job is to translate a solution to a problem into a language that a computer can understand. This ability, of course, is not enough. To have a successful career in the game industry, you must be able to write or "cut" code that is efficient, fast, flexible, and reusable.

Furthermore, code must not only be flexible, but Programmers must be as well. Frequently, you will be expected to complete a task or create new technology in an area that is unfamiliar to you. This will also take place in a production environment, which means that not only will you be learning, but you will also be learning under a deadline. It is part of both the challenge and beauty of being a Game Programmer. An additional positive aspect of this is that you will rarely find yourself bored. Every new project promises exploration into new and uncharted territories. You can expect to find the same Programmer working on a game engine in one project, building tools in another, and developing a game's core logic routines in yet another. And, above all else, Game Programmers must be absolutely passionate about making games and solving problems no one has seen or even thought of before.

YOU LOVE GAMES AND POSSESS A NOTED KNACK FOR THE TECHNICAL, SO, WHERE DO YOU SIGN UP?

Landing a programming job in the industry requires effective demonstration of your ability to create well-balanced software applications. To transition into or a get a job as a Game Programmer, you must demonstrate game programming skill and knowledge. To put it quite succinctly, if you want to be a Game Programmer, start creating games!

DO GAME PROGRAMMERS EARN LESS THAN BUSINESS APPLICATION PROGRAMMERS?

Generally, there does seem to be a lower average salary for Programmers in the game industry when compared with business Programmers from equal positions of experience and education. If that is the case, why would anyone want to work for less money doing the same job?

In reality, the skill of programming may be the same or similar, but the jobs are completely different. On a game project, you have a good time working on a piece of entertainment. You also have more liberal hours and you don't have to wear a suit to work. The bottom line is to imagine whether you would want to work on a project writing drivers for printers or on a project making the next *Doom*. Most people who love making games make the sacrifice of money for a job they love to work at every day.

Your best opportunity to get into the industry lies in creating a demo that show-cases your coding ability and strengths, as well as your grasp of current game programming techniques and technologies. But creating attention-grabbing code is not unlike a full-time job in order to get a full time job (think of it as college). You have to work hard, learn from your mistakes, and always remember that, in creating your code, you have the ultimate control. Your demo will be as compelling or as disappointing as you require it to be, and a good gauge of how you'll perform can probably be found in your reaction to that statement.

So, what makes a good demo good? In your quest to create job-getting code, the first thing you must learn is the fundamental programming hierarchy. What do you ultimately want to do as a Game Programmer? How much of a drag is this part of my life really going to be? For how long? And, by the way, what will your business card say?

TYPICAL JOB TITLES AND FOCUS

Although a Programmer's most difficult task is converting a Game Designer's creative description into working game code, there are plenty of different types of problems to be solved in a game project. As quarter to half a million lines of code go into a typical video game today, a programming team will consist of members with different specialties.

When dreaming those shiny, new business card dreams, the following sections overview the typical job titles to which you may aspire.

Associate/Junior Programmer

Euphemistically known as a "newbie," the initial focus for a Junior Programmer is adding small elements to the game project. Many game companies design their own scripting tools and languages to provide an easier interface for the non-technical contributors to a game's development. The Junior Programmer often uses these tools to program events or actions in the game. A Junior Programmer position is usually an opportunity to demonstrate abilities and prowess before getting into a more complicated set of tasks. An entry-level Programmer typically has a BSCS (Bachelor of Science, Computer Science) degree, equivalent Computer Science Associates degree, or specialized training in game programming from a school like Full Sail Real World Education or Digipen. Note: For more information on schools, see the "Resources" part of this book.

AFTER I GET A JOB, WHEN DO I GET TO WORK ON THE 3D GRAPHICS ENGINE?

It will depend on your specific skill set, but probably not on the first couple of projects that your company develops. The game industry works on a system of respect among developers. When you come in as a newbie, you have to work hard and prove yourself. If the company has an engine team, those people have a lot of responsibility to the whole company. Just work hard and good things will come to you.

Engine and Tools Programmer

This Programmer creates the core code from which the game itself will operate and designs tools to assist the non-technical members of the team incorporate their work and ideas into computer code so it can be included in the game. For example, an Engine and Tools Programmer creates things like map or level-editors to help Game Designers create game designs for the different missions or worlds that a player can visit in the game. In addition to creating the very code that is used to draw 3D graphics to the screen, this type of Programmer may also write plug-ins for graphics software like 3D Studio Max and Maya so Artists can more easily work their magic. The primary distinguishing character of this programming position is that an Engine and Tools Programmer is more of a support Programmer. That is, rather than working on a single game, an Engine and Tools Programmer is responsible for making the job of creating the games working with specific technologies easier. This type of Programmer needs a solid understanding of math, physics, graphics programming, and collision detection. This position also calls for knowledge of the programming languages C/C++ and Assembly. There will be more on these programming languages coming up.

Graphics Game Programmer

A mix between a Programmer and an Artist, this person understands code animation and effects using a 3D graphics API (Application Programming Interface) like Direct 3D or Open GL. These tools will be discussed a little later. The Graphics Game Programmer is responsible for designing algorithms or programming solutions to specific graphical game issues. This person could work on dynamic lighting for a 3D scene one day and the next day, create a particle engine to draw each little piece of an explosion. A Graphics Programmer must also be an optimization wizard who gets all of this information to display "optimally," or in real time.

Networking Programmer

Massively multiplayer online games (MMOGs) are the current rage in game development. In fact, most PC and console games also have a multiplayer component. To work on massively multiplayer games, Network Programmers must have an understanding of database management. This includes setting up client and server architecture, developing security, writing code using basic network protocols like TCP/IP, Winsock, or UDP, as well as understanding synchronization, latency, and DirectPlay (the DirectX interface to networking). Depending on the particular project they are working on, Network Programmers also need to have basic knowledge of wireless protocols like BlueTooth and Infra-Red.

Artificial Intelligence (AI) Programmer

In a word, this Programmer gives the game "intelligence." A beginning AI Programmer must study basic algorithms for games and concepts behind AI, such as tracking and pathfinding, before moving on to more advanced AI concepts such as deterministic automata, finite state machines, neural networks, genetic algorithms, fuzzy state logic, and a-life. Although it is important to understand these concepts, an AI Programmer must also be able to code and implement these ideas, which is not always an easy task. An AI specialist will likely have done some academic research and study on the subject as Game AI and traditional AI concepts begin to merge in ways that are useful to creating competitive opponents in games.

Audio Programmer

This Programmer must effectively access the sound card, load different sound formats, and program music for the game. The Audio Programmer must also take care of implementing music into the game, which is not easy. As audio technology becomes more and more immersive, audio programmers need to know the latest codecs and how they can be useful to the audio components of the game.

Miscellaneous Programmer Positions

Other programming positions may include the following:

- **Physics Programmer.** Responsible for research, development, and optimization of efficient physics and collision systems.

- **Interface Programmer.** Responsible for designing and creating expandable, customizable graphical user interface systems.

- **Game Engine Programmer.** Handles development of core game engine systems that other specialized engineers don't. The Game Engineer Programmer is frequently separated from the Engine and Tools Programmer.

- **QA Programmer.** Develops tools for QA to test product releases. Works on automated testing tools, defect tracking system customization, and so on.

OVERVIEW OF PROGRAMMER RESPONSIBILITIES

The following sections detail the responsibilities of programmers.

Game Programmer

The primary function of the Programmer is to write code that fulfills the functional, graphical, and technical requirements of the project.

GAME PROGRAMMER

RESPONSIBILITIES

- Develop C++ and/or micro-code, as assigned and scheduled by the Lead Programmer including the following aspects of code development: architect, implement, debug, document, and maintain.

- Provide the Lead Programmer with feedback regarding the time allotted to assigned tasks.

- Work with proprietary existing software technology, and build new technology, to fulfill the project's technical requirements.

- Focus on making the best possible game, which requires adaptation to changing requirements.

- Adhere to the project's coding standards (for example, commit process, version control, documentation, and so on).

- Ensure that the code is clean, easy to use, free of bugs, and reliable in the game.

- Ensure that the code is efficient (CPU, memory), as required by the project's technical requirements.

- Ensure that assets are stored and processed optimally.

- Research coding techniques and algorithms.

- Keep current with technological developments and advancements in the game industry.

- Identify technical and developmental risks and obstacles and generate solutions.

SKILLS

- Mathematics (particularly linear algebra, trigonometry, and vectors).

- Deep understanding of one or more of the following specialties: physics, 3D graphics/rendering, audio (particularly real-time streaming, Digital Signal Processing [DSP], and Midi), game logic, AI, cameras, networking, creature animation, and game tools.

- Ability to write or aptitude to learn micro-code is preferred.

- Willing and able to work closely with Game Designers and Artists.

REQUIREMENTS

- Passion for playing and developing games.

- Proven ability to architect, program, and optimize object-oriented C++.

- Technical experience with the PC, PlayStation 2, XBox, and/or GameCube.

- Experience in building new software technology and/or tools.

- Experience as a Game Programmer is preferred.

RELATIONSHIPS

Reports to: Producer

Managed by: Lead Programmer

Supervised by: Project's Technical Director

Project Lead/Lead Programmer

Part Manager and Part Programmer lead the programming team in development issues and decides what work to assign to different members of the team. The Lead Programmer is responsible for overseeing all aspects of the programming involved in making a game. Generally speaking, this person has shipped multiple games, can jump in and code almost any portion of the game, is skilled in several programming languages, and has worked on a variety of operating systems and platforms. The Lead Programmer usually has an expertise in Tools or graphics libraries development, client/server multiplayer, 3D graphics (physics, rendering, animation, and so on), or AI. Typically reporting to the Executive Producer, this person also works closely with the other Leads on the art, design, and production teams and helps develop schedules and determine milestones.

PROJECT LEAD/LEAD PROGRAMMER

DESCRIPTION

The primary function of the Lead Programmer is to manage and contribute to the development of the software for the project.

RESPONSIBILITIES

Take responsibility for breaking down the vision of the Game Designers, visual design of the Art Director, and production requirements of the Lead Artist into technical requirements:

- Establish and enforce the code development pipeline (for example, coding standards, commit process, version control, documentation, and so on), within the standards of the software department.

- Author and maintain technical specifications that document the development process, requirements, and risks of the project's software. Collaborate with the Technical Director and Technical Writer, as needed.

- Update the technical specifications in response to changes made to the game design by the Lead Game Designer and approved by the Technical Director.

Take ultimate responsibility for the successful completion of code-related tasks:

- Schedule and delegate the implementation, debugging, documentation, and maintenance of the code to the team's programmers.

- Track programming resources and the development of code; verify that programming tasks are completed on time and meet the requirements of the game.

- Maximize the productivity of the programming team by avoiding redundant development, utilizing the specific skills of individuals, and evaluating their performance regularly.

- Establish clear, project-specific roles for all programmers on the team; co-define the details of the relationship between the Lead Programmer and Technical Director.

- Provide any needed direction, guidance, assistance, and feedback to the programming team; ensure that the team members clearly understand their tasks in relation to the overall project.

- Ensure the involvement of the Technical Director at every level of code development. Defer to the Technical Director on matters of architecture and technical approaches, within the constraints of budgets and schedules.

- Delegate the implementation of technical support (for example, testing and tuning tools) as requested by the project's Leads, within constraints of schedule and budget.

- Establish and maintain the development environments of the team's programmers.

- Share the project's technical approaches, tools, and so on, with the Leads of other teams and departments.

- Call meetings as needed—including code design, code reviews, and periodic technical reviews—in collaboration with the Technical Director.

- Provide training and orientation for new programmers on the team.

- Collaborate in timely reviews of the project's Programmers.

- Pass along performance issues to the project's Producer and HR.

- Participate in external and internal recruitment for your programming team.

PROGRAMMING

- Develop C++ and/or micro-code, including the following aspects of code development: architect, implement, document, maintain, work with proprietary existing software technology, and build new technology, as required to fulfill the project's technical requirements.

- Merge the code of other Programmers contributing to the project.

- Ensure that the code is clean, easy to use, free of bugs, and reliable in the game.

- Ensure that the code is efficient (CPU, memory), as required by the project's technical requirements.

- Research coding techniques and algorithms.

- Keep current with technological developments and advancements in the game industry.

- Review competing products from a technical perspective.

- Anticipate technical and developmental risks and obstacles, and generate solutions early.

SKILLS

- Organization and management.

- Mathematics (particularly linear algebra, trigonometry, and vectors).

- Deep understanding of one or more of the following specialties: physics, 3D graphics/rendering, audio (particularly real-time streaming, DSP, and Midi), game logic, AI, cameras, networking, creature animation, and game tools.

- Ability to write or aptitude to learn micro-code is preferred.

- Willing and able to work closely with Game Designers and Artists.

REQUIREMENTS

- Passion for playing and developing games.

- Strong background in management.

- Proven ability to architect, program, and optimize object-oriented C++.

- Technical experience with the PC, PlayStation 2, XBox, and/or GameCube.

- Experience building new software technology.

- Minimum of 5 years programming for games, including the completion of one full cycle of game production.

RELATIONSHIPS

Reports to: Producer

Manages: Project's Programmers

Supervised by: Software Director

Technology Director

Responsible for research and development, the Technology Director reviews current and emerging technologies for incorporation into a game's development. This person decides what technologies will and won't be supported in the game, sets company coding standards, develops and maintains libraries, reviews new software and hardware, and keeps up-to-date with the latest technical developments. This position often involves slightly more management and somewhat less hands-on coding. Most technology group charters are fairly broad. On one end, you can deal with graphics, while on the other end you may see low-level process control and memory management. In between, for example, you may work on the tool chain that supports the art for the game.

TECHNOLOGY DIRECTOR

DESCRIPTION

The primary function of the Technical Director is to create the technical design for the project and oversee its implementation through all phases of development.

RESPONSIBILITIES

Technical Design and Development

- Help break down the vision of the Game Designers, look and feel of the Art Director, and production requirements of the Lead Artist into the technical requirements for the project.

- Determine which technical approaches have the strongest potential for success, within the constraints of schedule and budget.

- Analyze and manage the risks of the technical approaches that are chosen.

- Take ultimate responsibility for the creation and successful implementation of the software architecture and technical approaches for the project.

- Design and/or approve the initial software architecture of the project to fulfill its technical requirements and optimize the quality, performance, reliability, and reusability of the code.

- Oversee the technical development of the project. Encourage input from team members, but make final decisions on which technical approach to take to achieve the goal of making the best possible game within the constraints of technical feasibility.

- Communicate the software architecture and technical development of the project to the programming team and client through verbal discussions and appropriate media such as technical specifications, sample headers, testers, flowcharts, and class and state diagrams. Contribute to technical specifications that document the project's technical requirements and risks, in collaboration with Lead Programmer and Technical Writer.

- Evaluate the technical feasibility of changes to the game design and visual design, as proposed by the Lead Game Designer and Art Director. Make final decisions relating to the technical impact of proposed changes, within the constraints of schedule and budget.

– Evaluate the technical feasibility of requests by the Lead Game Designer and Art Director for technical support, such as testing and tuning tools.

– Direct and mentor programmers on the team before and during production via discussions, written analyses, and code reviews.

– Work with the Lead Programmer and other leads of the project to maximize technical innovation, quality, and resources, within the constraints of schedules and budgets.

– Co-host meetings as needed—including code design, code reviews, and periodic technical reviews—in collaboration with the Lead Programmer.

PROGRAMMING

– Architect and/or implement the most critical and complex technology for the project.

– Assist the team's Programmers with solving difficult problems and fixing complex bugs.

– Optimize the code (CPU, memory) as called for by the project's technical requirements.

– Research coding techniques and algorithms.

– Keep current with technological developments and advancements in the game industry.

– Review competing products from a technical perspective.

– Anticipate technical and developmental risks and obstacles, and generate solutions early.

SKILLS

– Thorough understanding of software architecture and best practices.

– Extensive scope of various technical specialties relating to game development.

– Mathematics (particularly linear algebra, trigonometry, and vectors).

– Familiar with different technical approaches for many types of games.

– Willing and able to work closely with Game Designers and Artists.

– Highly self-directed and proactive.

– Analysis and risk evaluation.

– Problem solving.

– Provide critiques and feedback.

– Evaluate talent.

REQUIREMENTS

– Minimum of 10 years programming.

– Minimum of 5 years programming for games, including the completion of two full cycles of game production.

- Proven ability to architect, program, and optimize object-oriented C++.

- Technical experience with the PC, PlayStation 2, XBox, and/or GameCube.

- Experience building new software technology.

- Ability to write or aptitude to learn micro-code is preferred.

- Passion for developing innovative software technology for games.

RELATIONSHIPS

Reports to: Producer

Supervises: Project's Programmers

Development Director or VP of Development

Responsible for directing research, development, and development-process, Development Directors utilize engineering experience and methodologies for managing Programmers, Artists, Animators, and Audio Developers to maximize the game-development process. This position is primarily technical-management, with little hands-on coding.

DEVELOPMENT DIRECTOR

DESCRIPTION

The primary function of the Development Director or VP of Development is to improve the process, quality, and productivity of software development throughout the company.

RESPONSIBILITIES

- Take ultimate responsibility for the quality of all software developed by the company.

- Manage the Lead Programmers on projects.

- Review all Technical Design Documents (TDDs) and programming schedules for projects.

- Work with the executive staff and Leads to determine allocations for new projects.

- Prioritize resources for project development, and research.

- Work with executive staff to maintain an environment conducive to high productivity (for example, space planning, separation of Programmers and Artists, equipment, and so on).

- Make the final decision on proposed additions, terminations, and allocations for the software staff.

- Set up and maintain guidelines and quality standards for the software department.

- Preview employee review forms prior to their being presented to employees.

- Provide feedback to the executive staff regarding the scope of proposed projects during contract negotiations.

- Attend Programmer and Leads meetings.

- Talk with all Lead Programmers weekly.

- Mentor all Programmers, especially Leads.

- Oversee the initial technical development of prototypes and new projects.

- Analyze proposals for future projects from a technological perspective.

- Oversee the research and development (R&D) of miscellaneous technology.

SKILLS

- Fair and objective in all proceedings.

- Management of technical staff.

- Communication.

- Mentoring.

- Thorough understanding of software architecture and best practices.

- Extensive scope of various technical specialties relating to game development.

- Familiar with different technical approaches for many types of games.

- Willing and able to work closely with the game design and art departments.

- Analysis and risk evaluation.

- Problem solving.

- Evaluate talent.

RELATIONSHIPS

Reports to: CCO

Supervises: Lead Programmers (directly), all Programmers (indirectly)

TOOLS OF THE TRADE

Compared to animation and audio jobs, one of the great things about programming is that there isn't a load of expensive software packages you need to get started. You just need a few tools and a basic understanding of programming languages, operating systems, and game platforms.

The Tools You'll Need

The following sections describe the basic tools you'll need as a Programmer.

Compiler

The compiler takes the source code that you write and translates it into lower-level machine code that the computer can understand. The compiler also makes sure that every statement is at least syntactically correct. When you have built the framework of a program and are ready to see it run, you compile it. If it compiles properly, you should be able to execute the program. If it won't compile, there is some problem in the syntax of your program.

There are a large number of compilers available. Each language has its own. Some of the more common ones in the C/C++ arena are the open source GCC and Microsoft's Visual C++. In terms of differences, GCC corresponds to the existing standards for C, whereas Visual Studio corresponds to the same kinds of standards but also gives access to programming in the Windows platform. User interface also differentiates the two. GCC is a command-line interface, which means no pretty windows; whereas Visual Studio is an IDE or Integrated Development Environment. The IDE will be discussed shortly.

There are a large number of compilers available, each with its own strengths and weaknesses. Some of the more common ones in the C/C++ arena are the open source GCC, Metrowork's Codewarrior, and Microsoft's Visual C++. Keep in mind that compilers and languages are different. For example, although C++ is a standard language, there are many C++ compilers for many different platforms such as Windows, Mac, and UNIX. Most platforms also have their own, platform-dependent libraries that provide features specific to that platform, such as DirectX under Windows. Here are some of the compilers on the market:

- **Microsoft Visual Studio** (and .NET environment) supports a host of languages and tool sets, and has a capable and user-friendly interface. Visual Studio is optimized specifically for Microsoft APIs and libraries, for MS-Windows and MS-XBox development. For more information on Visual Studio, visit msdn.microsoft.com/vstudio.

- **Metroworks Codewarrior** development environment supports a vast array of languages and platforms, includes a capable user-interface and tool set, and is also well supported. For more information on Codewarrior, visit www.metrowerks.com.

- **GCC compiler** is a part of the GNU Project, which is supported by the Free Software Foundation—a long-standing supporter and icon of open software development. The GCC development effort uses an open development environment and supports many languages and platforms, targeting multiple architectures and diverse environments. The compiler and tools are downloadable and free. The basic development environment is command line, but there is support for GUI add-on environments. GCC is typically the compiler of choice for Linux game development. For more information on the GCC Compiler, including information on the GNU Project's rich history, visit gcc.gnu.org.

Typically, the questions asked about compilers and development environments are as follows:

- What languages, platforms, and operating systems are supported?

- What tools (profilers, debuggers, source-managers, and so on) are included or available, and how capable are they?

- What is the user-friendliness of the editor, the help system, and the development environment?

- What is the quality of the generated code? How well optimized is it?

- How well is it supported for changes in coding standards and external libraries?

- Finally, how much does it cost?

Debugger

The debugger is a Programmer's best friend. After a program compiles, there will still be bugs in the system that need to be fixed. In many cases, the problem is very elusive. The more complex the program, the harder to find the solution. This is where the debugger comes in, allowing you to look into the values that are stored in particular variables, and walking you through the program line-by-line watching what happens behind the scenes. Debuggers can set break points to stop the execution of a program, or set a watch on a particular variable to be notified of any change. All of these are powerful tools are used to find bugs.

Debuggers are easily found on the Internet, and many, like GNU Visual Debugger, are free. Visual Studio has a visual debugger built in. GDB is the most common command-line debugger under UNIX systems. Many visual interfaces are available for GDB. In short, each programming language has its own debugger, so make sure that you get one that will work with your language.

IDE

The Integrated Development Environment is a particularly useful tool, allowing increased productivity for the Programmer by not forcing time-wasting swaps of applications. Typically, IDEs allow the user to set preferences on font sizes and keyword coloring. Most contain a compiler as well as a debugger and some other useful tools. All of these tools are centrally located, which makes working much easier.

Some of the more popular IDEs are sold by Microsoft and Borland, and demos are usually available on those companies' web sites. Prices range from $50 to $800 or more. Additionally, there are a number of freeware, open source IDEs available on the Internet. RHIDE is an example that will work with the freeware compiler DJGPP.

API

The Application Programming Interface is a set of methods designed with a specific focus in order to make a Programmer's job easier. An API offers a Programmer some specific ways to make requests of the operating system or a program that has resources needed. Offering pre-built solutions, all the Programmer has to do is learn to use the tool, not the underlying code. There are APIs for almost everything, and most are tested prior to release, which means in most cases they should work as designed. But don't forget the adage about not trusting anyone's code!

Two of the most popular APIs used within the game industry are Microsoft's Direct3D and OpenGL from SGI. Many games use both APIs to develop cutting-edge graphics.

The Open Graphics Library or OpenGL was first made available in 1992. It provides support for 2D and 3D graphics systems. In particular, OpenGL offers a very flexible and powerful methodology to render high-quality graphics in a number of ways. The flexibility of OpenGL comes from the open architecture of its extensions. Used by simulation companies as well as game companies, OpenGL works on numerous platforms including Windows, BeOS, Mac, and Linux systems.

First made available in 1995, Direct3D (or DirectX) is composed of a number of foundation classes that handle everything from 3D graphics to force feedback for joysticks. Direct3D is the primary 3D rendering tool available with the DirectX SDK (see the following). In comparison to their OpenGL counterparts, early releases of Direct3D were criticized for lesser performance; the DirectX team listened to game developers and released a growing list of incredible features. Now, Direct3D stands out as an excellent API to work with in the Microsoft family of operating systems, as well as the XBox.

SDK

A Software Development Kit, or SDK, is a set of tools designed to help with development for a particular technology. When a company releases an SDK, it's designed to increase the productivity of the Programmers who are working with that particular technology. Most console platforms come with an SDK that will introduce the developers to the nuances of working with the advantages and limitations of the platform. SDKs usually come with some sample applications that outline how the technology is organized. When developers want to learn the new technology, they need only read the SDK documentation and cross-reference it with these sample programs. DirectX, for example, is released as an SDK. It is so varied that it is considered a multimedia SDK that can handle most all aspects of game programming related to graphics, input, or sound. Approximately once a year, Microsoft releases a new version of DirectX to take advantage of the latest trends and advancements in hardware and gaming software. DirectX works on the Windows platform as well as the XBox gaming platform.

Popular Programming Languages

A programming language is the tool that bridges the gap between the user and the machine. Computers work in a binary framework and can only interpret 1s and 0s (ones and zeros). Needless to say, writing endless lines of 1s and 0s to program a game would be not only mind-numbingly boring but also extremely easy to make a mistake that would cause the whole roof to crash in. Rather than take that risk, Programmers avoid machine code whenever possible and, instead, use languages that abstract or "talk" to the computer at a higher level. By the way, this is not a challenge, but you do get full geek points if you tackle a game in machine code.

Programming languages were built as a way to step back from this binary business, while remaining a non-ambiguous form of communication that gets work done in a way that is not only more appealing, but also more productive. Programming languages can be compared with a language that is almost completely subjective and terribly ambiguous: English! Languages that we use to communicate are called natural languages. English is a natural language. With natural languages, it is difficult to communicate in a way that is not ambiguous. For example, if Bob describes something to Jane as being "scary," he is putting his definition of the word "scary" into his attempt to communicate. Jane's interpretation of the meaning of the word "scary," however, might be 10 times what Bob is thinking.

A computer is a simple machine. It will do what you tell it to do to the best of its capability, and hopefully, when something is wrong, it will tell you so you can fix the mistake. Many times, however, a computer will not notify you that something is wrong, and you have to go on a bug hunt. If you told your friend to "go jump in a lake," you most likely don't want her to actually do that; but if she takes your statement literally, she would act accordingly. The computer does the same thing. It takes a Programmer's statements literally, and if something goes wrong, the Programmer has to get into the code and try to find out where he made a mistake in telling the computer what to do. It is a given that you should know how to code in C, C++, Visual Basic, and Java. See Chapter 2, "Common Tools of the Trade," for a complete overview of some of the more commonly used languages in the game industry. These are by no means the only languages that exist, simply the more common ones.

Popular Operating Systems

Operating systems are a hot topic in today's computing industry, and no less so in the game industry. If you want to be a professional in the game industry and continue to draw a paycheck, check your attitude on any particular operating system (OS) at the door. It is an important consideration when deciding when and where to build a game. Factors like popularity have to be considered in the world of commercial games. Although sometimes people would rather play it cool and talk about the art and making games, it can come down to people losing their jobs and projects being canceled if a poor choice is made as to the platform for a game.

The fundamental job of an OS is to give a basic framework on which other applications run. It serves as a layer between the user and the system, giving the user control over devices like the hard drive and CD-ROM. It also allows you the ability to move, delete, and exchange information. The OS is responsible for managing memory, providing a way for the user to work and interface with the machine, and maintaining control over programs that are already in memory. No simple feat. The following provides a nutshell overview of the more popular OS versions available along with current gaming platforms.

Windows 95/98/2000, Windows XP, and Windows NT

The primary operating system in today's personal computers, Windows employs a graphical user interface, greatly simplifying computer use. Windows 95/98/2000 and XP are designed more for personal use, whereas NT employs security and networking features common in networked business environments. DirectX and many other programming tools are written to run specifically on systems that use the Windows operating system.

Windows CE

Windows CE is the compact edition of the Windows platform. It is used as the base of gaming systems like Dreamcast and XBox. Windows CE is also used in the Pocket PC line of PDAs (Portable Digital Assistants). It is reliable, small, and gives access to specialized versions of the standard tools that are available on the full Windows platform.

Macintosh (Mac)

A computer, or a religion depending on whom you ask, the Mac uses its own operating system, frequently called "OS *(number here)*." The most recent version is a spin off of UNIX called OS X. The Mac also employs a very intuitive graphical user interface. Although many games are written for the Macintosh, some of the most popular applications associated with Mac are graphical programs and digital audio workstations. Many Animators and Modelers use Mac tools to deliver high-quality artwork for the game industry.

UNIX

An open architecture operating system with several variations, including Linux, HPUX, and many others, UNIX is written almost entirely in the C language and is used in servers and networking. UNIX is an important operating system because all of the source code is available to the user. This allows people to modify the code to fit their particular needs. Many Programmers have spent a great deal of time accessing and hacking the UNIX code in an effort to learn and improve.

Linux

One of the many UNIX spin-offs, Linux is very popular in the Open Source community. Many games, as well as many sets of development tools, are ported to run to Linux. Indeed, Linux is growing with regard to its gaming functionality. Currently, projects are underway to port the DirectX API to work with Linux. Linux is also available in smaller forms for PDAs. Sony has recently released a set of tools to allow for programming on the PlayStation 2 that run on a special version of Linux.

Gaming Platforms

The power of the gaming platform has surged in the past few years. As a developer-to-be, it's important to keep in mind that you are trying to hit a moving target when deciding the platform for which to develop your games. The following provides an overview of some of the more popular gaming platforms in recent history. And although the technology of the game industry is moving quickly—Dreamcasts will come and Dreamcasts will go—there are many things, like game play, that directly translate across platforms.

Sony (PlayStation [PSX] and PlayStation 2 [PS2])

Sony entered the games market in 1995 with the PSX platform. Within two years, Sony established itself as one of the dominant video game developers having sold approximately 80 million PSX units worldwide. Sony's next generation console, the PS2, has sold millions of units and is expected to maintain Sony's dominance in the console games market.

PROGRAMMING FOR SONY

The PSX is a 32-bit gaming system. There are some important advantages associated with those bit values. Although an 8-bit machine can yield 256 values to be used for calculation and the color palette, a 16-bit machine can yield 65,536 values. (Obviously, this is significantly higher than an 8-bit machine and allows for more precise calculations as well as more cool colors). A 32-bit system, however, can yield 4,294,967,296 values. This is a major leap from the 16-bit machine and it shows in the improved quality of games on systems like the PSX. Now, just try to imagine how many values can be represented by a 128-bit system like PlayStation 2! The PS2 is as powerful as a PentiumIII 600MHz computer. To take full advantage of the powerful hardware, PSX and PS2 games are programmed predominantly in C and Assembly.

Nintendo (GameCube, Nintendo64, Dolphin, Game Boy Advanced, Color Game Boy, SNES, Game Boy, NES)

Nintendo entered the American gaming market in the late 80s with the Nintendo Entertainment System (NES). This cartridge-based, 8-bit system quickly became the most popular gaming system available. Its success was followed by the 16-bit Super Nintendo Entertainment System (SNES). The Nintendo64 (N64) was Nintendo's answer to the SEGA Saturn and Sony PlayStation. This 64-bit system is still cartridge based, restricting the available development memory, and making it difficult to compete with the CD-ROM based PSX and Saturn systems.

The Game Boy, Color Game Boy, and Game Boy Advanced (GBA) are hand-held systems. The Game Boy set of handhelds stand high as the most successful platform of all time. The limitations of the machines have been offset by the incredible design of games like *Tetris* and the *Zelda* series. The GBA marks a big improvement in the capabilities of the Nintendo handhelds. The games for GBA look awesome and still maintain a high level of game play.

PROGRAMMING FOR NINTENDO

The NES and SNES systems were programmed almost exclusively in Assembly language. The N64 is programmed in C and Assembly. As its primary development language, GameCube uses a combination of C, C++, and, Assembly. The Game Boy platforms are mainly programmed in Z80 Assembly, C, and C++ for later versions.

Microsoft (XBox)

Microsoft's entry into the home gaming console market was with XBox. The bulk of Microsoft's development in the gaming industry to date has been PC games. Because PCs are still not as plug-and-play oriented as the dedicated console platforms like the PlayStation, Dreamcast, and N64, users are confronted with issues such as driver capability and involved system configurations. The XBox allows developers to market a title that could be played on PC in an environment where users won't have to worry about things such as drivers.

SEGA (Dreamcast, Saturn, 32x, SEGA-CD, Genesis)

SEGA entered the games market with the SEGA Genesis, rivaling Nintendo's NES and SNES console systems. Prior to the introduction of the PlayStation, SEGA was the second most popular gaming platform behind Nintendo. SEGA tried to push the technology forefront by releasing the SEGA-CD to compete with the SNES and Panasonic's 3DO platforms. Next, to compete with PlayStation, SEGA introduced the 32x, a cartridge-based expansion component designed to increase the SEGA-CD to a 32-bit platform. SEGA then introduced the Saturn, a 64-bit, CD-ROM based gaming system, as a more viable rival to the PlayStation. SEGA's next generation console, the Dreamcast, a 128-bit system, was introduced in the autumn of 1999 and discontinued in January 2001, in large part because game publishers abandoned the platform.

PC and Online/Multiplayer

Massively multiplayer online games (MMOGs) have dramatically increased in popularity over the past few years. Prior to that, most online play was either combat flight simulations or text-based MUDs (multi-user dungeons), which evolved from the popularity of *Dungeons and Dragons* and other paper-based role-playing games (RPG). Today, the multiplayer market is growing at an incredible pace. Popular games like *Everquest* and *Ultima Online* have allowed players to join in RPGs with other players from all over the world. Most MMOGs are developed in C and C++. Most PC games have a multiplayer component these days.

Other Popular Game Console Platforms

The preceding section covers some of the more popular game consoles, although the following "blasts from the past" consoles are still around and in use:

- **Arcade/Coin-Op.** Pretty much self-explanatory, don't you think?

- **Colecovision**. Cartridge-based system developed by Coleco in the mid-1980s.

- **Intellivision**. Cartridge-based system developed by Mattel in the early to mid-1980s.

- **Atari 2600**. Cartridge-based system developed by Atari in the early 1980s.

- **Amiga**. One of the first PCs for which games were developed in the UK.

- **Commodore 64**. Basically, the first commercially available PC.

- **3DO.** The first 32-bit gaming system. Although very advanced for its time, this system never caught on because of its hefty $700 price tag.

HOW TO GET THERE

Almost everyone in programming is at a different place because there is just a whole lot to learn. Nevertheless, just because you don't have the experience working on particular tools or algorithms, don't discount your abilities and skills as a Programmer. Although people are often at different skill levels, there are certain core skills that all Game Programmers should possess.

Skill Levels

The following takes three sample cases of different skill sets and gives some basic ideas as to how to move forward from those points. Although you might not think that you fit directly into one of the categories, read through each of the listings and identify the skills that you have at each level. There might be some things that you've overlooked or forgotten. Most game companies do not have formal training or internship programs; it is just the nature of the beast. Game companies use advanced technologies on the bleeding edge, and they seek people who can jump in and immediately contribute to a development project. If you can do all of the things listed in each category, you are on the right track. For all levels, there are suggested books in the back of this book that should help.

New to Programming

You have either just started or are beginning to start working with a new language. You could be a high school student or someone casually interested in programming. If this description fits you, do the following:

- Select one language to learn at a time. A good one to start with is C++ or Java.

- If you have a textbook associated with a class you're taking, read it! This is something that a lot of people don't do well. There is valuable information and code samples to review in books—don't ignore them.

- Type in all the sample programs in your textbook and experiment with them.

- Experiment with the code listings to learn how different operators work.

- After you start to learn conditional statements, like *while* loops, see if you can make a Guess the Number game.

- Make a game of Hangman.

- If using C, C++, or any language that uses pointers, make sure that you are comfortable with the concept and usage of pointers fully and are comfortable with using them in a variety of ways.

- Learn as many aspects of the language that you can. After you have made a Guess the Number or Hangman game, see if you can change or re-implement the workings of your program to use new techniques that you are learning. This is one of the best ways to learn a language because you know the expected outcome of your game. Modifying it will make the game better and more robust. You will also be improving your programming abilities at the same time.

TIPS FOR NEW PROGRAMMERS!

- Get ready to be frustrated. This is an integral part of programming and it will stay with you long into the future. Every Programmer makes mistakes; you will too.

- Don't give up when something gets hard. This might sound like an old cliché, but all Programmers go through the early stage problems and have to power through them. Giving up too easily might be a sign that game programming is not the profession for you.

- Learn how to use the debugger.

- Comment your code! It's really hard to help someone when you have to take 40 minutes to figure out what that person is doing. Commenting helps considerably and is key to becoming a professional Programmer and working in a development team.

- Read everything you can on the language. Watch and learn from the mistakes you make. These are prime ways to improve your skills. You will always keep learning from a language even if you have been using it for a long time.

- Look at other people's code and ways that they organized it. How easy is the layout to read through? How easy is your code to read through for another Programmer? Frequently peruse other people's code in the game industry.

- Be consistent in the style that you use to write your code.

Some Experience Programming

You have completed a course or been studying a language for a little while, probably more than nine months. You can write programs that will solve simple problems, and perhaps, you have written a few small text-based adventure games. At this point, the next step is to start working with some game tools to get things going. Look into gaming libraries and SDKs like Allegro (www.talula.demon.co.uk/allegro) or CDX (http://cdx.sourceforge.net). These libraries contain many functions that will be used in games. They are free or shareware and can be downloaded from the Internet. If you are at this stage, the following is your To Do list for improvement:

- Read through the documentation on the game library of your choice. Look through sample source code and get some ideas of how things work in the organization of the library. The game industry is a busy place and everyone has a job to do. Reading documentation is an important skill to have. If you come across something you need but don't know about, you will have to have the ability to research and learn as you go. This ability to adapt and overcome makes you a valuable component in a development team.

- Work with the game library to solve some basic problems. You should write test or "driver" programs to solve problems like the following:

  - Drawing a single sprite to the screen.

  - Moving the sprite across the screen.

  - Testing for collision with the objects on the screen.

  - Playing some sounds.

  - Testing the input mechanism for the keyboard, mouse, and joystick.

  - Finding an existing tile engine (a representation of a game using small blocks with bitmaps similar to *Super Mario Bros.*) and making some basic maps.

- Working with those tools and programs you have now built, write a basic game. A game similar to the original *Asteroids* would be perfect. After you have solved the problems above, *Asteroids* should take around two weeks. Don't sweat it if it takes longer, just make sure that you finish.

Programming for Some Time

Perhaps you started programming in high school and have progressed into college. At this point, you might be a Junior or Senior in a Computer Science or Computer Engineering degree program. You could also be an enterprise developer looking to make a transition from database programming to the game industry. Your knowledge of syntax and data types will help you write better programs and games. In any case, you should be able to complete all of the tasks that have been listed in the previous sections and now you need to tackle the bigger problems. A background in Computer Science or a game training program will be very beneficial. My suggestions for you are as follows:

1. Write a bitmap and wave file loader.

   Problem Description: A bitmap is a simple image data file, and one of the basic elements of game graphics. To get started, don't worry about compressed bitmap formats; rather, concentrate on loading and displaying a simple, uncompressed bitmap format such as a Windows BMP. The program should have three parts: the user interface (command line or windowed), the input (loading the bitmap file), and the output (some way of displaying the bitmap you have loaded).

Wave (WAV) files are the audio analog to bitmaps in programming. Analogous to the bitmap program, this should have three parts: the user interface (command line or windowed), the input (loading the WAV file), and the output (some way of playing the sound).

2. Write a tile map engine.

   Problem Description: Tile mapping is a technique that stitches textures together to display a larger and more complicated graphical mosaic. This well-established method is used for creating the backdrop in older style side-scrolling games (*Mario*) and in modern pseudo-3D games (*Xcom*). If you already know how to load and display textures, you have the basics. All that remains is the following

   a. You'll need a number of tiles (textures) that represent logical graphical areas. For example, in a basic Mario-style game, perhaps you have all-brick tiles, all-sky tiles, and some brick-sky border tiles. For the border tiles, you would have horizontal, vertical-left-brick, and vertical-right-brick tiles. Each of these types will need to be referenced by some pre-assigned "tag" value.

   b. Now you'll need some logic to tag each tile, so that you can organize them in a meaningful graphical layout. For example, the image wouldn't appear correctly if you have any all-brick tiles adjacent to all-sky tiles. You'd need to ensure that all-brick tiles and all-sky tiles are separated by brick-sky border tiles. Remember, you're not rendering the entire background from a single bitmap, you're composing it from a collection of bitmaps. If you don't stitch these together carefully, the background will look horrible! So, you'll need to organize the tiles in a map-array, which is used to render out the entire background.

   Note that this is an interesting way to create incredibly diverse background graphics, with less memory/storage requirements for textures.

   c. After you have the basic display logic, the tile-tags, and the map-array worked out, you'll need to be able to load the tagging information from a (text) file format, which will allow you to load editable levels. This file should simply be the data that represents the entire map and gets loaded into the map-array to select which tiles are displayed.

   d. To take this a step further, you can experiment with different rendering techniques. Change to isometric by rotating the tiles and rendering X down-right and Y down-left. Change viewing angles by manipulating the ratio of Y to X pixels drawn. For larger maps, you may want to add scroll bars to your display window.

3. Create a state-based AI engine.

4. Try to simulate some basic Newtonian physics models in 2D games.

5. Write an RPG in the vein of the classic NES games.

6. Learn Windows MFC and basic Win32 programming methods.

7. Learn basic assembly code for Pentium processors.

8. Learn DirectX.

9. Learn the basic concepts of 3D.

10. Work with an existing 3D engine and try to get some basic concepts down.

11. Start a larger project with some friends. Focus on laying out a plan to follow during the course of production and stick to it as best as you can. Make sure that you note where your plans went bad and try to figure out ways to anticipate and prevent similar mistakes in future projects.

TIPS FOR EXPERIENCED PROGRAMMERS!

- Try to emphasize the robustness of your design. Make things as elegant as you can without causing issues in performance. Don't hesitate to use object-oriented programming methods, unless the platform prohibits it.

- Make sure that you have strong group skills. This is one of the most critical skills to have in the game industry. Often, studios won't hire you if they think they could not effectively live with you for three months at a time, even if you have an impressive skill set.

- Read as much as you can on the game industry and the techniques used therein.

- Write clean code. Ask someone to review your code to see if it is easy to understand.

The Well-Rounded Programmer

A Programmer has one main job in the game industry: translate algorithms or instructions into code that works with the game. Although achieving excellence in this area takes time and dedication, there are other skills that a Programmer should have, many of which can be learned through the study of different subjects. Even though your professional skills will be used for the implementation of programs, there are many non-technical subjects that keep your mind open to different ways to solve problems. Some of them are also good hobbies, too. Simply put, the more you know, the better.

Education

A BSCS (Bachelor of Science, Computer Science) supported by a portfolio of your own games, makes you most attractive to a game company. Several schools today offer game training programs, such as Digipen and Full Sail Real World Education, a well-established 30-year-old technical school in Orlando, Florida. The 15-month degree program requires over 900 hours of C/C++ hands-on coding and real-world experience with project deadlines, team environments, and an attendance requirement of a minimum of 40 hours a week. In the game industry, it is not unusual, particularly during product release time, to find a development team chomping on pizza at 3:00 a.m. while having a coding party. Students at Full Sail reportedly do the same.

If you start your degree—get your degree. Don't quit three quarters of the way through unless there is a serious extenuating circumstance. Some employers may view it as quitting when the going gets tough. Moreover, to be a truly well rounded Programmer, you need a well-rounded education including Mathematics, Science, Arts and Humanities, and, yes, English.

Mathematics

Learning math is frustrating for many. Some people don't relate to math the same way that they do to straight programming. Nevertheless, math is a vital tool in games programming. Programmers use it for calculation of physics as well as performing 2D and 3D calculations in graphics programming. How much math you need to learn as a professional Programmer is largely determined by your precise role. Different jobs require different levels of math. Across the board, however, it's safe to say that every Programmer should have knowledge of trigonometry and basic geometry in addition to strong fundamental algebra skills. No need to panic at this prospect. It's amazing what a person can do when the brain is put to work. In addition to those basic math skills, there are some other levels of math knowledge helpful to specific programming jobs. Remember that the levels listed are just the skills themselves, not just completion of a class. There are numerous Programmers who have taught themselves how to manipulate matrices without ever taking a linear algebra class or any higher math for that matter. What you learn and the skills you have are more important than the way you get them.

How Much Math Do You Need to Know?

More than Einstein! This is a question that comes up quite a bit. At this point, you know at least something about math. You had to know a little math just to buy this book! One thing that can be said about math and in general about learning is that when you close the door on your need to know something, you put a definite timetable on the usefulness of your skills. If you were a Pascal Game Programmer, you could still get work somewhere in the online Pascal game club or something homespun and amateur. To be more precise on the math requirements, you should probably have a minimum of calculus. You will also need to be able to work with matrices. Knowledge of vectors is also important. Learn as much as you can and then learn more.

CAN YOU WORK IN THE GAME INDUSTRY WITHOUT STRONG MATH SKILLS?

If you have the desire to make something happen, it will happen. If you have to motivation to make it in the industry, you have the motivation to learn some more math to boost your knowledge. The amount of math you need to know will depend on your specific job, but a basic knowledge base will be required.

Suggested baseline math skills: Trigonometry, Analytic Geometry, and Algebra

Engine Programmer: Statistics, Calculus with continued studies into Calculus 2 and 3

Graphics Programmer: Statistics, Calculus with continued studies into Calculus 2 and 3, Linear Matrix Algebra

AI Programmer: Statistics, Calculus, Discreet Math with Inductive Proofs

Network Programmer: Statistics, some Calculus

Sound Programmer: Statistics, Calculus with additional study into Calculus 2 a major plus

Again, if you're panicking, stop! Most people are motivated to learn things that they need in order to do something that they want to. This is not any different with programming. When you start working on a game and get stuck, chances are you will go learn the programming components you need to fill in the gaps. Math for Programmers is the same way. When you need to get a component of physics working in your game, you will go looking for that piece. This is fine as long as you are an amateur, but when you take a professional position, your employer will expect that knowledge to be ready and available. For this reason, it's a good idea to learn these skills before you go looking for a job. However, when you are a "pushing-the-envelope" Game Programmer, learning on the job is inevitable.

FROM THE EXPERT

"Almost every entrance exam I have seen has some math question on them. This is not a really big deal in the long run. If you really want to earn a living as a Programmer, you will have to exert the effort to make it happen. Programming is a lot of fun, but it's also a lot of work."

– Dustin Clingman, Professor of Game Development, Full Sail Real World Education, and Founder of Perpetual Motion

FAQ

I just received a programming test from a prospective employer. How long should I take to finish it?

Many times, the person who gives out the test will specify some time frame about how long you have to complete and return the test. The best thing to do is to beat that time and get it back to them.

What if I can't answer all the questions?

Even if you can't answer all the questions, return the test in the time specified. Some questions are extremely difficult to answer and don't have a simple solution. Some of them are trick questions. Just do your best and make sure that you submit the test. Programming tests can gauge your skills and let you know what things you need to work on.

Science

A basic class in Chemistry or Biology teaches the Scientific Method, a way to perform experiments and analyze what happens. Experiments must be repeatable in order to follow the Scientific Method. Programmers, likewise, use the basic Scientific Method to find bugs in programs. There is also a tendency for Computer Science to follow nature and other scientific occurrences as inspiration for programming. Object-oriented programming, for example, is much like the cycle of life. When no longer useful, parents, children, and objects are deleted. It's important that a prospective Programmer have knowledge of the Scientific Method. Physics is also an important science for the Game Programmer as many of the best games offer really cool physics that make us believe we are really driving racecars. And, that's all based on the work of Newton.

Though there are far too many to list, here is a quick, tip-of-the-iceberg check-list of particularly useful areas of science:

- The Scientific Method and its implementation

- Basic Newtonian Physics

- Basic algorithm analysis

- Biology fundamentals

- Scientific Notation

Arts and Humanities

It's important to be aware of major Artists as well as major thought movements. Believe it or not, the history of a particular era might be useful to you as a Game Programmer. The Arts and Humanities are a primary outlet for creative people, and successful Programmers are extremely creative people. They have to work out problems on a machine that can act differently on the drop of a hat. Spend some time making sure that you are well rounded. Again, there are far too many to list, but here are some suggestions:

- Learn about the major art movements

- Study painters and their styles

- Learn about early architectural styles

- Know the geography of the world

- Study intellectual movements of history

- Listen to classical music and analyze its composition

English

Probably the most important skill anyone can have is the ability to communicate via spoken or written word. As a Programmer grows, an increasing need to delegate work to others arises. Making sure that the assignments are understood is critical to the success of the project. How you communicate to people will directly relate to how they perceive you. Proper format of memos and reports along with attention to grammar and spelling are very important aspects of communication that many people take for granted. Although this shouldn't sound like a lecture, it's important to know and execute these things. Here are a few things on which to focus:

- Learn to proofread without the spellchecker.

- Be able to identify the major components of a story.

- Practice speaking in front of others on topics you know about.

- Practice speaking in front of others on topics you don't know much about.

- Read fiction and non-fiction books (including comic books).

The purpose of discussing these things is not to force you into 10 years of schooling. It's important to be well rounded as well as an expert in your field. Amazingly, some of the most important influences in and out of a person's career have to do with something that is unrelated to their daily work. The more well rounded you are, the more of a prospect for employment you are.

Teaching Yourself

Although formal training is almost a necessity today, the creative hacker mentality that started the game industry is still alive and well. Books on C++ programming, Windows APIs, math, and DirectX, along with more focused game programming books are widely available. As you teach yourself, be sure to focus on becoming a good Programmer by creating small games that test the concepts of what you are learning. You will stand out from the crowd if you can demonstrate your creativity and willingness to push the technical envelope.

Ideal Programmer Qualities

When an employer begins a search for a particular Programmer candidate, there will likely be many different expectations about the ideal candidate. You will almost always find that there are some desired qualities specific to that particular company (such as the ability to speak French), but there are some general qualities that will always make you an extremely valued employee at any company.

Team Attitude

Probably the single most important quality in a production environment, team attitude implies a type of selflessness and dedication to the team and project over your own personal interests. If people on your project are more concerned with what title they will get on a project, petulantly establishing who is "right", or spending their time pointing fingers at others, the chances of your project making it out the door and onto the shelves are not all that bright.

There is an almost tangible magic that takes over a team when the majority exhibits a team spirit. When you see people behave with a strong team attitude, it can be infectious. The cohesiveness of a solid, dedicated team can be what separates the mediocre games from the great games.

FROM THE EXPERT

"When you get that very first Game Programmer job, your education doesn't stop! For example, a good place to start learning script programming is to study scripts from games that provide open source to their scripts. Learn how scripting engines are built and learn other programming languages that are used as scripts. Study level design and design a few levels for a game. Create scripts for the game."

– Dustin Clingman, Professor of Game Development, Full Sail Real World Education, and Founder of Perpetual Motion

Self-Starters

These are the Programmers who do not need constant supervision. When given a task, they will supervise themselves. They will ask another Programmer on the team for information when and if they need it. They will go to the Designer and ask questions relating to the implementation of their task. They will go to the Artists and track whatever assets are needed for their task. This ability to self-start allows a Manager to assign a task and walk away knowing that they do not have to oversee all the different aspects of accomplishing that particular task. Most employers consider self-starters worth their weight in gold.

Follow-Through

The ability to see tasks through to the end, on both a micro and macro level, is a highly valued quality. There is a thrill with the beginning of every new task you take on. It is something new and exciting and you generally don't have any difficulty getting started on it. Sometimes, however, the last 10 percent of a task can take 90 percent of the time. When you are working on that last 10 percent of a task, it can be a bit painful at times. There are the times when you will be getting feedback from Designers and Artists that forces you to retread old ground, revisiting the same code/functionality over and over again. It can become tedious, but rarely do you nail something such as AI character behavior the first time around the block. Perfection will come with time.

Communication

FROM THE EXPERT

"Programmers usually exist in one of two states – either diving deep, or coming up for air. When they come up for air, they need to be able to explain exactly where they have been, what they have seen, etc. When they get ready to go down again, they need to have a good description of where they are going to go and what they are going to do while they are down there."

– Bran Kelly, Chief Technical Officer and Vice President, Tremor Entertainment

Communicating with others in a team environment is extremely important. The goal is not only to communicate, but to communicate well. One of the biggest tendencies that Programmers have when communicating is to slip into "Programmer speak." This can glaze over the eyes of nearly any Artist, Designer, or Producer on the planet. You could be explaining the inner workings of the particle system to a Designer in incredible detail that any Programmer would understand, but if he doesn't get "Programmer speak," you may have just wasted both his time and yours. It is a rare and valued gift for a Programmer to be able to communicate to others in a language that they understand. This is not always easy. It can take time to perfect, but it is well worth the effort.

Responsibility

Taking responsibility for what you have done or what you are supposed to do goes hand in hand with all the other qualities. Those who embrace responsibility and, in fact, seek more are those who rise to Lead Programmer status and become one of the cornerstones of any team.

Chapter 6

Artists

There are several aspects of the game industry that work in pretty much the same way as any other business. Ideas require structure, structure requires planning, planning requires a shop of some sort, and the shop requires funding to keep it in light bulbs, coffee, and 22-inch monitors. There are people who are involved in every aspect of this process, and every one of them is crucial to a game's ultimate place on shiny, store shelves. Without the support of each segment of the process, the games just would not happen.

But perhaps you're cut from a cloth of altogether different—perhaps even *unique*—textures. Perhaps you're the creative sort, always have been: the two-year-old making play dough sculptures, the high school freshman with the ink soaked spiral-bound notebook, or the girl who never slept because you were too busy breaking down the graphics of the first *Quake*. You're an Artist—in more ways than one. And whether or not you're currently employed, that's what you want to be. You have to be. You'll do anything. What now?

The game industry offers perhaps the only creative artistic career in the world not yet diluted by the draw of worldwide celebrity or teenaged groupies. Game Artists are here because their creative and professional backgrounds make them particularly well-suited to the industry or, as for many, they just flat-out love games and they'll do whatever they can to make the coolest, most inventive experience the world has ever seen. Ask someone in the film industry how many people there are operating at that level of commitment. Ask a rock star.

So why isn't everyone working as a Game Artist?

It may sound odd, but not everyone has a clear vision. Perhaps they also never had the right encouragement or artistic training. Nor is everyone tenacious in their job search, or at least they don't start out that way. Your best opportunity to get into the industry lies in a stunning demo reel and effective self-marketing. Although the specifics of a demo reel will be addressed just ahead, in short, a demo reel is a compilation of your best work, put together in a montage and presented either on video, CD, or online.

Creating the right reel and marketing it, and you, is not unlike working a full-time job in order to get a full-time job (think of it as college). You have to work hard, learning from your mistakes and always remembering that, for example, in creating your demo reel, you have the ultimate control in the output and flow of the images. It will be as compelling or as disappointing as you require it to be, and a good gauge of how you'll perform can probably be found in your immediate reaction to that statement.

Unfortunately, but not surprisingly, most tend towards the latter. For example, Andrew Paquette, Art Director for Sony says he's only seen five extremely compelling reels out of the thousands he has reviewed—a daunting yet clarifying ratio. What's most interesting, and of course elusive, is what makes a good reel good. In your quest to achieve *fivedom*, the first thing you must learn is the fundamental structure of the industry. What is the hierarchy? What do you ultimately want to become? How much of a drag is this part of my life really going to be? For how long? And, by the way, what will your business card say?

TYPICAL JOB TITLES AND FOCUS

As they say, "a rose is a rose," but in the game industry an "Artist is an Artist, Animator, Modeler, Texture Artist, Character Animator, Skins Artist, 2D Artist, 3D Artist, and more." Generally speaking, Artists create character and environment designs and storyboards. Their design sketches are used as references by Modelers who then create the 3D models of the game's characters. Character Animators then animate the models by creating frames or poses for every movement the character will make in the game. Artists are also responsible for creating the skins and textures that make a game environment pleasing to the eye.

When dreaming those shiny, new, business card dreams, the following are typical job titles to which you may aspire. Please note that the various areas of expertise will be addressed in greater detail later in this section.

Art Director

Responsible for the entire art development team, Art Directors have paid their dues and worked their way through the ranks. Generally speaking, Art Directors are responsible for the operations of the art department with duties including scheduling development, budgeting, and hiring. Art Directors may also be very hands-on, contributing to the development of the title on an individual basis as an Artist or Animator.

Simply stated, the duties of the Art Director in game production revolve around building and actualizing a team of professional Artists to construct the art assets for the product (on schedule and within budget), whatever the genre or platform for the game. The Art Director is also largely responsible for directing the entire style of the art, determining the mood, look, and feel.

ART DIRECTOR

DESCRIPTION

The primary function of the Art Director is to improve the process, quality, and productivity of art development throughout the company.

RESPONSIBILITIES

- Take ultimate responsibility for the quality of all art developed by the company.
- Manage and mentor the project Lead Artists.
- Review all art specs and art asset schedules for projects.
- Work with executive staff and Leads to determine allocations for new projects.
- Prioritize resources for art development.
- Establish and enforce processes for art department development.
- Make the final decision on proposed additions, terminations, and allocations for the art staff.
- Set up and maintain guidelines and quality standards for the art department.
- Preview employee review forms prior to their being presented to employees.
- Provide feedback to the executive staff regarding the scope of proposed projects during contract negotiations.
- Attend Artist and Leads meetings.
- Talk with all Lead Artists weekly.
- Mentor all Artists, especially Leads.
- Oversee the initial artistic development of projects and proposals for future projects.
- Oversee the artistic aspects for research and development (R&D) of miscellaneous technology.

SKILLS

- Thorough understanding of art department architecture and best practices

- Extensive scope of various art specialties relating to game development

- Familiar with different artistic approaches for many types of games

- Willing and able to work closely with the game design and software departments

- Analysis and risk evaluation

- Problem solving

- Evaluate talent

RELATIONSHIPS

Reports to: CCO

Supervises: Lead Artists (directly), all Artists (indirectly)

FROM THE EXPERT

"A Lead Artist's drawings must be clear enough for Modelers and Texture Artists to work from. Often, these Artists do not work much in color, but I prefer to see color as it is so important to the end result. This person always has a strong understanding of the 3D tools and is available to assist Artists with their tasks. Lead Artists may have been senior Animators before attaining this position, so they know how to build, texture, and animate models. They can get models into the engine, and they understand the pipeline inside and out."

- Andrew Paquette, Former Director of Art, Sony Pictures Imageworks

Lead Artist

Often described as equivalent to the Production Designer on a film, Lead Artists should be the most experienced and talented Artists on the project—typically responsible for modeling and texturing of the objects and environments in the game. Lead Artists must also have the skills of personnel management and positive motivation to get the best from the team, along with the project management experience to accomplish this all within the allotted schedule and budget.

LEAD ARTIST

DESCRIPTION

The primary function of the Lead Artist is to manage the implementation of art and animation.

RESPONSIBILITIES

Take responsibility for breaking down into required art assets the game design established by the Game Designers and stylistic look and feel established by the Art Director:

- Establish and enforce the art production pipeline, within the standards of the art department.

- Author and maintain art specifications that document the production process, requirements, and risks of producing the project's art assets. Collaborate with the Art Director and Technical Writer, as needed.

- Update the art specifications in response to changes made to the game design by the Lead Game Designer and to the style and mood by the Art Director.

Take ultimate responsibility for the successful completion of art-related tasks for the project:

- Schedule and delegate the creation and maintenance of art assets to the team's Artists.

- Track art resources and the development of art assets; verify that art assets are completed on time and meet the requirements of the game.

- Maximize the productivity of the art team by avoiding redundant development, utilizing the specific skills of individuals, and regularly evaluating the performance of the art team.

- Establish clear, project-specific roles for all Artists on the team; define the details of the relationship between the Lead Artist and Art Director.

- Provide any needed direction, guidance, assistance, and feedback to the art team; ensure that the team members clearly understand their tasks in relation to the overall project.

- Ensure the involvement of the Art Director at every level of asset development. Defer to the Art Director on matters of look and feel, within constraints of budgets and schedules.

- Share the project's artistic styles, processes, techniques, and so on with the Leads in other teams and departments.

- Host art reviews in collaboration with the Art Director to obtain external feedback and suggestions for improvements.

- Provide training and orientation for new artists on the team.

- Review competing products from an artistic perspective.

- Collaborate in timely reviews of the project's Artists.

- Pass along performance issues to the project's Producer and Human Resources.

- Participate in external and internal recruitment for the art team on your project.

- Use 3D packages, such as Maya and/or proprietary software, to create high-quality art assets that fulfill the requirements of the project's game design and visual design.

- Understand the requirements and constraints of game design, engine, and platform.

- Proactively seek feedback from the Art Director in style and mood.

SKILLS

Ability to use commercial software for 2D and 3D art production (for example, Photoshop and Maya) and administrative tracking (for example, Microsoft Office and FileMaker Pro)

REQUIREMENTS

Experience as an Artist or Lead Artist on several published titles.

RELATIONSHIPS

Reports to: Producer

Manages: Project's Artists

Supervised by: Art Director

Lead Animator

The most experienced and talented Animator on the staff, the Lead Animator generally makes guideline animations for other Artists to use as a standard, and animates the more prominent characters. Lead Animators will also set up the animation pipeline in accord with the senior engineer, Lead Artist, and Art Director. Generally speaking, all Animators must have an acute sense of timing combined with visuals.

LEAD ANIMATOR

DESCRIPTION

The primary function of the Animator is to bring characters and environments to life through the use of several proven methods of animation—from traditional process to the latest state of the art tool sets available on the market.

RESPONSIBILITIES

- Use 3D animation packages such as Maya, 3D Studio Max, and/or proprietary software to animate 3D characters and environmental objects.

- Work closely with the Art Director and Lead Artist to develop animation assets that fulfill the requirements of the project's game design and visual design as documented by specifications, style guides, and appropriate reference material.

- Follow the schedule determined by the Lead Artist.
- Use tracking and management tools.
- Understand the requirements and constraints of game design, engine, and platform.
- Proactively seek feedback in style, direction, and technique.
- Proactively seek feedback from the Art Director in style and mood.

SKILLS

- Animating creatures and environmental objects
- Ability to use, or aptitude and willingness to learn, Maya and/or 3D Studio Max for 3D
- Skeletal rigging and skinning in 3D animation software
- Traditional animation and drawing:

    Timing, weighting, and conveying emotion

    Expressions and blend-shapes

    Forward and inverse kinematics

- Background in one or more of the following specialties: bipeds, quadrupeds, or cinematics
- Willing and able to work closely with Modelers, Game Designers, and Programmers

REQUIREMENTS

- A 2- or 4-year degree from a qualified animation school
- Deep understanding of animation principles, as demonstrated by a strong portfolio
- Completion of at least 1 full cycle of game production

RELATIONSHIPS

Reports to: Producer

Managed by: Lead Artist

Supervised by: Art Director

Lead Concept/Storyboard Artist

Traditional pen-and-paper Artists, Lead Concept/Storyboard Artists are accountable for character design and storyboard artwork. These Artists work with the Art Director to design all elements of the game so that a coherent style is adhered to, objects are buildable in 3D, and all 3D elements are appealing. In short, the art team bases the in-game artwork on the Lead Concept/Storyboard Artist's concepts.

Before attaining Art Director or Lead status, Artists must put in their dues in senior- and entry-level positions. A Senior Artist/Animator, for example, typically has two to four years of game industry experience and is involved in multiple aspects of art, whereas an Artist/Animator is an entry-level position in the art department and is responsible for only one or two elements of the game's art. Artists working in these particular elements are covered in the following sections.

2D Artist

The 2D Artist must have traditional 2D drawing and painting skills for conceptual work on characters, worlds, and objects, plus the ability to utilize digital texturing software to prepare texture assets for production use on models and environments. Pre-render compositing for cinematics and special effects is often the responsibility of the 2D Artist, as well. Proficiency with Adobe Photoshop, AfterEffects, and Illustrator, along with Painter, DeepPaint3D (with Texture Weapons), and other texture generation/application software packages are required.

Pre-rendered compositing is essentially the function of editing together sequences of computer animation and visual effects that have been generated separately from either off-the-shelf software packages, like 3D Studio Max or Maya, or captured directly from the game engine. The editing is normally performed utilizing a variety of software, ranging from Adobe Premiere and Adobe After Effects to Discreet's Combustion and Flame packages. The layers of art elements are combined (composited) through the use of these digital editing software programs.

2D ARTIST

DESCRIPTION

The primary function of the 2D Artist is to create and refine 2D art assets.

RESPONSIBILITIES

- Use 2D packages, such as Photoshop and similar commercial and proprietary software, to create high-quality 2D art assets that fulfill the requirements of the project's functional, art, and technical specifications: create textures, apply lighting, and make sprites and other types of 2D art assets.

- Follow the schedule determined by Lead Artist.

- Use tracking and management tools.

- Understand the requirements and constraints of game design, engine, and platform.

- Take direction in style and technique.

- Proactively seek feedback from the Art Director in style and mood.

SKILLS

- Proven ability to create textures for characters, environments, and props

- Ability to use Photoshop or equivalent commercial software for 2D art production

- Willing and able to work closely with Game Designers and Programmers

- Ability to take direction

REQUIREMENTS

- Experience in fine art, as demonstrated by a strong portfolio

- Willingness to learn commercial and proprietary software

- Game experience preferred

RELATIONSHIPS

Reports to: Producer

Managed by: Lead Artist

Supervised by: Art Director

3D Artist

Traditional art skills, plus a facility at dimensional visualization such as sculpture and construction, enable the 3D Artist/Modeler to create the environments, objects, and characters used in the game.

3D ARTIST

DESCRIPTION

The primary function of the 3D Artist is to create and refine 3D art assets.

RESPONSIBILITIES

- Use 3D packages, such as Maya and similar commercial and proprietary software, to create high-quality 3D art assets that fulfill the requirements of the project's functional, art, and technical specifications: Model geometry at multiple Levels of Detail (LOD—versions of the same model with less polygons and textures), map textures, and set up lighting for 3D art assets.

- Follow the schedule and pipeline established by the Lead Artist.

- Use tracking and management tools.

- Take direction in style and technique.

- Understand the requirements and constraints of game design, engine, and platform.

- Proactively seek feedback from the Art Director in style and mood.

SKILLS

- Model, texture map, and light real-time 3D characters, environments, and props

- Ability to use Maya or 3D Studio Max for 3D art production

- Background in one or more of the following specialties: creatures, vehicles, and environments

- Willing and able to work closely with Game Designers and Programmers

- Ability to take direction

REQUIREMENTS

- Experience in real-time 3D modeling and lighting using Maya or 3D Studio Max, as demonstrated by a strong portfolio

- Willingness to learn commercial and proprietary 3D modeling software

- Game experience preferred

RELATIONSHIPS

Reports to: Producer

Managed by: Lead Artist

Supervised by: Art Director

Character Animator

The Character Animator should have a firm foundation in the traditional 2D-cell character animation process. This is the process of generating a series of single art frame elements, which include separate instances of an action, defining a personality and motion of a character, when combined in a continuous visual stream. This style of animation is well exemplified by the works of the Walt Disney Studio and other companies' animators. Skills in this traditional method, when combined with the skill to translate this knowledge into such 3D character animation packages as 3D Studio Max, Maya, SoftImage, LW/Messiah, and so on, become the basis for creating moving creatures, humans, and other characters for use as game assets or cinematic movies.

Environment Modeler

The Environment Modeler is a 3D Artist/Modeler who constructs landscape and structures in either proprietary World Editors, or in such 3D packages as 3D Studio Max and Maya.

Skins Artist

The "Skins" Artist is a 2D Texture Artist who generates, then applies texture maps onto character and object models for the game. The process of making these maps may include a mastery of both 2D and 3D texturing utilities to appropriately prepare the object models with correct mapping coordinates, as required by the game engine technology.

ENVIRONMENT MODELING VERSUS CHARACTER MODELING

The major differences between environment and character modeling become quite apparent when you consider that environments include landscapes, skies and other atmospheric effects, buildings and other structures, plants, water, rocks, and so on; and characters are human bodies, animals, fantasy creatures and other life-forms with personality and emotion, some of which might normally be viewed as inanimate objects like furniture. The Environment Modeler creates the "stage," or world, that is then populated by the characters and other objects expected to live in that world. Each type of modeling utilizes similar, and sometimes the same, tools, yet the approach to each is unique and varied. The Environment Modeler must have a good understanding of structures, both natural and man-made, in addition to an awareness of lighting, texturing, and effects, in order to create the world set out in the production designs. The Character Modeler must have a solid knowledge of anatomy, both human and other creatures, as well as costumes, and body and facial types, plus the ability to prepare models that are technically set up for use by animators.

Texture Artist

Responsible for adding color, personality, and style to the entire game, the Texture Artist focuses on generating 2D maps, which are applied to the 3D elements created by the Modelers. This Artist brings dimension and an aesthetic element to the game.

Cinematics Artist

This Artist creates the story-telling cinematics for the game project. These art assets normally draw from in-game content, but may include exclusive cinematic content that is unique and new. The Cinematics Artist may well be a Character and World Modeler, as well as a Texturer and Animator, in order to fulfill the duties required. Composite editing and effects work may be required, as well.

Package Design and Marketing Artist

Every game product needs package design, inbox printed materials, and marketing support. This may include web design and animation for the product web site. In most cases, these tasks are handled by a separate department or company entirely, but may include several in-house or development team Artists.

TOOLS AND SKILLS YOU'LL NEED

After you've decided your primary art career focus (or at least your initial focus), it's important to start learning the software. 3D and 2D art packages have zilch to do with normal office software like word processors or spreadsheet programs. Although learning on the job is a possibility for some aspiring artists, it simply may not be a practical training solution for many, and you can't fake your way through this stuff. It's impossible to guess why anyone would try, though of course they do. As a staff artist candidate, you must know the tools of the trade to be successful. Everyone has a preference as to the best or worst of what programs and tools are out there. Although consensus does not exist, majority certainly does. Discover what software packages are being utilized at the companies you want to work for, and why they prefer to use them. Then set out to learn this software through school, vendor, or retail sources. By proving your knowledge of this software, you become a more viable and valuable candidate for the target company.

2D artists still put pen to paper. And traditional skills, such as the ability to paint texture, simulate dimensionality, model and sculpt, animate (sense of timing), design and composite, and set lighting and proportion, are all valuable assets. But getting an art job in the game industry also requires experience with at least a few 2D and 3D software packages. A great way to familiarize yourself with software currently being required by the big game companies is to look over their job postings. Also, you can refer to Chapter 2, "Common Tools of the Trade," for a complete overview of some of the more commonly used programs.

Artistic Abilities

Traditional art skills may be the least discussed topic on the agenda in most situations in this industry because, in many instances, developers are continually mastering the latest technology in their game engines and in the latest version of their software tools. Nevertheless, traditional art skills are, in fact, the most sought-after by production heads and Art Directors who expect a high degree of traditional visualization skills; the ability to draw, paint, animate, and sculpt are the fundamental grounding of the successful technological art toolset.

Art production groups do not attain aesthetic excellence simply by having the latest and greatest 3D or 2D package and mastering its many intricacies—far from it. The ability to visualize and construct a cohesive production design for the next major game project clearly and effectively, to the team, demands the mastery of traditional methods. After the design is implemented, it is these same traditional methods that are utilized in conjunction with the technical mastery of the software to yield the highest quality production values to the final product. Do not underestimate the power of a drawing! It is the conceptual design that inspires the ideas, at first, but the successful transition from idea to actuality relies on each Artist's skill as interpreter to bring it to fruition. Balance of composition, color, anatomy, architectural/industrial design, and even line quality are all drawn from traditional art training. These are the fundamentals on which all, great game art productions are based.

THE ART PRODUCTION PIPELINE

The art production pipeline in game development begins by coordinating the art group with all other project team members—Designers, Programmers, Testers, and so on—to ensure that the team dynamic is a positive, supportive one, and conducive to great communication. The goal of the art group is to clearly and accurately visualize the game concept from initial creative spark through the final stage polish before it goes to manufacturing.

Concept Phase

During the early discussions leading up to a fully realized game concept document, the first real manifestation of a potential game product, the art team assists the core team with sketches, color comps (design sketches that have been colorized through the use of markers, paints, or digitally through Photoshop), storyboards, and possibly, preliminary art assets such as models and environments, animatics (animated storyboards), and simple animations for early testing of the concept or technology. Artists are tasked with designing characters, costumes, objects and vehicles, environments (including architectural structures and natural landscape forms), potential game play diagrams and mockups, interface designs, and storyboards.

In preparation, Artists gather visual resources related to these tasks including source materials in architectural and industrial design, natural environments, costumes, style, anatomy, and culture, among a myriad of other topics. And they begin to draw. In some cases, the initial conceptual visions of products are scrapped for something else, based upon the first pass elements and new discussion, resulting in a mountain of artwork, which becomes archive material. Many first-time Artists find this a bit frustrating, but it is much more reasonable to use this phase of production to work out the vision for the game before more costly production methods are utilized. The added benefit of a full pre-concept and then full-concept design phase in game production is that all segments of the team get to test their ideas, driving both game design and technology to more concisely define the production goals for the product.

After the game concept has been defined, visually, verbally, and hopefully, technically, a full Game Concept document is generated that, in essence, is the "bible" for the game production cycle. This Game Concept document has sections that discuss and define all aspects of the game, from story content and game play descriptions to full-on asset lists, scripts, and market comparisons to competitive products. Additionally, a Technical Design Document (TDD) is formally delineated, based upon the goals defined in the Game Concept document, which reveals, in extreme detail, how the programming team plans to implement all aspects of game play.

The art team's main focus for these documents is to discuss and define the visual needs and goals of the product, as defined by the concept, and generate a production method for the assets that coincides and supports the technical necessities and limitations, as defined in the TDD. In many cases, the art assets created

NOTE

For more information on game design documents, see Part III, "Preparing for the Career You Want."

during the Concept Phase become embellishments and visual examples in these project documents, assisting in fully communicating the overall vision intended for the game.

Prototype Phase

With the information gathered, an early production schedule is discussed and agreed upon amongst the full project team, with contingencies and dependencies defined and accepted. In some cases, this is enough to move forward to Full Production of the game assets, but in many other cases, it is wise and warranted to prototype the concept to further delineate risks of production and prove method. The additional information that the Prototype Phase gives the team in terms of time and materials needed to generate and implement the assets, potential pitfalls of the decided method, and whether the game play prototype meets its playability goals will result in a tighter, more realistic schedule and help to better define project goals. When creating a prototype of the full game concept, the project team decides on the core aspects of implementation that fully define the game play, thereby generating a list of tasks that must be performed to complete a working version of the product. The art assets called for during prototyping vary from product to product, but normally include a limited version of the full assets required for the entire game production cycle, with assets chosen from all major categories, so that accurate time and materials scheduling examples will result, along with the working prototype.

Prototype art assets normally include character models with animations, objects, environments, effects, and interface design. They may include examples of storytelling in the form of animatics (animated storyboards)—a full pre-rendered or real-time implemented cinematic. Through the process of creating these art assets, the art team formulates a production procedure and art deliverable schedule for the entire product, by simply multiplying the Prototype Phase art production timeline by the final number of art assets delineated in the Game Design document. Barring accidents and the inevitable snafus that occur during full production, the timeline defined during prototyping will act as a solid guide to project planners as they create the final production schedule.

The Concept and Prototype Phases of development normally yield the first working demo for the project and a formal presentation of the product and its potential with full documentation. This information is critical for selling the idea internally for a project go-ahead, or for actually selling the game to a potential publisher. Concept continues through much of the project cycle as the ideas are refined, but the preliminary Concept and Prototype Phases can take from two to six months, depending on the scope of a project and the level of tech development on the product at inception. Concept and prototype Artists will generate hundreds of assets during this time, most of which, while guiding the vision of the game, may well be left by the wayside as the project moves forward. Some of the assets, if managed correctly, will stand as the paradigm for all other assets as they are created.

Full Production Phase

After the documents, prototype, and deliverable schedule are approved, the team moves into the Full Production Phase of product development. The art team gets organized along deliverable types of assets and begins making the visual elements of the game. Before moving forward with the process, the team structure should be defined and personnel resources allocated. They are normally set up along the following lines, with many of the positions noted being filled simultaneously by the same Artist, such as a Lead Modeler for all models, rather than for characters only, and so on. Larger teams may very well have staff filling each of those noted:

- Art Direction/Art Lead

  –Concept Artists

  –Schedule oversight

  –Personnel Management

  –Coordination oversight

- Character Models/Textures/Animations

  –Lead Character Modeler/Modelers

  –Lead Character Texturer/Texturers

  –Lead Character Animator/Animators

- Object Models/Textures/Animations

  –Lead Object Modeler/Modelers

  –Lead Object Texturer/Texturers

  –Lead Object Animator/Animators

- Vehicles/Other Models/Textures/Animations

  –Lead Modeler/Modelers

  –Lead Texturer/Texturers

  –Lead Animator/Animators

- Effects Models/Textures/Animations

  –Lead Effects Modeler/Modelers

  –Lead Effects Texturer/Texturers

  –Lead Effects Animator/Animators

- Cinematics Models/Textures/Animations

  –Lead Cinematics Modeler/Modelers

  –Lead Cinematics Texturer/Texturers

   −Lead Cinematics Animator/Animators

   −Lead Compositor/Editor

 • Environment/Level Models/Textures/Animations

   −Lead Level Modeler/Modelers

   −Lead Level Texturer/Texturers

   −Lead Level Animator/Animators

 • Interface/GUI Design Models/Textures/Animations

   −Lead GUI Modeler/Modelers

   −Lead GUI Texturer/Texturers

   −Lead GUI Animator/Animators

A full production art team can number from a handful to a small army of full-time and part-time contract members during the complete project schedule. An average project has between 10 to 15 Artists working on it at all times, according to most game credits but many have expanded staff for pre-rendered cinematics and other special services.

To keep this analysis of the process simple, the type of tasks are broken down as follows:

 • Modeling

 • Texturing

 • Animating

 • Interface Design

In this way, the various skillsets are as unique categories, along with the type of assets generated that would require them. Rather than presenting each category with method tutorials, because superior versions can be found in many books, web sites, and magazine articles, this presents merely an overview of these tasks to make you familiar with how they work together to make the rich game worlds found in most games.

Modeling

Modelers in game development are charged with creating just about all of the tangible assets used in constructing the game world and all of the beings and elements within it, unless the technology is a sprite- (2D-) based system. Even so, the graphic aesthetic demands of the marketplace sees most game assets being modeled, even if the actual asset will be a 2D render of it in the final product.

Basing their work upon the initial concept drawings from the early stages of the project, Modelers create the 3D assets of the game: characters, weapons, items, objects, environments, landscapes, structures, and so on. They translate the initial 2D drawings into fully realized three-dimensional versions, closely following the style defined by the project art direction, and through the optimal method the tech allows. Modelers must coordinate with the texture and animation Artists to make sure that the geometry will accommodate their needs.

A modeling assignment may be the Lead character, an environmental object such as a statue or architectural structure, or the world landscape. The Artist who is assigned to this task must have the requisite skills with the modeling tools of choice to even begin to succeed at creating a viable art asset usable in the game. In many instances, the choice of tool is dependent upon the ease of use with the technology that makes up the game engine. Some technologies will accept models from only one 3D package upon export but may allow models to be completed in other packages, as long as they are exported from the acceptable tool and various tasks are completed in that tool, such as UV mapping, setting up the skeletal armature, and animating.

Although it is difficult to master all of the available 3D software packages, the general principles of modeling are the same, and the Artist should be well-versed in this general knowledge. If the particular package being used at a company where you want to work is known, proficiency in that toolset should be uppermost in your priority list.

Modelers of characters and objects will sometimes also be the Texturers, or at least apply the textures supplied by another Artist. They may also be the Animators assigned to these characters and objects. However, on larger teams, Modelers do the sculpture and other specialists create the textures and motions applied to the models. Models have tech limits and specifications that they must meet to be fully implemented within the game engine. Sometimes, this includes single skin structure, or it may allow for segmented elements. Morph objects may be allowed requiring certain vertex controls and management among the iterations of the models, polygon limits, and other special circumstances. If these guidelines and limitations are not considered and adhered to, the models may not function properly when brought into the game engine. It is extremely important that the geometry is tested and found acceptable before textures and animations are applied, otherwise a great deal of expense of time and money will be spent on needless retrofitting of geometry, retexturing, and in some cases, reanimating.

Modelers who build worlds (Level Builder/Level Artist) do not only create the geometry but also, in most cases, apply the textures supplied by other Artists or themselves and complete the environmental lighting and animated world effects within the level they have built. In some engines, these Modelers also set up general game play layouts within the level, working closely with Designers and Programmers. These Modelers must adhere closely to the game play design specs from the "bible," the game design document, as well as work within the tech limitations of the game engine as set out in the TDD. All engines have limitations, polygon counts, texture caches, animation node counts, number of characters and objects on screen, clipping distances, level of detail, and more. It is imperative that the art team and, specifically, the Level Builder Modeler, is fully aware of these limits and the targeted asset density expected in game play so that the world building process can be well managed and balanced, allowing for enough space to accept all other game assets, while meeting the design and aesthetic expectations as laid out in the game design document. This is true whether the levels are constructed with a proprietary or commercially available world editor.

All modeling assignments have a time frame attached to them, scaleable from several objects a day, up to a week for an average environmental character, a couple of weeks for a Lead character, and perhaps, a couple of months for a world level. The length of the overall schedule, when evaluated with budget and allowable staff, determines how many art assets can be generated for a particular project. The goal is to maximize content for the project, so every modeling assignment must adhere to these preset limitations while still fulfilling all game play functionality and aesthetic expectations.

The basic skillset of all Modelers includes excellent spatial relations and structural logic, a sense of the 3D world space, anatomy and proportion for creatures and other natural forms, a working knowledge of design and construction for architectural elements, including a solid grounding in art history, a good grasp of mechanical constructs for the physical puzzles and other environmental animations, and reasonable industrial design for "man-made" elements in the game world. Although the concept Designers must have a grasp of these elements when the preliminary design drawings are made, the Modelers must possess an equal understanding in order to build fully realized versions of the 2D concepts and be prepared, with inside knowledge, to adjust the initial concept logically to create the "real" 3D assets.

Texturing

Texture Artists focus on generating the 2D image maps that are applied to the 3D elements created by the Modelers, bringing the aesthetic elements to a visual completion from raw geometry. Many Texturers are also 3D Artists and actually apply the textures in the 3D packages on both models and environments. The texture style defined during the Concept and Prototype Phases of development drives the work of the Texturers.

The Texture Artists, working with the Art Director and Conceptual Artists, further refine the visual detail and palettes, as each tile set is completed. The technical limitations of game engines and various hardware platforms define the limits for texture size and quantity that will be able to pass through the processor while still maintaining adequate framerates supporting game play. The Texture Artist is challenged to fit the conceptual goal into the practical reality of the final texture specifications.

Hundreds of individual texture tiles and tile sets are created for every game project, taking several dedicated Artists months to complete. It is imperative that the overall aesthetic vision is maintained consistently through the resultant style of each Artist's output.

Animating

The animation process in game development can be broken out into distinct phases including armature setup and rigging, skinning and weighting, testing, and finally, animating. The individual tech process and production paradigm of a project will determine various limitations and caveats that the Animator must take into consideration at every step of development. For example, an engine may only take Forward Kinematic setups with minimal node counts, made up of Dummy objects rather than Inverse Kinematic (IK) bones. The Animator must be able to rig the character model accordingly and successfully animate the final model, when prepped. Likewise, another engine may only take a particular IK setup from a particular package, like Max or Maya. The Animator must ensure that the model is appropriately rigged and tested before taking the production time to animate the model.

FK VERSUS IK

Forward Kinematics (FK) is a mode of animating wherein the joints of a character's bone structure are simply linked and must be animated by each individual bone in sequence. As an example, for the character to move his arm from a hanging down position upwards in order to scratch his head, the animator must animate the shoulder, elbow, wrist, and fingers separately to complete the motion.

Inverse Kinematics (IK) is a programmatic setup that links the arm joints into a chain-like assembly, so that the animator can drag the finger and the rest of the arm joints will automatically move to the proper physical position to complete the move. In some systems, dummy objects are used as linkage points, or end effectors at the end of IK chain assemblies, but are not considered literal "bones" on a character; whereas in other systems, animators use armatures of these dummies instead of programmatic bones, because the requisite game engines may require an extremely conservative joint, or node, count for the character to operate properly.

These concepts, although basic to all CG animators, may be new to the reader, and we recommend further research in animation instructional books and web sites, such as New Rider's latest book releases on Animation and tutorials on the Gamasutra, Maya, and 3Dstudio Max training web sites noted in Appendix A, "Resources."

MOTION-CAPTURE, OR MO-CAP

If you care anything about games (and if you're reading this book, you probably do), you have probably seen some behind-the-scenes footage of, say, Tiger Woods or Michael Jordan being *mo-capped*. Motion capture is used to create game characters by capturing the motions of real people. Special markers are placed on the joints and key points of the real person, and these markers track the movements of the marked person to create 3D motion data.

After the armature is set and the model has been attached and properly weighted, several methods for actually animating the model may be utilized. First is straight-ahead keyframing, where the Artist makes each pose of a movement and sets sequential keyframes to generate the animation files. Second, a series of motion-captured movements can be applied directly to the model and cleaned up for the performance. Third, in either keyframed or applied mo-cap animations, the movements can be motion blended to create new animations

111

and new variations. This last method can also be used to create the movements of composite creatures and monsters, such as a centaur, combining the motions of a mo-cap horse with either the keyframed or mo-capped upper torso of a man. Because of the sheer volume of work required to keyframe individual performances, many product cycles are including more and more motion-capture animation to help speed production, and add to the realism of the title.

For most projects including animated characters, the performances are divided into separate files, each including a distinct move, or segment, of a composite move. The details of these breakdowns are normally driven by the engine technology and how it implements animations. The Animator must work closely with the Programmers to ensure that the files are prepared and exported properly. Each animation file might consist of less than 100 frames of an action and require hundreds of similar files to completely animate a character's performance for the game. Multiply it by the hundred, or so, unique characters in the average game production and each game project may have thousands of animations in the final product.

Animators also get involved with environmental objects and effects work, wherein a similar set of phases is applied to these specialized models for animating. This may also include particle effects for explosions and atmospherics, dynamic cloth and water effects, and other real physics animations if the technology supports them.

Besides the customary in-game motions and performances, Animators also get involved with story content cinematic sequences, either real-time, in engine, or pre-rendered, composited movies. These sequences follow storyboards from the Concept Phase, which further the game's story and character development and sometimes are drawn from the pre-existing game play animations, but many times necessitate unique animations to be generated specifically for the cinematics. These movies are used for several main purposes: basic story and game play setup information, character and story development, an enhanced visual payoff for the player when she has successfully passed some major hurdle in the game, and finally, enhancement of the overall production value of the project.

Animators must have an understanding of the traditional 2D cell animation techniques in order to further embellish their 3D performances, along with quite a bit of acting sensibilities to come up with the personality, mood, and attitude appropriate to the character being portrayed.

GUI—Interface Design

The menu system and other screens for interaction with the game, including the HUD (Heads Up Display), are generated by the Interface Designer who may be the Concept Artist, a Texture or Model Artist, or the Art Director. The HUD is the portion of the game screen utilized by the program to communicate situational data (score, tasks, and such) to the player. Normally, these screens are simple 2D overlays, but several different styles of implementation have been utilized in game products over the years, including fully 3D mini-levels built in the game engine.

The importance of the GUI (Graphical User Interface) is often understated, but this aspect of communicating with the player is another opportunity to enhance game play and the overall aesthetic of the project, if designed and implemented wisely.

The Interface Artist must work very closely with the Programmers implementing this aspect of the game to get the most bang for the buck and to make sure that the many elements of the game mechanics linked through the interface are adequately represented.

Art Integration—Putting All of the Art Assets Together

These are the major elements of game art production:

- Concepts
- Models, including characters, objects, and worlds
- Textures
- Animations
- Effects
- Cinematics
- Interface design

Integrating these elements to make up the full visual content of the game is an ongoing iterative process of importing, testing, revising, and editing. World levels are often revised as game play implementation is tested and refined. Character models go through similar stages of metamorphosis as the elements are brought together in engine and tested. After all assets have been placed within the game, there may be some surprises, such as texture limits exceeded, number of unique characters exceeded, and so on. In these cases, various optimization passes are attempted to either reduce the total number of assets in the game or some other edit is performed on the assets themselves, polygon reduction or a reduced number of animations, to bring them in line with tech limitations. Through optimization of game content, the development team is able to improve the performance of the project by making the game assets fit within the memory and processor specification limits on the target platform (PC, Console, and such).

This phase of development begins during the Prototype Phase in microcosm and is continued on the macro level for the balance of the production cycle. During integration, Designers, Programmers, Producers, clients, and marketing may have input, which redirects the art asset creation process, resulting in new elements being created or old ones being revised.

It is not unusual to revise throughout the product cycle, but Art Direction attempts to minimize this through careful review and implementation of the design specs in close communication with other team Leads and personnel, including the client, as each revision and retrofit costs additional time and

113

expense for the project. The Art Production Pipeline normally results in all art assets integrated into the product by the Alpha deadline, with only bug fixing and corrections being implemented during the Beta Phase, and all art fixes completed by the Beta deadline. However, many projects have art assets being finalized all the way until the Gold Master date, though this is not recommended.

PHASES OF TESTING

- **Alpha**. First phase of testing for the game. Usually done in-house.

- **Beta**. Second stage of testing. Typically done by "real world" users. You may have seen game developers looking for Beta testers. They want gamers to find out what is wrong with their game before bringing it to market.

- **Gold**. When you read that a game has "gone gold," this refers to the Gold Master CD from which the thousands of games are manufactured.

FROM THE EXPERT

"If an aspiring Artist wants to get his or her 3D education at a school, please get your traditional education down first. The 3D tools are very easy to learn compared to drawing, animation, and color skills. Once you start without the basics, you may get a job and at that point it will be very difficult to go back and get the education you should have had. The net effect of such a scenario is that you significantly limit your potential."

- Andrew Paquette, Former Director of Art , Sony Pictures Imageworks

HOW TO GET THERE

Now that you know exactly what you want to be and how to achieve the goal mechanically, you're ready to create the five-in-a-thousand reel that will get you the job you want. It's possible you'll get the job even if your demo isn't perfect, but there are definitely some fundamentals you should keep floating about your head as you create and refine your images.

Education

First, to be able to create that righteous demo and become a successful Game Artist, do you need a special game degree?

In general, traditional art schools and university art programs provide the game industry with talent on the art/aesthetic side. These talented people then need training in particular methods and software packages used in game production. Recently, however, additions have been made to the curriculum in several art schools, such as the BA program in Game Art and Design at The Art Institutes International at San Francisco. Also, there are a few schools such as Ringling, in Florida, that have developed candidates better prepared to take on full Artists tasks straight out of school.

The Skills You'll Need

With the art team job descriptions, a general tools overview, and a greater understanding of the entire art production process now in your pocket, a clearer picture of where you want to start contributing to this creative effort should be in your mind. Do you want to be a conceptualizing Artist? Or would you prefer to create models and textures? Or are you an Animator? Perhaps you want to drive the whole process. Well, first things first.

In addition to the following information, you should read, or re-read, the earlier section regarding the ideal qualities for programmers in Chapter 5 "Programmers," as several comments about follow-through, communications, and responsibility are most appropriate to all team members embarking together to create a Game Production.

Aspects of the ideal Game Artist, no matter what your chosen specialty, are covered in the following sections.

A Team Player

Every game production cycle is successful because of the combined efforts of the entire production team—that is, the coordination and cooperation of Designers, Programmers, and Artists. Every Artist *must* have this fact uppermost in her mind. Although individual egos cannot be fully negated—nor should they be because they lend personal pride in your own work—the group is only fully successful when everyone connects with the *team ego* and success as the top priority, even above the individual team member's feelings and ego. This attitude supports consistent cooperation among all team members resulting in higher quality and quantity output from all production cycles.

Polished Art Skills

Every Artist should have basic, traditional art skills. The ideal Artist will have taken the extra time to polish these basics so that they are, by second nature, the highest professional quality possible. All other success is founded on these prerequisite abilities as an Artist and visualizer. Solid drawing, painting, and sculpture skills; good color and compositional abilities; and a knowledgeable grounding in art history for style and cultural trends should be every Artist's mantra.

A Positive Force

Self-motivation is the prime energy source for all great game development teams. It enables the team to move the project forward faster and, more accurately, and allows the team to focus on pushing the envelope on the project. With encouragement and enthusiasm, the team contributes more than the anticipated assets and game play due to the added efficiency of a team plugged into each other at all times. This not only motivates you, but it also causes everyone to rise to the occasion and do their best work.

Adapt and Succeed

When it seems like the only answer to a problem is not the one you want to hear, don't stop moving forward. The best teams, when faced with seemingly insurmountable obstacles, continue to refine and adapt their production process to incorporate new directions into the path towards success. It is this stress and potential chaos that has fostered some of the most exciting, elegant solutions that have driven the game industry thus far. Never get discouraged; be challenged by adversity.

Open to Enlightenment

Everyone has his own skills, ideas, and knowledge that he brings to the team. Unless you are a savant, most, if not all, of that knowledge came to you from someone else. From a class lecture, a book, an article, a colleague, all knowledge starts somewhere else. Don't hoard what you know. Share it as freely as the one

FROM THE EXPERT

"After turning down a full, 5-year scholarship from Carnegie-Mellon's School of Architecture, I spent a year at the Pennsylvania Academy of Fine Arts before going to the University of Pennsylvania for a Bioengineering program, with an English/Art History dual-degree end result. Sometimes a varied background of education will still get you to your goal!"

- Matt Scibilia, Founder and Art Director, BigSky Interactive, Inc.

who gave it to you. Likewise, accept knowledge from other teammates graciously. Listen, if you want to be heard. Such a positive dynamic not only is more efficient and honest for team communication, but it actually feels better.

Endurance

The game development process is exhausting. You should be prepared for the realities of production—delays, reworks, tech problems, design flaws, deadlines, lack of resources, more retrofits, broken something or other…you name it. But, not one of these realities is a valid excuse for missing the final deadline. You have to endure and hold yourself to a higher standard of performance to overcome the inevitable chaos that ensues during almost every production cycle.

After you are confident that you have the above-named traits, you should evaluate your current abilities and decide what career path is most acceptable to you and begin training for success to meet that goal. For example, if you have always wanted to create the best character models, study anatomy and sculpture, along with Maya, Max, or some other modeling program. Observe projects from other development companies and study the solutions they came up with to create the character models; read production notes and post-mortems, describing problems their team encountered so that you can work around them. Build upon the proven success of finished titles, so that your methods and results will have that much more likelihood of generating a superior version.

Define a Career Goal and Prepare Yourself

With a detailed knowledge of how the "machine" works, you will be able to define your desired career path, judge what skills are needed to successfully attain the starting position, then train and polish these abilities before attempting to enter the job market. This is a highly competitive industry. To succeed, you must understand the production process, define your target level of proficiency and expertise, and hone your abilities before presenting them to the decision makers. Be completely honest with self-critiques as you compare your current, proven art abilities to examples from professionals in the industry, as seen on company web sites and in the games themselves. This is your competition, and the closer your current work quality, and output rate quantity, can come in line with your competition, the more likely that will lead to your dream position.

Marketing Your Talent to the World

Armed with the right knowledge and refined skills, you now face the daunting task of presenting them to prospective employers with the highest potential for success. The tools of marketing to the industry include demo reels, resume/brochures, CDs, and web sites. After all your research and training, this stage is extremely critical. The marketing presentation is the first, and potentially only, time you will have to pique the interest of the prospective employer and garner a face-to-face interview if not the position itself.

To set up for success, this stage of career development must have as high a priority as your art training, with as much attention to detail and honesty in self-critique:

- Will the work represented in the presentation reveal the best overview of your abilities?

- Will the presentation hold the viewer's interest?

- Is it too long? Is it too short?

- Are the abilities represented on a level of quality expected by the viewer?

- Are the abilities represented in line with the art positions to be filled by the viewer?

Landing a Job and What Happens Next

The game industry is an exciting, fulfilling, frustrating, exhausting, and enlightening environment that has endured through the energy and abilities of the teams that make the games and the players who buy them. As newer technologies have been developed over time, the quality and quantity of game art assets have increased exponentially. Although the market demand for extremely great looking games has increased, making it possible for many more Artists to be employed by the industry, you still have an obligation to coordinate with Programmers and Designers to not only deliver excellent art assets, but to continue to push for excellent game play, which is the foundation for the further success of this business.

CHAPTER 7

Producers

What is a producer?

pro-du-cer *n.* 2. One who finances and supervises the production of a play or other public entertainment. 3. A furnace that manufactures producer gas. (*The American Heritage Dictionary*)

pro-du-cer *n.* Often this is someone from a game's publisher who will be the liaison between the publisher and the game development team. It is really crucial that this person knows how to communicate between both teams as otherwise a lot of problems can arise. Sometimes this is the title of someone in the game development company who is working as the project lead. (*GameDictionary.com*)

If you want to learn about furnaces producing producer gas, this is not the section for you. However, if you want to learn the basics of being a Game Producer, read on.

Producer careers range from the entry-level Assistant Producer position to Executive Producer. The following is a sampling of recent Producer job openings from GameRecruiter.com: Producer, Producer/Director, Associate Producer/Localization Manager, Senior Producer, Executive Producer, Online Producer/Webmaster, Development Director (Executive Producer), Producer (External), and Producer (Internal).

Read this description for a Producer job with a prominent California game company:

> Responsible for planning, scheduling, and directing the timely creation of projects from inception to final submissions. Ensures that various project specifications and milestones are met. Supervises the production staff (internal and external). Serves as the primary contact during the product development stages from inception to approved TDD with external developers. Responsible for all phases of the product development cycle including programming, graphics, continuity, music, quality assurance, documentation and packaging. Responsible for product concept submissions and all associated approvals. Excellent written and verbal communication skills. Ability to communicate effectively with developers and within the organization. Strong time management skills with a proven ability to focus on priorities, solve problems, handle multiple tasks, and meet deadlines. Proficient use of PC and all console-based platforms. Working knowledge of MS Office. Minimum of 5 years of production experience. Must have 3-5 years of experience in software product management.

JOB TITLES AND FOCUS

Although Producer positions can become more specific and include titles such as Project Manager, Senior Producer, Line Producer, and Lead Producer, the following are the primary titles.

Executive Producer

The primary function of the Executive Producer is to ensure the general efficiency and smooth management of all projects and take ultimate responsibility for their successful completion. The Executive Producer oversees other Producers, consulting with them on evaluation of production risks and anticipation of potential problems. This person also works with the other Producers and Leads to resolve project conflicts, as well as participate in client communications. Along with negotiating new products and reviewing existing ones, the Executive Producer also obtains funding and provides direction for new projects and consults with console manufacturers regarding updates, training seminars, and the submission process. And even though this is the top of the Producer totem pole, the Executive Producer must also have the ability to maintain project-related documents, schedules, lists, and more using commercial software such as Microsoft Office or FileMaker Pro.

TIP

Management is an exhaustively studied topic and this book is only one example. To learn more about the "Art of Management," you should consistently read, listen to tapes, and watch videos. As you develop your management skills, you will advance in your career. Unfortunately, only a small percentage of the workforce actively takes the initiative for personal and professional growth.

EXECUTIVE PRODUCER

The primary function of the Executive Producer is to ensure the general efficiency and smooth management of all projects.

RESPONSIBILITIES

PRODUCTION MANAGEMENT

– Oversee Producers.

– Regularly consult and work with Producers to evaluate production risks and anticipate potential problems.

– Work with Producers and Leads to resolve project conflicts.

– Be involved in client communications.

PROPOSAL AND PROTOTYPE MANAGEMENT

– Negotiate new and review existing contracts for product development, game services, and so on.

– Obtain funding and provide direction for new projects.

– Collaborate with involved employees to define the scope, perform initial risk management, and help establish the prototype plan for new projects.

– Function as the Producer for research and development (R&D) demos and prototypes.

PROJECT SUPPORT

– Consult with console manufacturers regarding updates, training seminars, and submission processes.

– Provide mentorship and training opportunities for Producers and Associate Producers.

– Prepare and present reviews of Producers.

– Attend regular Project Lead's meetings.

SKILLS

– Thorough and accurate management and communication

– Problem solving

– Ability to maintain project-related documents, schedules, lists, and so on, using commercial software (for example, Microsoft Office and FileMaker Pro)

REQUIREMENTS

– Minimum of 5 years managing a large team composed of members from diverse disciplines

– Professional experience working in the game industry, including contributions to 5+ shipped titles

– Experience communicating with external clients

RELATIONSHIPS

Reports to: CEO

Manages: Producers, Lead Programmer and, depending on structure of company, Game Designers

Producer

The primary function of the Producer is to manage projects, ensuring that the goals for the project—quality, timeliness, budget, and so on—are met. The Producer reports to the Executive Producer and manages the Leads of assigned projects. Establishing the policies, goals, and values of the development team and ensuring the entire team knows its highest priorities and due dates are key responsibilities. The Producer must also make certain all contractual requirements are met in each milestone delivered to the client, as well as validate and authorize milestone payments to third parties and contractors. And, like the Executive Producer above him, the Producer must also be proficient with commercial project-management software.

External Producer

External Producers work with the third-party developer/studio, making sure the project on track and on schedule. They also have budget responsibilities in addition to engaging in contract negotiations and licensing agreements.

Internal Producer

Internal Producers manage in-house staff, working more hands-on with the Artists and Designers to maintain the creative vision of the product while keeping the project on schedule.

PRODUCER

RESPONSIBILITIES

- Ensure that the goals of the project—quality, timeliness, budget, and so on—are met.
- Establish the policies, goals, and values of the development team.
- Ensure that the entire team knows and focuses its highest priorities and due dates.
- Ensure that all contractual requirements are met in each milestone delivered to the client.
- Validate and authorize milestone payments to third parties, contractors, and service providers (for example, music, motion-capture, and so on).
- Effectively use all resources for production and testing.
- Maintain forecasts of the project's budget; anticipate, identify, and resolve overruns.
- Constantly evaluate and create contingency plans to deal with risks and potential obstacles.
- Interact with clients, as appropriate.
- Provide status reports about each project to upper management and manage their expectations and concerns.
- Identify and track the responsibilities and dependencies of clients.
- Manage potential conflicts between internal and external expectations for the project.

- Oversee the creation and maintenance of all project-related documentation: milestones, schedules, contracts, design documents, specifications, and so on.
- Work with the team and Technical Writer to develop project specifications that define the scope of the project, requirements of the prototype, and deliverables of milestones.

STAFF SUPPORT

- Assist and counsel marginal performers according to Human Resource policies.
- Complete the performance reviews of team members on time.
- Help settle project-related conflicts and disputes.
- Ensure that the team's work environment is healthy and facilitates productivity.

SKILLS

- Thorough and accurate management and communication
- Problem solving
- Ability to maintain project-related documents, schedules, lists, and so on, using commercial software (for example, Microsoft Office and FileMaker Pro)

REQUIREMENTS

- Minimum of 3+ years managing a large team composed of members from diverse disciplines
- Professional experience working in the game industry
- Experience communicating with external clients

RELATIONSHIPS

Reports to: Executive Producer

Manages: Leads of assigned projects

Associate Producer

The primary function of the Associate Producer is to document, track, test, bug hunt, and research for the production team. Indicative of the title, the Associate Producer assists the Producer in day-to-day maintenance, organization, and management of the project with tasks such as helping maintain the task and bug databases. The Associate Producer oversees the Game Testers, but also burns CDs as necessary, makes client deliveries, takes meeting notes, distributes meeting notes, picks up lunch, as well as performs, supervises, and documents the testing and analysis of the game. Other responsibilities consist of writing test plans, including milestone acceptances, play tests, and focus tests, as well as researching and analyzing competitive products, and inputting findings in the appropriate database.

ASSOCIATE PRODUCER

RESPONSIBILITIES

PRODUCTION ASSISTANCE

- Assist the Producer in day-to-day maintenance, organization, and management of the project (for example, help maintain the task and bug databases and so on).
- Maintain daily builds; ensure that artists have good builds with which to test assets.
- Burn CDs as needed.
- Provide deliveries to and from the client, as needed.
- Take meeting notes and distribute them within one day of meetings.
- Assist with setting up and tracking equipment for the project.
- Run errands for the project (for example, order and pick up meals), as needed.
- Assist in organizing events (for example, parties) for the team.

PRODUCT TESTING

- Perform, supervise, and document the testing and analysis of the game, including verification of all testables in commits and otherwise.
- Assist the QA Lead Tester with writing QA test plans, including milestone acceptances, play tests, and focus tests.

RESEARCH

- Research and analyze competitive products, input findings into the appropriate database, and keep the team informed of key discoveries.
- Assist in locating and organizing reference materials for the team.

SKILLS

- Ability to maintain project-related documents, schedules, lists, and so on, using commercial software (for example, Microsoft Office and FileMaker Pro)
- Organization and communication
- Detail orientated

REQUIREMENTS

Interest in and general knowledge of video games

RELATIONSHIPS

Reports to: Producer

Supervises: Game Testers

Supervised by: Executive Producer or Lead Game Designer

TOOLS AND SKILLS YOU'LL NEED

Were you the kid in school who actually utilized the organization features of your Mead Trapper Keeper? Are you the one who plans, schedules, and directs weekend game tournaments for your friends? Although the rest of the world may, on occasion, get slightly annoyed by your Julie McCoy-your-cruise-director attitude, it's those very traits that could make you a premier Game Producer.

Virtually every job listing for Game Producer requires the following attributes:

- Great scheduling ability

- Exceptional organizational skills

- Excellent leadership consensus building abilities

- Skilled at conflict resolution and consensus building

- Ability to direct development of a project from start to finish while meeting deadlines

More tangible tools include a working knowledge of office software such as MS Office, as well as familiarity with the latest game systems. And, generally speaking, you should be an avid gamer.

Further, if part of your job is to review Technical Design Document (TDD) schedule and design and direct revisions as needed, make sure you understand the fundamentals behind a TDD. Simply put, a TDD specifies all the programming steps which must occur in order to develop the game.

The "Double Check" Technique

The United States and its Constitution are based upon it and most of the world's accounting systems use it, so perhaps you should consider it. I'm talking about checks and balances—the basis of double entry bookkeeping. The way a producer can employ and leverage this powerful principle is as follows:

> Double-check all of your important work. And in very rare circumstances, triple-check it. This means, go over the results of your work a second time. Read it again, analyze it some more, rethink it, count it again, edit it…what have you. This does *not* mean you have to waste a lot of time checking it multiple times. The idea is to check your work exactly two times—do the work first and then review it all again.

To illustrate, let's say you are a meticulous, efficient Producer. But because you are a human, you will sometimes make mistakes. Let's say you do any given task correctly 90 percent of the time and make errors the other 10 percent of the time. By double-checking your work one extra time, 90 percent of the time, you are going to catch 9 out of 10 of any of those errors. So by just checking your work a second time, you've gone from getting it right 90 percent of the time to 99 percent of the time! Now that's an excellent return on your investment in time. It's generally not worth the effort to spend a lot more time reviewing your work, with the hope of catching just the extra 1 percent of errors. Unless, of course, what you are working on is extremely critical. In that case, with a third review, it's possible to reduce your likelihood of errors to just one tenth of 1 percent! So remember to use this tool often and get in the habit of double-checking your work. It is especially productive to use it to review things you have written down, like reports, emails, employee reviews, and other important writing.

The Triangle of Game Development Factors

When you make a game, there are three factors you have available to work with and must frequently balance: time, money, and quality. These three factors are closely interrelated—given more time, the quality and cost usually will increase, and so on. The problem is oftentimes there will be unreasonable expectations; there will be an expectation that you must make an awesome game on a shoestring budget, to be delivered in a few months!!

One of *the* most important tasks of a Producer is to identify the true order of priorities for each project, given the realities of the current circumstances, and emerge victorious by delivering very accurately on your first priority, while striving to come close to delivering on the other two. The ideal situation is when only *one* of these factors is fixed and you are given reasonable latitude with the other two. You should strongly avoid getting into a situation where all three have been defined by someone else. Don't play that game; you're likely to lose. So, if quality is job number one, you should be sure to get ample money and time. Similarly, if being on time is of paramount importance, you should seek to get plenty of resources and also significantly reduce management's expectations of the game's quality.

Time

Time is a very valuable resource, arguably the *most* precious. There are many kinds of time: the time to get your product to the market before your competitor, the time your boss says to get it done by, the time your boss's boss says to get it done by, and so on. No one on this planet can sell you even one second of time, for any amount of money. The other two factors will often be subject to interpretation, but time is not. An exact date is that exact date, easily measured, and successful completion on time is easy to judge.

DELIVERING GAMES ON TIME

If you want to know very precise information about a particular particle (its position and velocity, as per Quantum Physics), you will have to take the particle out of the realm of mathematical probabilities and into our reality, by observing (*measuring*) it. But as per The Uncertainty Principle, the very act of measuring a particle effects and alters *both* the particle *and* the measurer. As a result, this principle effectively says you cannot simultaneously and accurately know both. The more accurately you measure the position, the less you can be sure about its momentum, and *vice versa*.

Believe it or not, making a game with time as the number one priority is a very similar (and difficult) undertaking. Making a *great* game is part science (easy to quantify and measure) and part art (*not* easy to quantify or measure). So, delivering a great game, on time and on budget, is a minor miracle! On the one hand, you have to measure results reasonably enough to know what's going on and where you are. On the other hand, you cannot go overboard with measurements and metrics, or you end up interfering with the process or making erroneous decisions based upon spurious or misleading data.

Harnessing the power of time requires a great deal of precision, finesse, and hard work. First and foremost, if you want to know if your game is on time, you have to make reasonable measurements of your progress. And in the subjective world of games business, that's not easy. A feature or program that *looks* like it's done during a demo or even in a Beta state can yet have serious bugs hidden in the 90 percent that's below the surface of an iceberg. The second most difficult task is *predicting* or estimating time for some specific task, in the future, especially on long-term games that can take two or even three years to develop.

It is very difficult to accurately forecast a year or two into the future. Conversely, it is so much easier to forecast a task that lasts a few days or a week. The maxim to use here is "take care of the pennies and the dollars will take care of themselves." Divide and subdivide again all tasks into small, manageable chunks of time. If all of your daily tasks get done on time, you are sure to be on time each week. If you are on time each and every week, you are very likely to be on time each month, and if you take care of the months, the years will take care of themselves. Rarely give much credence to task estimates that are more than one week in duration. One week is a good benchmark: Work diligently to be on time *every* week, and if you are, it will be much easier to deliver the project on time many months and years into the future.

Money

Ironically, this is the *least* precious and easiest to get resource of the three. Usually, there is some way in the world to find just a few more dollars or resources for your project, and if you deliver a *great* (Quality) game *on time* (Time), your sin of being over budget will be soon forgiven. But obviously, there are times, in some companies, when it would be a disaster to be significantly over budget. Of course, if you have significant shortcoming in key resources, it may be difficult or even impossible to deliver.

Quality

The most *popular* factor. This is what everyone is seeking—The Holy Grail. Everyone wants Quality and they spend a lot of Time seeking to create it in order to make a lot of Money. In businesses in general, "Sales cures all evils," and in the gaming business, Quality *usually* cures all evils. If you create an awesome game, failing to deliver on the other two factors is not often an issue. But on the other hand, there have been numerous instances in the games industry where a really great game was created but did not succeed; because it cost so much money that it bankrupted the company (lost out on the Money issue) or it came out so very late (lost out on the Time factors) that it no longer was viable, and so on. So it's fair to say, if you asked most people in the games industry, the ideal situation is when you can deliver an awesome game on time and on budget, prioritized in that order.

FROM THE EXPERT

"With regard to software, a good start is Excel. Then, when you find yourself doing a great job with your tasks, all the while making neat little color-coded columns and excellent macros, and too many columns to fit on a page, then it's time to move on to MS Project. Simultaneous to this, get familiar with MS Developers Kit. Find out what your artists are working with and get comfortable with it (3D Studio Max, Adobe, etc.). Then, find out the current coding software being used and acquire enough proficiency in it so that when the time comes, you can help tow the line to Alpha.

- Randy Beverly, Vice President, Digital Dimensions

Tools of the Trade: A Simple and Effective Project Tracking Worksheet

For tracking progress of many small and medium sized projects that take less than a year or so, it's probably overkill, and overly complicated, to use heavy-duty project management programs like Microsoft Project. The investment in time needed to learn it and keep the tracking sheet up-to-date may not be worth the effort. For these kinds of projects, a simple Microsoft Excel spreadsheet is more than sufficient.

Here are some tips for using the Project Tracking Worksheet:

- **Dates.** For calculating dates, be sure to use the WORKDAY spreadsheet function (look up the Excel Help topic). This function calculates dates by ignoring Saturday and Sunday. You should almost always calculate your dates ignoring the weekends and use the weekends as padding, in case you get behind. Be sure to list each person's task, in the order in which she is to perform her tasks. Then (except for the date of the initial task for each person), use a formula to have Excel calculate all other dates. If you make a change to one date, all the other dates will also change automatically. Finally, as mentioned earlier, wherever possible, keep each task to five days (one work week) or less. If a task will take longer, break it down into sub-tasks and track them separately.

- **Sorting**. Each time you put in changes or additions, do it in the first Section ("Tasks (sorted by Name)"). Then, when you are all done with your current changes, simply copy all the rows in that section to the next Section ("Tasks (sorted by Due Date)") and then sort those rows by the due date column, in ascending order. This should only take a few seconds and now you have two ways of looking at the same data—all the tasks due by each responsible person, as well as all the tasks listed in the Due Date order.

- **Functions**. Modify the spreadsheet to satisfy your particular requirements. For example, you could add a Function column to indicate if the task is a Programming or Art or Design task, and so on. Also, you could write a simple formula to automatically highlight all tasks that are past due (relative to TODAY()).

- **Risk Factor**. There are many simple and complicated ways to assess and implement risk. This example uses a simple but effective technique. Each task is assigned a Risk Factor Number from 1 to 4. This number is used as a multiplier to adjust the task's time estimate (rounded up) and thus to calculate a risk-adjusted due date. A 1 is unadjusted, 2 is adjusted by +50 percent, 3 by +100 percent, and a 4 risk factor is adjusted by +200 percent. Obviously, you can change these multiplier effects to suit your own assessments.

  1. This is a very low risk task. It's something you feel confidently will be done properly, because this type of task been done by that person many times in the past.

2. This is slightly more risky. Your company has done this type of task before, but not by the person who currently has to implement it. That person should be able to implement it without too much difficulty, perhaps with some consultation with other people in the company who know this type of task very well.

3. Much more risky. No one in your company has ever accomplished such a task before. There will be a substantial amount of research and trial-and-error needed in order to accomplish this task.

4. The most risky task of all. No one in the entire industry has ever done anything like this before! You are trail blazing into uncharted territory. Good Luck! There will be lots of research, trial-and-lots-of-errors, and so on. Obviously, you must have *some* confidence your team can do this task; otherwise, it should not even be on your official task list.

- **Circulate**. To maximize the effectiveness of such task tracking, be sure to circulate the spreadsheet to all key members of the development team. That way, every person on the team knows precisely what their tasks are and when they are due. This is also very helpful when one person is dependant on another person's task. And last but not least, peer pressure is a very effective tool, so use it! Every person on the team will know that every other person on the team is looking at his progress. You can use the Comments column as a polite tool to inform team members when certain tasks are getting behind, compliment someone on a task, and so on.

- **Accountability**. Although it is certainly more efficient to update the status of each task by going to each person one by one and checking up on their work, a more profitable method is to do the status updating during team meetings (usually conducted once a week or so). You may want to update some of the simpler and more mundane tasks offline, but bring up the important tasks *during* the team meetings. This makes the responsible person openly accountable to the entire team for the completion of her tasks. In addition, it highlights any team member interdependencies, and most importantly, prevents a team member from "bluffing" about the state of completion of a task. For example, if Jim says he has completely finished coding a certain task, another person may chime in to correct him and point out that, in fact, certain key features are not yet implemented. Go through the task list openly during regular team meetings, and even though it may not be as productive time-wise, you will reap many other valuable benefits.

- **Maintenance**. As you make progress on your project, obviously, tasks will get done. You can either delete those rows as they are done (simplify and unclutter the task list) or leave them in and indicate *clearly* that they are done—for example, by crossing them out. Just be sure it is not confusing. It's usually a good morale booster to leave in a completed Task for one week, with a "Done" indicator somewhere, and then take it out after one week. Finally, as a bonus, during project post-mortem, you could go through all the old task list worksheets and review how accurate your time and risk assessments were and so on. Such a task list worksheet is a gold mine for data mining purposes.

Demonstrating Your Abilities

For the Game Producer, a well-organized résumé is a must. If you can't organize a simple résumé, how could you possibly organize the production of a game? Also, because meeting deadlines and attention to detail is key to your position, if you get the interview, make sure you're on time, bring another résumé with you (along with a complete title list), and be organized!

As part of your preparations for the all-important interviews (by phone or in person), it's very important to anticipate and rehearse the entire interview process. You should anticipate an initial phone interview, followed by one or more personal interviews. Prepare for these interviews by thinking up common questions you are likely to be asked and then writing up great responses. In addition, you should also prepare questions to ask during the interview for each specific employer. The exact questions you ask will not only provide you with the answers you seek, but the very nature and thrust of your questions should in themselves create a positive impression with the interviewer. And, if you have prepared some excellent questions and answers and the interviewer does not ask you those questions, you should seek opportunities to credibly segue their questions into the responses you've prepared. Remember: The better prepared you are, the more likely you are of being relaxed, self-assured, and not being caught off-guard during the interview process, which can greatly help to create a positive impression.

The following are some examples of common questions/requests you might anticipate:

- Please elaborate on your management style.

- How do you motivate yourself and your employees?

- Why do you want to work here? What are your opinions so far of our company?

- What kind of games do you like and play? What kind of games do you want to make?

- What are the components of a great game? How do you create a great game?

- Tell me a little bit about yourself (a very common request).

- Where do you think our industry is headed? What are the significant new trends you see emerging in this industry in the near future?

- What are your key strengths and your key weaknesses?

Here are some examples of questions you might consider asking the interviewer:

- What kind of person and skills are you seeking for this position? (Ask this question early in the interview. Then, throughout the interview, be sure to highlight your applicable skills.)

- What kinds of opportunities for learning and growing are there in this company?

- What are your company's three most important priorities currently?

- What do you think are the top two or three challenges your company faces in the future?

- What do you feel are your company's top strengths? And weaknesses? (Remember, you should be interviewing them, just as much as they are interviewing you.)

- What's your timeframe for making a decision on this position? (Ask this towards the very end of the interview.)

- How have I done during this interview? Your feedback would be greatly appreciated. (Believe it or not, this is an excellent closing question to ask at the very end of your interview. If you have done well, you will get the interviewer to review all your good points again in his mind, reinforcing his positive impressions of you. And, if you've done poorly, gather his feedback so you can later reflect, learn, and thus improve on your interviewing skills.)

Finance

Finance and accounting is the language of senior management. Even if your job is not primarily finance oriented, if you are leading a team, it is essential to understand the basics of finance and accounting. Operating budgets and project analysis are a constant part of any supervisor or manager's day. *Finance & Accounting For Nonfinancial Managers,* (Prentice Hall, 2002) by Steven A. Finkler, will help you get a basic handle on these concepts. The results will be greater power, reach, and influence on your part within your company.

THE ABCS OF RUNNING A DEVELOPMENT PROJECT

If you want to be a Game Producer, you need to understand the job fundamentals. From the initial game concept and "selling" the idea to management to the boxed game rolling off the assembly line, the Producer is part of just about every aspect in the development of the game. Don't panic at the detail in the following; this is just to familiarize you with what you'll tackle in your professional life.

The Concept and Selling It to Management

It is important that your project begin with a solid foundation. In the case of a creative effort such as a development project, a solid foundation is the essential heart-felt vision or high concept that will serve as the "spirit" of the project. This vision will be the driving, motivating force that will spur you and your team on

> ### TIP
>
> Project Management is also part of every Producer or Team Lead type job. You need to learn the basics of Gantt or PERT charting and project organization. You need to know how to "think" like a manager to meet the challenges you will face when you *are* in charge of any size group of people. The most common situation within a game company is that you find Managers, Producers, and Team Leads working on multiple projects simultaneously. *The Jugglers Guide to Managing Multiple Projects* (Project Management Institute, 1999) by Michael Dobson is a helpful tool for honing your skills in this area.

to its manifestation through the sleepless nights and the real-world constraints. When Alan Ball, Hollywood Screenwriter, pitched three projects to his agent, his agent could tell the one project that Alan was most passionate about and suggested that he pursue it further was *American Beauty*. Any great work, anything worth doing, especially a project that will consume perhaps two years or more of your life, must begin with this spirit.

As a Producer, your initial job is twofold:

- **Step 1.** Conceptualize, or otherwise recognize, a concept that you believe in.

- **Step 2.** Sell the idea as a sound business opportunity to the executive staff at your company.

Undoubtedly, you will be asked to present your concept as a business opportunity to management. This may be necessary, for example, to secure funding for prototype development of the concept. Consider preparing the following materials for your presentation (each will be covered in the following sections):

- Concept paper

- Sample artwork

- Executive summary

Concept Paper

The concept paper acts much like a résumé as it serves to briefly identify the high points of the concept. It is also the important first impression that many will have about the concept. Start by creating a memorable working title by which to refer to and then note the genre, hardware platform, and target demographic. Provide a one-line visual description of the product. (Marketing people will appreciate this.) This could be something simple like, "This game is *SimCity* meets *Quake*." Then, elaborate some on the concept in the body of the paper. The personality of the game and characters should be defined, as should the general macro design (for example, number of worlds and levels). An example of play control is useful to give the reader an idea about the interactivity of the game. Defining the art and music style with reference to other games is also beneficial.

Here is an example:

Big Time Rodeo

Concept Paper

Genre: Arcade Sports

Platform: PlayStation 2

Target demographic: Male/Female 12 – 24

High Concept: The sport of Rodeo meets Nintendo's *Punch Out*

You are rugged cowboy Jack West or cowgirl Amber Gayle competing against a host of eight other cowboys and cowgirls vying for the Rodeo National Championship.

The goal is for Jack/Amber to work his/her way through the Rookie, Semi-Pro, and Professional circuits. There are five competitions in each circuit. Each competition features four of eight rodeo events, including bull riding, barrel racing, and calf roping.

Human opponents, bulls, and broncos will all have personalities of their own. In bull riding, you will start by riding relatively tame bulls with meek personalities in the Rookie circuit and evolve to take on Black Bart, the meanest bull of them all, in the Pro circuit.

Play control is unique and requires dexterity and learned skill to be successful. For example, when a bull bucks, the player must push down (back) on the controller to counter and stay on the bull.

Art style is cartoon, much like *Punch Out* or *Hot Shots Golf,* in attempt to lighten the mood of the game and establish it as an arcade game.

Music is up-tempo, sing-along, Western, a bit goofy perhaps.

Sample Artwork

Given the visual nature of "video" games, it will be invaluable to include sample artwork with your concept paper. In the case of *Big Time Rodeo*, still sketches of Jack and Amber, Black Bart, and perhaps a mock screen shot of Jack aboard Black Bart will help to convey the style of the characters and the arcade/cartoon nature of the game.

Executive Summary

This document should convey an overview of the business points of the deal. This should include the name of the developer; the development costs and royalty rates; marketing commitments; the anticipated Gold Master date; the results of an ROI (return on investment) analysis that notes the breakeven point and potential profits for moderate, good, and great sales; and data on competitive titles. Though beyond the scope of this article, you may want to include the actual calculation of the ROI that accounts for development costs, marketing costs, costs of goods, overhead, and so on for support. Consider including sales data for competitive products, such as that provided by the NPD group, to show the marketability of a successful game in the genre.

Here is an example:

Big Time Rodeo

Executive Summary

Developer: BestDigital

Deal Points:

- $200,000 prototype fee advance against $5 royalty for 3-month effort

- Additional $1.5 million advance against $5 royalty per unit for full development assuming $32 wholesale

- Marketing guarantee of $500,000

- Gold Master target: September 15, 2003

ROI:

75,600 units breakeven

100,000 units + $250,000

250,000 units + $1,750,000

500,000 units + $4,000,000

Competitive Analysis:

- Direct: None

- Indirect: Rumor that Company X is making a 3D Wild West adventure title

- Sales data: Bronco Bust Up 431,230 units Company Y PS2

The Development Company and Team

Whether you are looking for a team to develop your concept, or a team has come to you with an intriguing idea, it is essential that the developer and team are thoroughly evaluated. Think of this as an interview. The company and team are, of course, just as important as the vision—they will bring the vision to life. Find out how the developer is financed. Is it going to be living paycheck to paycheck, or does it have some reserve cash? This will be important when considering milestone descriptions and the accompanying payment schedule for the developer. It is also important to spend quality time with the team and individual members of the team. Know each member's strengths and weaknesses. What drives them? How do they work together? In getting to know the team, you can assess potential risks for the project. See that the team is passionate about the vision and has the skills to execute it. Technical considerations are significant as well. Will the team be able to use an existing engine to develop the game? Does it have adequate tools?

A key at this point is to define the roles for the team, including that of you, the Producer. Good communication is more than essential. Each member of the team should have a clear understanding of who is responsible for each task on the project and who has authority in a time that a tough decision needs to be made. Discussing this up front and having this understanding will help to prevent conflicts throughout the course of development.

It is recommended that the following information about the developer and team be obtained as part of the evaluation process:

- **History and interests of the company**

    –When was the company founded?

    –What products has the company developed?

    –What were the products' original forecast ship dates? And what were the real dates the products finally ended up shipping on?

    –Are the company's past projects similar to your currently contemplated project? If not, the current project may be a stretch for the company and your risk can go up substantially, as it learns on your dime and time.

    –Which companies/products did the developer enjoy working on most and why?

- **Assets and Intellectual Properties**

    –Does the company own assets (buildings, equipment, and so on)?

    –What intellectual properties does the company own? Game engines? Characters?

- **Financial Matters**

    –Financial statements and accounting processes are useful in gaining an understanding of the developer's monthly costs and determining the financial security of the company. A good developer will not resist supplying a breakdown of the monthly cost for a development team. Also, inquire about long- and short-term debt.

    –If there are external investors, determine their interest and expectations in the company. Are they knowledgeable of the industry? Do they believe in quality product?

- **Legal Matters**

    –Determine if there is or has been any litigation between the company and other companies or former employees.

    –What is the company's lease agreement? You do not want your team looking for a home at the end of the project.

- **Team**

    - **Size of team.** Is the size and constituency of Project Managers, Designers, Programmers, Artists, and Musicians sufficient to realize the vision on time and within budget?

    - **Capabilities of the team members.** A résumé or detailed profile of each team member can be useful. Determine how each team member will contribute his strengths, weaknesses, interests, and so on.

    - **FMV and music**. Does the Developer have internal resources to develop these assets or will he contract this work out? With whom has the developer worked with in the past? If music is to be licensed, who will be responsible for the costs?

- **References**

    - Ask for references, especially those of other Producers who have worked with the team. Then, call each and find out what you can about the team's interaction with these Producers, their work ethic, how they are motivated, and so on.

Pre-Production: Design, Technical Design, and Playable Prototype

As budgets for game development have and will likely continue to increase, it is often best to consider one or two stages of pre-production before full development. In these stages, the full design, technical design, and playable prototype on target hardware should be completed and together define and prove the fundamental game play, character animation, and underlying technology. Not only does this phase of development give you, the Producer, an opportunity to see if the team "gets" the vision, you will learn how the team works together—if the team can meet milestones and if your targeted development budget and schedule are realistic. Develop monthly milestones for the Prototype Phase to track development and get a sense for how the team interprets and responds to these milestones. This will facilitate the process of drafting milestones for full development of the project.

The Development Schedule and Milestone Descriptions

A full development schedule with detailed milestone descriptions should be drafted as part of the technical design in Pre-Production. The purpose of this document is to provide structure and a method by which to measure the development effort, not to be a detailed blueprint for construction. Consider a format that, for each milestone, defines the following. Descriptions of each task should be objective, though— neither too detailed, nor too vague;

- Objective
- Design tasks
- Programming tasks

- Art tasks
- Music tasks
- Other tasks
- Completion test
- Risk assessment
- Due date
- Payment due upon completion

Tool development and core engine technology should be accounted for in the milestone schedule. It is also important that the core game play features and technology (those which may not have been proven in the Prototype Phase) be addressed early in the milestone schedule. For example, in an action, platform game, it is important to prove early on the basic mechanics and move set parameters of the main character, such as jump distance, so that levels can be constructed accordingly. It is best to take time early in the project to determine these details, rather than backtrack later in development. After this has been achieved, development of other levels can be completed with relative ease. The milestone schedule needs to also account for work from outside vendors, such as FMV or music production. Signing music artists often takes a considerable amount of time. You must account for this.

Development of demo versions, tradeshow versions, and marketing materials, as well as vacations and the inevitable holiday and flu seasons are often overlooked but should be accounted for when drafting the milestone schedule. These are realities.

Here is a sample milestone schedule for *Big Time Rodeo*:

Big Time Rodeo

Milestone Schedule

Milestone 1

Objective: Complete tool and engine development. Bull riding and barrel racing play mechanic is responsive and fun.

Design: Refine bull riding and barrel racing play mechanics. Anims for Opponents 5-8. Bulls 6-10, Broncos 6-10, Semi-Pro locales.

Programming: Complete edits to animation tool. Edit camera logic to track player properly. Complete bull riding and barrel racing play mechanic.

Art: Alpha art for artwork completed during Prototype Phase: Opponents 1-4, Bulls 1-5, Broncos 1-5, Rookie locales.

Jack and Amber anims on bull and on horse for calf roping.

Concept art for Opponents 5-8, Bulls 6-10, Broncos 6-10, Semi-Pro locales.

Music: Identify three potential music composers.

Completion Test: Animation tool is fully functional. Camera logic tracks the player properly when riding bull and barrel racing. Player can ride bulls 1-5 and barrel racer on broncos 1-5. Controls will properly respond. Jack/Amber will fall from bull appropriately. Jack/Amber will knock down barrels. Basic timer works for both events.

Concept art for Opponents, Bulls, Broncos, meet theme.

Profiles of three music composers obtained.

Risk Assessment: Jack and Amber's anims in bulls and broncos are dependent upon completion of the animation tool edits due first week.

Due: May 31, 2002

Payment: $100,000

2–12 … Define these similarly.

Alpha

All circuits, events, and characters are fully functional and playable, though game play needs to be tuned some. Game artwork is near final. Glue screens, tally screens, and FMV sequences are included, though placeholder artwork and FMV may be included in some cases. Music and sound effects are near final.

Due: May 31, 2003

Payment: $100,000

Beta

The game is fully tuned. Artwork and music is final. All known standard and class A bugs have been fixed. Game is ready for final bug testing.

Due: July 31, 2003

Payment: $100,000

Gold Master

The game has passed test and is ready to send for manufacturing.

Due: September 15, 2003

Payment: $150,000

PAL

The PAL version of the game has passed test and is ready to send for manufacturing.

Due: September 30, 2003

Payment: $25,000

Japan

The Japanese version of the game has passed test and is ready to send for manufacturing.

Due: October 15, 2003

Payment: $25,000

International Appeal

The Prototype Phase is also an ideal time to give consideration to the international appeal of the game. If possible, receive input from Japanese and European counterparts and tailor the design and prototype to allow for broad appeal. This obviously is beneficial to the global success of the product and for all parties involved.

After pre-production is complete, and the game has been green-lighted by the executive staff for full production, the fun can really begin. Though there still is a mountain to climb, an important plateau has been reached. The "framework" for your project has been built upon the original foundation, or spirit, of the project. There should be a sense, even at this early stage, that something special is in the making.

Full Production: Tracking Progress

Your game is now in full development. The spirit of the game is alive, the framework is in place, and it's now a matter of execution. However, as we all know, not all goes as planned. It is the role of the Producer to be the pillar of strength through the inevitable storms.

Good and frequent communication with your team will be your greatest asset. It is important for your team to know that you are there for them and that information is articulated as objectively as possible. Over-communicating is better than not communicating enough. Remember that the world is not as it is, but as one sees it. The way you see the world will undoubtedly be different from that of the members of your team, especially given that you are dealing with both extreme left and right brained people. As the Producer, you need to always be aware and understanding of this.

Though payable milestones are generally due on a monthly basis, it is best to track progress regularly on a weekly basis. If you are working with an external development group, consider asking for weekly objectives on Monday and then reviewing progress on Friday. If the team is slipping, get to the source of the problem immediately. Encourage the team to work that extra weekend now to make up for a slip in the weekly schedule rather than cram at the end of the month to make the milestone delivery. This will help to keep the development process consistent rather than one with peaks and valleys that ultimately contribute to fatigue and burnout. Further, this intermediate weekly communication will help the developer keep on the correct creative path and facilitate prompt approval upon submission of the completed payable monthly milestone.

As necessary, update the design and development schedule. Make it known to the developer that this is an important task and a practice that is to be maintained regularly from the beginning of the project.

During development, respond to the needs of your developer with a sense of urgency. Whether it is a piece of equipment that your developer needs or feedback to a payable milestone, regard it as a hot potato. Your developer is awaiting your leadership and feedback, often nervously, so better to relieve this stress to your team sooner than later to keep the team motivated and happy.

Keeping the Team Happy Through the Good, the Bad, and the Ugly

In running the project, you will need to keep the team—this living, breathing, organism that is realizing the vision—happy. Here are a few suggestions.

Praise

It can go a long way, if given sincerely and when deserved, especially when the team or an individual has gone beyond the call of duty. This positive feedback lets the team or individual know what you like, and the team will generally respond with more of the same.

CALLING POTENTIAL PROBLEMS TO THE TABLE EARLY

A developer may mention something in passing or in a very polite and conversational manner. If there is any thought that something is askew, pry a bit to see if there is something more irksome beneath the surface. This may be just what your developer wants you to do. I once produced a gambling game and noticed that one of the more respected Programmers in the company seemed uncharacteristically less than enthused about his work and reluctant to talk about the game. I asked him if he enjoyed working on the project, and he confided that, though his work was important to him, as a Mormon, he objected to gambling. This was a conflict for him. As there wasn't another project to which he could be assigned, we agreed to not put his name in the credits. This was sufficient, in this case, to ease his mind and he then worked much more effectively on the project.

Resolve Conflict Through Open Communication

Conflict is usually a symptom of miscommunication, or lack of communication. It could be that the Lead Programmer is irritated with a design decision that was made, for example. Because he is especially tired near the end of the project, he is not holding his feelings back. It is important to get to the root of the conflict quickly, without getting sucked into the conflict itself, so that matters do not escalate. You, as the Producer, need to be that pillar of strength during these times and find creative ways to resolve conflict. This often requires some psychology on your part, recognizing the human element. Get into the heads of those in conflict. It may be that you need to give the Programmer a day off to get some rest and regain perspective. Or it may be best to bring the Designer and Programmer together to openly discuss the issue. You may need to remind the Programmer of the earlier discussion (and agreement hopefully) of each person's role on the project and ask that he trust the Designer to do his job.

Bringing in Marketing, Public Relations, and Sales

It is important to see Marketing, Public Relations, and the Sales force as your allies throughout the development of the project. It is best to educate them from your perspective on all aspects of the game. It is just as important to consider their input on the product. Marketing, for example, can help in defining the

TIP

From a pure management perspective, take the time to learn about management from "gurus" like Ken Blanchard and Peter Drucker. Blanchard is co-author of *The One Minute Manager Builds High Performance Teams*, (Quill, 2000), which covers goal-setting, motivating, training, praising, and even reprimanding employees. Drucker is with The Drucker Graduate School of Management and is the well-known author of such books as *The Practice of Management* (HarperBusiness, 1993), and *Management: Tasks, Responsibilities, Practices*, (HarperBusiness, 1993). Another excellent book (reportedly required reading at Microsoft) is *The 7 Habits of Highly Effective People* (Simon & Schuster, 1990), by Stephen Covey.

main character for the target market. They should also be consulted to determine when demos and marketing materials will be needed from the developer. Marketing can also assist in providing market research and gathering data through focus testing. Sales can provide valuable feedback from retailers. The more educated and familiar these parties are about the product and the more you consider their input, the better the chance for the success of the product.

Final Production: Alpha, Beta, and Gold Master Milestones

Undoubtedly, you will need to let go of some of those great ideas you had at the beginning of the project. Ideally, the milestones have been prioritized such that the ideas to be left on the shelf are not core elements of the game. At the Alpha stage of development, it is time to reassess the remaining work to be done, give consideration to new ideas that have germinated over the course of the project, and incorporate them into the schedule if they are viable. This may help to motivate the team through to the end.

Just before or as your game reaches Beta, is also an excellent time to conduct Focus/Play testing. It's best to present your game and gather feedback from both game professionals (such as other gamers and testers in your company), as well as newbies in your target audience from outside your company. Frequently, people completely outside of the game development team provide many excellent ideas that can help you fine tune the final product.

It is especially important that you nurture the team through the final phases of development. Final testing can be an especially difficult time. The bugs seem to never end and some are seemingly impossible to fix. The Programmer may have some anxiety as to the integrity of a piece of code. As the Producer, this is yet another storm to weather. Do so by facilitating in any way possible. Consult with Technical Support, for example, to help solve technical problems. Send a care package to your development team, or better yet, to the families from which they have been absent of late. "Whatever it takes" should be your motto at this stage of development.

Testing

It is important that the Producer define a method with the developer for bug reporting.

Developers often like to receive bugs as soon as they are found versus waiting a day or more for full testing of a version. With a proper procedure in place, this can be accommodated. Consider a live database that includes Open, Fixed, and Waived bugs. Bugs might be prioritized into four categories:

- **Standards.** Platform holder or Publishers standards. Must fix.

- **A.** Crash bugs and bugs that severely impair the game experience.

- **B.** Obvious, but less severe bugs. If fixed, improves the polish and overall impression of the game.

- **C.** Minor bugs. Fix these, if done easily.

It is also important to note the tester that reported the bug and the version of the code on which it appeared.

The Producer should review the bug report and filter bugs before they are sent to the developer. The bug report should be well structured and easy to read. Descriptions of the bugs should be clear and concise. Avoid submitting redundant bugs to the developer. If there is any question as to the nature of a bug, try to re-create it yourself to understand it more fully so that you can convey it clearly to the developer. Know what bugs are important to fix and those that can be let go for the sake of time and sanity. Resist your temptation for perfection and accept excellence.

Rejoice!

When it's all over, remember to celebrate! Allow yourself and the team time to acknowledge the hard work and long hours, and appreciate the opportunity you have been given to do what you love to do.

Part III

Preparing for the Career You Want

Images courtesy of Gunilla Elam

Chapter 8

Getting Organized and Networking

You know your skill level and now you know what you need to do to improve it, but you've also got rent to pay. How do you get a game industry job?

Think of that roller coaster ride of emotions you feel when playing your favorite game—that series of ups and downs, frustrations, and elations as you face obstacles and overcome them. Your job hunt is much like that game.

After hearing the word "no" over and over and over again, it is easy to succumb to an overwhelming sense of inadequacy. Do not succumb! It's not personal; it's business. Although it may sound cliché, it is the truth. A job rejection usually means you did not set yourself apart from the other candidates. Even a shiny new Computer Science or specialized game degree will not guarantee success.

If getting a dream job were easy, everyone would have one. You don't accept defeat when playing your favorite game; you keep at it until you reach the next level. The same should hold true for you and your job quest.

Along with technical and creative prowess, job hunting is a skill you must develop to get employed and stay that way, particularly in a high tech field such as games. Job-hunting requires practice, planning, patience, and persistence.

A structured, organized job search campaign will increase your chances of getting the job you want. An organized system relieves the natural anxiety about what you should be doing next in your job search. Structure provides peace of mind as it discourages confusion and allows you to rationally assess where you stand.

The average game company receives over 100,000 unsolicited résumés every year. Although this may sound like a discouraging fact, remember that people do, indeed, get hired. And, typically speaking, those hired are the people with the most organized and effective job-hunting campaign. But what about talent? Oh, you'll need that, too, but unless you're effectively marketing that talent, you're the proverbial tree falling in the woods.

Job hunting can be broken down into a series of steps starting from the first, which is targeting your search, and ending with your first day on the new job. In this chapter, you will learn how to take those steps.

GETTING ORGANIZED

Getting a job is really about *getting noticed*, and getting noticed is about getting organized and staying in control. You will be creating lists of companies to approach and lists of people currently working at your target companies, as well as maintaining records of interviews, conversations, and their results. Finally, you will be generating the steps you need to perform for each company. Sound overwhelming? It's not. As long as you start out organized and stay that way.

Using a Database

To get suitably organized, you need to get your hands on, and learn how to use, a simple database program such as Microsoft Outlook, Act!, File Maker Pro, or GoldMine. These products keep you organized, allowing you to track target companies, individuals within each company you wish to contact, and the corresponding contact results. Additionally, you may need an accompanying paper file system for physical correspondence, research information, and so on. But as this is a computer savvy industry, the basis of your organization systems needs to be computer based.

These database programs allow you to pull together contact information and then use that information—for example, to track contact history, as well as monitor pending activities and appointments. It is a very powerful organizational tool to have all job-hunting related communication and activity relate back to a contact. This database will be used for the entire life of your game industry career. In addition to job-hunting purposes, you will utilize your database to keep in touch with personal contacts you make in the industry. You never know, you may eventually use your database to hire someone.

So, how much will this cost you? Well, how much is your career worth? Most database software programs such as GoldMine or Act! are available at your local computer stores or through online retail outlets such as Amazon.com. The programs range in price from $100 to $200. Whichever one you choose, make sure you are comfortable with the software and its capabilities, as it will be your "friend" for life.

Coding Leads in Your Database

Think of your database as your new telephone book. This telephone book, however, holds much more information per person than just names and contact information. You will want to have all your personal and professional associations entered into it, no matter who they are. Feed your database with the names of everyone and anyone you know. Don't overlook contacts like friends, family, and the people you hire to service you professionally, like your doctor or lawyer. Even lawn service or maintenance people may be able to network you, so consider all the people in your world. And yes, include your grandmother. You have no idea who she may meet at her weekly card game or who her doctor knows. If your grandmother boasts about you as much as most do, you can focus her natural skill at promoting you.

Coding your leads is an important aspect of using a database. To code, you include category keywords along with the name and contact information. This way, you can quickly isolate just a few records out of the thousand or so names you will accumulate over a lifetime of networking. Some suggested categories include the following:

- **Family**. All your family contacts.

- **Friends**. All your personal contacts.

- **Passive**. Leads who may know other people for you to network with.

- **Active**. Game industry people.

- **Job Prospect**. Specific names of hiring managers.

- **Game Company**. Specific game companies.

TIP

Compile a list of 100 people. Don't forget people like schoolmates, your insurance agent, fraternity/sorority types, and school alumni.

You don't know 100 people? Start listing everyone you know who fit in the following categories: Personal, Family, Work, and Other Acquaintances.

Targeting Your Search and Gathering Leads

As with most things in life, job hunting works best when you have a focused plan of action. You've created your initial database, now what job do you want? Who do you want to work for? Where do you want to work? Which companies are viable targets for your job search? What type and size of a game company would you be most comfortable working with? A small third-party developer? Large publisher? A company whose product mix is sports only? Online games? Traditional coin-op games? If you're new to the industry, you should consider being as flexible on location as possible. After you have gained industry experience, you will gain more control on geographical preferences.

AUTHOR NOTE

"It's fairly easy to get a job; it's getting the right job that's the true task. To find the right job, you must ask the right questions and do the right research for a company's past, people, and products."

- Marc

Develop a list of all game companies that match your criteria, Do your research! Learn the names of the product lines or major selling titles, be familiar with what the companies are currently developing, and find the names of anyone you may know who works at each company. Identify people by researching the company web site, press releases, trade publications, and industry organizations.

Trade publications, both online and print, like *GIGnews.com*, *Gamasutra*, *Gamedev.net*, *GameDaily*, and *Game Developer*, will dial you in to the industry trends that will help you fine tune your job search and identify people to contact. Professional associations such as the International Game Developers Association (IGDA) and the Academy of Interactive Arts and Sciences are also very useful resources.

Organize the list of companies you wish to approach. Who surfaces as your top target company? Who are the second and third choices? By the end of your research phase, you should have a nice long list of companies to approach and the order of importance to you and your career goals.

TIP

Use this book's appendix, "Resources," to start gathering your leads.

Another tool for targeting your job search is a game itself. Go out and buy a target company's latest game. If you interview with this company, you will need to know about its games anyway. Having experience playing them will only make you more credible. Usually, there is a list of credits buried in the game or the accompanying instruction manual. However you get the names, these people can be utilized as contacts to approach when you are ready to talk to your target company.

Research pays off not only in terms of creating a tailored résumé or having plenty of interview fodder, but also in terms of discovering opportunities before they become official. When you read industry and company news, pay close attention to clues as to a job in the works. For example, if you read a press release that says Marc Mencher was just promoted to Project Lead, you can bet a Programmer spot is likely to be open to fill the old spot. Matt Scibilia is now Art Director? Who will fill the Artist position? Also, keep track of newly hired managers. They often want to have new staff and create their "own team."

THE WAY HR DEPARTMENTS REALLY WORK

Thousands of people apply for a single advertised job! Job postings are easy to identify and locate on the Internet or through the local newspaper. If you find one you are interested in, you can be sure your résumé will be considered against the hundreds of other people who also applied. Who knows what kind of blitz campaign the Human Resource (HR) department chose for advertising the job you just found? Who knows how old the job posting really is? More advertising results in more résumés.

AUTHOR NOTE

"According to the Department of Labor, *more than 80 percent of jobs are obtained by networking.* You will not find these positions advertised in newspapers nor posted on the Internet. Only 10 percent of open jobs are ever posted or advertised."

- Marc

HR departments typically receive so many responses to an open job posting that, on average, it takes two months for them to wait for responses and then sift through the results. In other words, about two months after the job was advertised, HR will present to the hiring manager a stack of 100 résumés of people who seem to qualify for the job.

That's right, résumés that *seem* to qualify. Typically, the HR people screening your résumé know little about the game industry. They are not Programmers, Artists, Producers, or Designers. That's not their job. At best, they only conceptually understand the game development process and probably don't even play games themselves. This should not be taken as an HR trash or rant. Rather, people who choose this line of work are generally very nice and love to help people. In fact, HR has a serious job. Companies could not survive without effective HR departments. But HR departments are trained to deal with insurance, stock, performance reviews, employee issues, and so on. They, quite simply, are not required to have game industry experience or training. They most likely have not even spoken to the hiring manager about the job he needs to fill.

Often, HR just utilizes a job order requisition that was signed and approved by another department located in another building. Therefore, HR can only cling to the buzzwords in your résumé and the description of the job advertised, and every word in the written job order is taken literally.

In short, HR has no idea when it reviews your résumé that because you reverse engineered a GNU compiler, this skill could be useful for the open PlayStation Tools position. If you do not use the word PlayStation in your résumé, you get disqualified even through it would be obvious to any engineer reviewing your résumé that you totally qualify technically for the job advertised. This is why in the résumé you will learn how to effectively utilize buzzwords and action statements to "sell" yourself.

Now, back to the stack of 100 résumés on the hiring manager's desk. Despite the title, hiring a new person is not usually a priority for the hiring manager. This person already has a full-time job and has little time or interest in reading through a stack of résumés. Sure, a few of the résumés mention PlayStation, which is why they were flagged for review, but in all likelihood, the hiring manager is facing a pile of marginally qualified people. And so the pile sits for another month.

The moral to this story is that HR must be used when the time is right. Answering job ads or Internet postings is more like playing the lottery than actual job-hunting. It is a lazy and ineffective way to job hunt. Sure, someone occasionally gets the advertised job, but the odds are stacked against you.

And if you're wondering about working with recruiters, loads of information is just ahead.

JOB HUNTING IS LIKE SELLING ANYTHING—IT'S A NUMBER'S GAME

In this game, you're selling yourself, and the more contacts you make, the more likely you'll get sold. Talking to people gets you jobs. In fact, many jobs are filled by word of mouth before a company advertises them, often before Human Resources even knows the position has been open.

The goal in your networking efforts is to position yourself to interview and, even better, get hired for these unadvertised jobs. You never know who can help you, so talk to as many people as you can. The most important information you want to get from people when you are networking is the names of other people you can contact.

As you move through the steps, it should be increasingly clear why initial research is so important. Later in your job search, when you actively network for a specific job, some of your identified contacts will turn into prospective job opportunities that you will move into job offers. One good place to start your research is the Game Development Search Engine (www.gdse.com).

TIP

Don't focus your job search on only 10 percent of the open jobs; rather, focus on the 80 percent of jobs not advertised. Take the time to uncover the "hidden or unadvertised job market" through networking. Position yourself to be only one of three people being considered for a job, not one of a thousand!

AUTHOR NOTE

"I am not a big fan of online job-hunting services. Who exactly has access to these databases? You lose total control of your job-hunting campaign when you post your résumé to the world. Even the services that guarantee privacy can't and don't police who pays to have access to their service. These companies need to make a profit. Do you think they turn away sales? Do you think they bother to investigate who is asking for access to your résumé?"

- Marc

AUTHOR NOTE

"As a professional recruiter, I know first-hand the value of networking and tapping the unadvertised job market. This is how I earn my living. I match people I know to the unadvertised jobs I discover through networking. You can do the same yourself."

- Marc

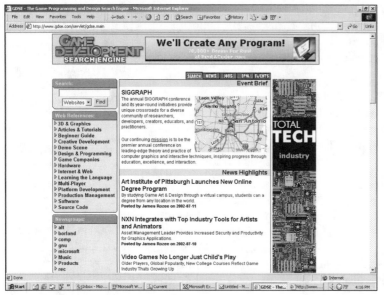

www.gdse.com.

As you get ready to network, keep in mind the following purposes you want to accomplish:

- Gather insider information and opinions.

- Make connections and get your name circulating.

- Find mentors—people who will help you in your target companies.

- Gather information to help tailor your résumé presentation to the target companies.

And, remember, this stage of networking is not about asking for a job, which will come later. Rather, you want to accomplish the above purposes, which will ultimately lead to that job.

YOUR PERSONALIZED NETWORKING CAMPAIGN

The advent of email has certainly made networking an easier process than it was just a few years ago. If it is easier for you to start via email, do so, but don't avoid the telephone. Making voice contact, or better yet, face-to-face contact, adds reality to you. It fosters a bond that words typed on a screen can never duplicate between people. Try to meet people at industry conferences or, if they're not in the same town and you've got the money and the time, go to them. Again, these meetings aren't about asking for a job, rather, they are for establishing friendly contacts, feeding your database, and getting your name circulating among industry professionals.

Networking—It's Just Focused Socializing. Do It for Life.

Don't let the prospect of networking scare you. Approach it as focused socializing. And for you types who don't like the socializing thing, get over it! This is something you simply must learn how to do. If you've taken the time to train yourself as a game developer, take the time to learn how to socialize.

Most of your focused socializing will occur with other game developers, so it should be easy to get a conversation going if you bring up some game development issue. Most likely, you have had these kinds of conversations already in the past. From this point forward, you're merely socializing with a particular goal in mind: To position yourself for the next opportunity. This does not mean the next job. It means the next opportunity. Networking also leads to business ideas and other opportunities. Who knows where your life's path will lead you?

Today, you're an Artist, but in the course of networking, you may find that life brings you to heading up a new kind of entertainment venture. *You're doing this for life!*

If you're truly uncomfortable speaking in front of people or uncomfortable socializing, you can train yourself to network and socialize by reading books, taking a speech class, and practicing walking up to strangers and introducing yourself. Start out slowly. You don't have to walk up to a group of people, rather, look for the loners in a social setting. Most likely, they are as shy as you, which is why they are alone. Generally, they will be easier to approach and eager to connect, and many will be great contacts.

Practice deliberately placing yourself in networking situations. Definitely practice on your friends and family. Then, after you have refined your skill, go out and talk to closer industry contacts. Play this game with yourself when networking: how many business cards can you hand out and exchange? Even if you're not working at the moment, create your own clever personal business card.

Marc Mencher – Game Programmer Gone Recruiter!

800-779-3334

www.GameRecruiter.com

Expertise: Career Coach & Fantasy Game Job Guru

Confidentiality Assured!

In addition, you need to get a permanent web site address and keep it for life: www.YourName.com works well! Along with this, you need to establish a permanent email address: YourFirstName@YourName.com works well!

Enroll People in Your Life Goals. Use a One-Minute Pitch.

You want to be a game developer so, by gosh, be one and tell people about it! Don't just share your dreams and goals with your friends and family; tell everyone you ever meet. Get together your own personal positioning "pitch" and use it everywhere you go. Does this mean that you can never socialize freely again? Will you always be performing? Well, yes and no. Don't hang with people you do not like or participate in activities you don't enjoy just because you think it will get a job. Be as authentic and honest as you can be in life. Be honest with yourself. Aren't you already "on stage" when you socialize? Just focus what you do naturally. You socialize, so do it with a purpose and a one-minute pitch in mind. This is a one-minute summary of who you are, what you have accomplished, and what you wish to accomplish. It will take you time to create and hone this pitch, so be patient with yourself. You will find it easier to network if you prepare yourself ahead of time for the experience.

For a moment, pretend that you're back in grade school. What was it that captured your creative mind then? Was it a fascination with science fiction? Was your room covered with science fiction posters and sci-fi books? Did every

AUTHOR NOTE

"Toastmasters is a non-profit group that meets on a monthly basis and trains its participants to speak in a public setting. When I was in high school, my mother also owned a recruiting firm, Helen Mencher & Associates. She was a single working mother, which meant that often I would accompany her to her Toastmasters meetings. It was odd at first being a generation younger than the rest of the group, but I learned to love those meetings. I learned that correct presentation and networking skills produce results! I learned how to confidently speak and engage any size audience. Participating in sales and networking seminars honed my skills at "working a room" at any sort of gathering of people. You can learn these skills as well. Apply yourself. It's really a lot of fun."

- Marc

relative in your family know to get you some sort of science fiction gift for the holidays? We enroll people in an image or belief about ourselves. I am a biker. I am a jock. I am a geek.

Enroll people in the belief that: "I am a Game Programmer." "I am a Game Artist." "I am a Game Designer." And so on.

You will create one kind of pitch for socializing and networking and another kind of pitch when in active job-hunting mode. Memorize your pitch! Be your pitch! This is why no one else but you can create it. It must be laced with your passion, and it will modify as you accomplish, grow, and change focus in your life. If your pitch begins to sound like a script, this is a sign that you may not be feeling totally in synch with what you are saying. If so, then rewrite your pitch. It is paramount that your body language, facial expression, and tone of voice all be congruent with what it is you are saying.

Sample One-Minute Position Pitch: Networking

This is the pitch I use to establish credibility and obtain clients/candidates when networking:

"Hi, my name is Marc Mencher. I am a Programmer who used to work for game companies like Spectrum Holobyte, Microprose, and 3DO, before establishing GameRecruiter.com, a Game Industry Recruiting firm. I have been involved in the games industry for over 10 years. I first started hiring people for my own development teams but then found myself staffing all departments within the game companies I worked for. I know games. I have created games. I am not just a recruiter who understands a few industry buzz-words. In fact, all the recruiters at GameRecruiter.com are former game industry professionals. This way, we have like-kind people talking to each other. Here is my business card, do you play video games?"

Sample One-Minute Position Pitch: Game Programming

This is a pitch I used when trying to establish myself as a Game Programmer. Again, notice how credibility is established and how I would obtain leads from people:

"Hi, my name is Marc Mencher. I've been programming games since high school when I got my first TI calculator. My dad was a Programmer and he began teaching me when I was very young. I love games and have developed over 25 of them on my own! It is my goal to get a job creating games. Here is my card. Do you play video games? You're welcome to visit my web page and download for free any of the games you like. What kind of a game would you play? Ever meet anyone who is a game fanatic like me? Who?"

Take notes. I always have a tiny notepad or use my PDA to store them. Later, I use the information I gain from this pitch.

Other Sample Pitches

Here's a pitch for Artists:

"Remember the guy in your high school who was always doodling and drawing images in his note books, actually on any surface he could draw on? That was me! Today, I have focused my artistic talents so I can become an Animator. Here is my card; my web site is listed and you can feel free to snag some of my images if you like them."

Here's a pitch for Designers:

"What was the first video game you ever played? I started playing games when I was 8. My favorite type of games is Action but I have played them all. In fact, I have put together several game designs that you can review on my web site. Here is my card."

It's also useful to have a couple of topics on general issues for conversation. Before a networking event, brush up on current affairs and visit a group of game industry web sites to update yourself on current game development issues. Be ready to engage in a conversation—several kinds of conversations. Know the top selling games for the last quarter and for the year. It's natural to feel uncomfortable socializing and walking up to strangers. Practice makes perfect. Be happy, upbeat, and positive. You're socializing, so be relaxed and have fun!

Can't think of an opening line when approaching people? Ask if they've had the opportunity to play the latest, hot game. That will get the conversation flowing. After the networking opportunity is over, sit down and see how you did. How many business cards did you give out? How many did you get? What did you do that worked for you? What did you do that did not work? Can you think of another way to increase your effectiveness next time?

Networking means talking to everyone you know—friends, friends of friends, family, friends of family, and professional acquaintances (like your doctor or lawyer). Remember the movie *Six Degrees Of Separation*? It was based on the premise that we are all only six people away from each other. Therefore, people in your sphere of networking will know people who will know people. Follow these trails; they lead to a pot of gold! Tell people about who you are and who you want to be. Enroll them in assisting you. Who do they know? Who do their aquaitances know? This is how you tap into the "hidden" job market.

A list of 20 people is simply not going to be an effective way to get you networking. You need a list of about 100 people to contact. Try not to pre-judge your contacts. You never know who knows who. That lead your 82-year-old grandmother passed along because one of her friends at the weekly card game had a grandchild working in the game industry may just pay off. Your list should initially include everyone you know. Again, this is your personal telephone book.

> ### AUTHOR NOTE
>
> "Before a networking experience, I run out and purchase the latest *People* magazine or *National Enquirer*. I find them easy sources for general interest topics. A quick glance at the front page of the *Wall Street Journal* brushes you up on current affairs."
>
> - Marc

Some useful sources of names:

- Trade journals

- Web sites

- Active members of game associations

- Active members of online gaming or MOD communities

- People chatting in game-oriented-technical forums

- Speakers at game industry events

- Online symposiums or classes given on Game Development

- Real estate or insurance agents (people who truly know the value of networking!)

- Alumni from your college, fraternity, sorority, or high school

Keep in mind that at the initial stage of networking, you're not job hunting. Rather, you're working your contacts with the goal of expanding your contact list. Who do these people know? Get at least two names of someone who may know something about game development or the industry.

Keep in mind that the Human Resources department at a game company is not the best place to network. You must include HR when you officially approach the company for employment, but one of the functions of Human Resources is to keep the outside world away from the hiring managers. Don't try networking with HR.

Cold Calling or Contacting

The hardest part of networking is cold contacting those people you found in your research. Yes, it's tough to call or email strangers to ask for advice or referrals, but surveys of the unemployed consistently show that those who keep calling and talking get the jobs. Although you non-sales personality types are surely cringing at this prospect, you will find that most people are as nice as you. Actually, they are flattered when asked for advice, aren't you? Generally speaking, people like to help others. The first call or email is the hardest; it will get easier and easier as you become more comfortable presenting yourself. Preparing an email or telephone script before you make contact also helps ease discomfort.

Begin Networking Now!

Begin your networking endeavors several months before you graduate, plan to enter the job market, or want to change jobs. Focus on people working at your top 10 game company choices. Alternatively, decide what specialty you wish to develop and start talking to the people who are in that field of expertise.

For example, let's say you read an interesting article on depth of field as a post process, written by Jamie Artiste, a Lead Artist at Hot Smokin' Games, Inc. You check his bio at the end of the article and, bingo! You've got his email address.

Send him a note letting him know how much you enjoyed the article and that Maya was of particular interest to you. Then, ask for his advice:

" Hey, Jamie, I read your article on GIGnews.com. Thanks for such an informative article. I had been wondering about depth of field as a post process. What do you think about using the sampler node info like a Z post process buffer?

Odds are that a flattered Jamie will return the email and you can then engage him in a dialogue. Don't bombard your contact with every question you can think of all at once, but over the course of the correspondence, you can elicit advice on programs, course studies, demo suggestions, and more. See where you are going with this networking thing?

What if the only contact you've been able to find at a target company is Sara Suit, the Product Marketing Manager? Although your identified contact might not seem terribly direct, this person can point you in the right direction. Try to develop a relationship as it may prove useful later on as an internal reference, or even as a source of data on other open, but unadvertised jobs.

Try something like the following when getting in touch with a seemingly unrelated contact within your target company:

Hi Sara,

I am a student studying game programming. I discovered your name while doing research on Hot Smokin' Games, Inc. Would you mind giving me some advice? I want to focus my skills correctly while I'm in school. I won't waste your time and would really appreciate your help!

Short, sweet, and to the point. Sure, some people you approach—not many—will reject you. But who cares? This is a numbers game and sometimes you just catch people at the wrong time in their work or personal lives. Don't take it personally, because it's not personal. These people don't know you. You were just another email or voicemail they didn't feel like returning on a particularly bad day. Move on to another person. Eventually, you will get to the right person on the right day.

Most likely, Sara will immediately confess that she is in product marketing and has limited ability to help you. But don't give up! Ask her for the name of a friendly employee who you can approach for advice. Don't mention the words "job hunting." You're still not doing this yet; you're just networking. If Sara won't network you, call the main number for the company and see if you can get the name of the VP of Engineering's secretary. Maybe this person will hook you up. *Get names!* Be a name-dropper. Talk to people. When you finally approach the person, you can reference Sara or the secretary, which will build your credibility.

After you've established these contacts, consider emailing a quick "quarterly review" of your game-related accomplishments like the following:

AUTHOR NOTE

"Although I will help you
organize your job search in
this book, it is important to
add your own personality.
Don't use the exact examples I
use or the same words.
Contribute your own unique-
ness, just as you would to a
game you're creating."

- Marc

Hey Jamie,

Just wanted to drop you a quick note and let you know how much I appreciate the support and advice you've given me. As you suggested, I tried using
Mirai and you were right! It's a solid modeler and has some very interesting
animation tools. Check out the work I did with it at www.YourName.com.

Are you still working on that new PS2 title? How's the project going?

Professional recruiters working their network of contacts make, on the average,
50 calls per day. You're not shooting for such a high number. Your goal should
be about 12 contacts per day, preferably via telephone but email counts as well.
This is why you need that initial list of at least 100 contacts. Sure, you will get
some rejections when attempting to network, but if done properly you will have
a constant source of leads to keep you motivated and excited about your job
search. We all have a choice each and every moment of the day to be positive or
negative. You can choose to focus on the five rejects you got or the eight new
leads you generated. Stay focused on the positive. Be excited about the new
leads. Focus on your success.

Send your résumé to your primary contacts. (More about résumés coming up.)
Send a copy to your sister. Sure, she knows you love games and that you want
to work in the industry, but unless she works in the industry herself, she probably has no idea what you really do or want to do. Providing her a copy of your
résumé and reviewing it with her will help you elicit names of people she may
know for your network. Reviewing your résumé and accomplishments with
your sister will also arm her with the knowledge and ability to go out and network for you as she does her thing in life. These second tier contact names will
get you closer to your target of a game job. As you progress to third and fourth
tier contacts, you're getting closer and closer to a specific hiring manager who
could offer you your dream job. You're *not* asking your sister for a game job;
you're directing and focusing her to help you. Who in her world does she know
who may be able to help you?

After you obtain names, ask permission to use the name of the contact that gave
you the lead. Use this person's name in your telephone and email contact. You're
networking and name-dropping. Personal references to others are the key to
networking.

Here's a sample networking email using a primary contact as a referral source:

Dear Joe,

Dana Button Berry, one of the founders of Electronic Arts, suggested I contact you. I am a Game Programmer who specializes in AI. Dana and I have been discussing creating more compelling competitive opponents. I understand that you have some experience in this area. Love to ask your advice or direction. I will connect with you via telephone this Wednesday, January 25th, at 3:15pm.

Best Regards,

Marc Mencher

WRAP-UP

If you're stymied in your job search, this is an indication you need to brush up on your networking skills. Stop job hunting. Retrain yourself to network. Then start again. Practice makes perfect.

Chapter 9

Preparing Your Demo

The days have passed when anyone can expect to find a job by simply sending out the same standard résumé to a hundred game companies, or posting a résumé on a job board. Mass campaigning either through email, snail mail, or job board postings produces horrible results. Today's market demands much more from job seekers. The candidate who is willing to go out of her way to demonstrate skills, get attention, and stand out from the crowd, is the candidate who will get the interview and the job.

Game Artists have always needed a demo to obtain a job. For this career, it is impossible to gain employment without one. Game Programmers, on the other hand, used to be so difficult to find that just showing interest in game development qualified someone for this job. Today, this is not the case. As the industry has grown, so has the availability of people who have industry experience. The use of demos has gained in acceptance as a way of self promoting and getting jobs.

Even experienced Game Programmers now must show samples of code or even take coding tests before an interview is granted. Yes, it is still possible for some people with strong industry experience to obtain a job without a demo but this is no longer the norm. If you are new to the industry or have limited experience, a demo is a must! Our industry still values creativity over experience and although prior game industry experience is a definite plus, it is not always the qualifying factor. So create a demo no matter what career you decide to pursue.

GETTING YOUR DEMO TOGETHER

The importance of your demo cannot be overstated. It can be in the form of a web site, CD-ROM, videotape, slide show, AVI, PDF, 2D images, paper and pencil drawings, and so on. Not only will the game company use your demo to evaluate whether it wants to interview you, it is also used to ballpark a salary range if you're hired.

Your Demo Must Capture Interest and Amaze the Viewer Immediately

This is challenging, especially when you are trying to grab the attention of people who themselves are experts. However, if you invest the time, energy, and patience, you will be able to create a compelling demo. If you do not have prior game industry experience and material for your demo, go create it for yourself! Demonstrate your talent as a Game Designer, Marketing Professional, Producer, and so on through a good body of work.

Materials get separated, so have your name, web site address, and contact information on everything you submit! The following are other items to consider including with a demo:

- **Cue Sheet**. Explain what the viewer is looking at, listening to, or experiencing. If the demo piece appeared in a previous body of work, explain briefly what it was used for. Any production notes used to explain your motivation for creating the piece may also be helpful. List all tools used in the creation of the piece. If you learned something valuable, consider mentioning it.

- **Promotional materials, brochures, and press clippings**.

- **Business card**.

Write and post articles about your craft. This shows that you have good written communication skills excellent for any game industry position. It also gets people visiting your web site and establishes credibility. Many industry web sites seek articles, and some actually pay for them. So get writing!

Remember that a demo is a work in progress because it expands as your skill level does. If your earlier work is weak compared to your latest work, take it off of your site! You're only hurting yourself with it if you leave it up.

Think Ahead of Time About the Impression You Are Trying to Make

Decide what market you are trying to enter and then customize your demo appropriately. A demo's purpose is to show your skills but also to generate interviews. From the look of the packaging to the impact of the material shown, it all fuses together to prove to your target companies that YOU are the best person for the job. Graphics and expensive packaging are not necessary, but you do want to make the demo look professional. Remember: From the moment the package arrives, you are making an impression.

When approaching a game company, it is useful to know specific information about the company. Make reference to anything that may indicate you have given serious thought to the content of your demo before blasting it out to the world. By knowing what titles the company is currently working on, you can position your demo, skills, and approach.

Determine to whom you should send your work and what format they prefer. Most hiring managers detest getting huge downloads. Having a limited window of time each week when they can review and interview new candidates, they may react negatively when their time is wasted.

Decipher what sort of demo your target companies may be looking for. If you have existing material, use it. If not, create it! A hiring manager working on a game that is to be marketed to 8- to 12-year-old girls is probably not interested in hearing heavy metal music, viewing sexually expressive images, or playing the sports game you just coded. Just like your résumé, it is best to customize your demo for the audience that will be reviewing it.

Show Your Best Stuff First and End It There

Keep your demo short and to the point. A classic videotape or CD-ROM demo is three to five minutes. Your web site should be the same. Game companies incorporate bleeding edge technology in their products. Showing a game using older technology will sound the death knell, as will poorly designed and sloppy code, or submitting an uncompleted game.

Think of your demo and web site presentation as a tightly edited sampler of your best work, in a structured, well-designed presentation that guides the viewer through a portfolio of your talent, as well as your potential. It's like a movie preview. Capture the viewer's attention in the minimum time necessary, showing just enough of the range and quality of your work to want the viewer to ask for a face-to-face interview.

Don't rely on self-editing. Your demo must be the best, most concise representation of the range and depth of your talent and experience, so get opinions from respected mentors and teammates. Sure, criticism may hurt, but unemployment is infinitely more painful.

FROM THE EXPERT

"A real demo turn-off is when the focus is self-centered and self-indulgent. In other words, the viewpoint and attitude of the viewer are ignored, and the samples are not appropriate to the reviewer's requested parameters. You should re-edit your content to better serve the purpose of presenting not just your best work. But your best work that fits your clients' needs."

- Matt Scibilia, Founder and Art Director, Big Sky Interactive

FROM THE EXPERT

Other huge negatives? "Lots of killer clowns, excruciatingly gory (and badly drawn) characters, and art with lots of satanic references. You'd be amazed by how much of that I see. The first thing that pops into my head when I see it is 'high school!'"

- Andrew Paquette, Former Director of Art, Sony Pictures Imageworks

FROM THE EXPERT

"I strongly suggest that your demo be several smaller games which you will be able to complete, rather than one large game which may never be finished."

- Dustin Clingman, Professor of Game Development, Full Sail Real World Education, and Founder of Perpetual Motion

FROM THE EXPERT

"I think the one thing that has made my career more than anything else is that I make sure I get good feedback. I always ask questions so that I can understand and evaluate what I've done."

- Andrew Paquette, Former Director of Art, Sony Pictures Imageworks

Credit Everything You Use

If you don't credit everything you use, you will appear to be trying to take credit for someone else's work, and your demo and résumé will quickly find their way to the trash. Think about it. If you found it on the Net or in a book, so did others, and it is a silly risk to try to pass it off as your work. For a quick example, let's say you're a Game Programmer and have found a neat routine that will determine how much memory is being used and will notify the user if the memory usage goes above a certain limit. You want to add this functionality to your program. If the code is available to be used by you or someone else for the purpose of learning, clearly credit in the file header comments as well as anywhere in your documentation where you mention this feature. Let's say you're a Game Artist and you find a model on the web. Although it is acceptable practice to utilize free models in your demo, it's best to mention where it came from. Oh, by the way, you Artist folk are not showcasing your modeling talent when using free models off the web. Create your own!

Create Original Content

After you obtain a game industry job, you will be creating plenty of original content for the projects you are working on. Do the same for your demo! Show your ability to be original. This is what the game industry is built upon!

No—Not the Same Senior Class Project or Tutorial

Of course you attended that fabulous school so you could get your dream job in the game industry, but graduates cannot live on degrees and class projects alone. You must create something new and unique to stand out from the other thirty students who graduated with you. When thirty people work on something, how can it be determined specifically what your contribution was in the first place? If you're applying for an entry-level job, odds are a few of your fellow graduates are as well. Hiring managers do not want to see the same demo over and over. Merely using your class project is a weak way to show your skill. As for the tutorials you did to learn a new software product or experiment with the use of a technology, do *not* put it on your demo. Learn the lesson the tutorial is teaching and apply the lessons you learned to your own original work.

Use the Internet to Display Your Work

After you have your demo ready to go, the Internet is an awesome tool for housing and displaying both your demo and résumé. It is the preferred way of presenting yourself, requiring no special software, technical expertise, or equipment to operate or review. A personal web site is a must if you want to be taken as a serious professional. You will not only be posting your résumé to this site, but you will be showing samples of work as well.

Try to register an easy name for people to remember. www.YourName.com works well. Besides creating and maintaining a site, get active on the Internet. Join forums and groups that relate to your game career. Participate in online discussions and contests and post work in online galleries or sites that relate to your field. Get visible and get your web site linked to as many game related sites as you can. Perspective employers are on the Internet and scouting talent. They are not looking for your résumé posted on some job board. They are looking for people who write articles, participate in forums, respond intelligently to queries, and so on.

When you design your site, make sure it is easy to navigate and does not trap the viewer into a long download experience. One way to accomplish this is to use smaller thumbnails to bigger images. Beware: Like a résumé, you only have one chance to dazzle the viewer and if he has a difficult time getting around your site, he will usually drop it and move to the next. So don't overload with graphics other than what is necessary to demonstrate your skills.

KEEP COPIES OF EVERYTHING YOU DO

I have a folder in my computer and also a paper one in my filing cabinet. These files hold copies of everything, and I mean everything, I ever created, wrote, designed, developed, or contributed to. When I am customizing my demo, I search through these files and utilize the assets I feel my audience wants to review. Don't get caught without samples of your work. Think ahead on this issue. Keeping copies of everything you do not only provides you plenty of assets to use in the creation of your demo, but it also provides you with plenty of interview fodder to take with you during the face-to-face interview. Sometimes, it's helpful to be able to do a "show and tell" during an interview, and your files should be full of stuff you can utilize.

REGULARLY UPDATE YOUR DEMO

Your demo will evolve and change as you do. A demo is a part of you, a representation. Make sure you are on at least a monthly schedule of improving and refining it. If you only update your demo when you are job hunting, you will be faced with a very daunting task during a time of stress and anxiety. How can you create an amazing demo under these circumstances? Don't find yourself scrambling to put together a demo. Most importantly, realize that to be the best at anything, you must practice, practice, practice. Practice makes perfect. Keep creating new work and don't be afraid to throw out old work.

IDEAS FOR DEMO MATERIAL

One way to create demo material is to extend a game that you already own and love like *Half-Life*, *Quake 3*, or *Unreal Tournament*. Add some new features into the game play and test it out to practice balance and build your portfolio of work. The freelance development teams that form to create free *MODS* are great places to learn. Many groups have successfully built fan followings, as well as lucrative deals with publishers. Projects like *Counterstrike* and *Team Fortress* have proven that a team of dedicated freelancers can make games on par with the pros. Many developers actively pursue and assist people who are building mods for their game. This is also a great way to get some experience working with an existing tool.

CREATING YOUR DEMO

Now that you're ready to create your demo, where do you start? The following sections walk you through the best ways to present your work.

Level Designer and Game Designer Demos

The best way to present your work is in the form of a designer portfolio. This can come in many different forms from a personal web site, CD, or videotape that covers your work. Even an Acrobat Reader file can work as a demo.

You should be able to clearly show and communicate your abilities in the areas of career focus. For example, if you are looking for a position as a full Game Designer, you will need to demonstrate the ability to generate all of the information needed to manage the creative vision for a game. A picture is worth a thousand words and if you have managed to keep copies of your past work, now is the time to clean them up for presentation. What most game companies expect you to demonstrate, outside of good communication skills, is the ability to generate clearly understandable design documents, diagrams, and AI designs. Game companies also want to see you demonstrate an ability to pace out the game play throughout the entire game keeping the player engaged, excited, and not frustrated.

Level Designer and World Builders should be able to not only show levels created in the area they are seeking employment in but also be able to walk someone through each level and explain why they designed it the way they did.

Some formats for demonstrating and presenting your 3D level and world mapping skills can come from off-the-shelf world editors like those found for Quake, Unreal, 3D Studio Max, or Maya. There may be some areas of experience that are more important to your specific target game company, so it's best to do as much research as possible before submitting your demo. Find out how your target company prefers to see 2D or 3D levels and make sure your demo is customized to this. Don't forget to add as many notes as possible describing your play mechanics and how they work. Sometimes, you will find several designers working on the same world or level. Therefore, it is very important that, in your demo, you clearly distinguish your specific contribution.

Here are top areas that you will be judged for each position:

	Lead Designer	Game Designer	Level Designer
Communication skills	*	*	*
Work ethics	*	*	*
Team work	*	*	*
Ability to take directions	*	*	*
Ability to give directions	*	*	
Writing skills	*	*	
Design scheduling skills	*		

	Lead Designer	Game Designer	Level Designer
Production tracking skills	*	*	
Concept proposal skills	*	*	
Ability to pitch concepts	*	(Sometimes)	
Design document skills	*	*	
Ability to communicate design to others	*	*	
Game play design skills	*	*	
Level design skills in 3D or 2D	*	*	*
Level design skills on paper	(Sometimes)	(Sometimes)	(Sometimes)
Understanding of AI scripting/understanding	*	*	(Sometimes)
Ability to design mechanics	*	*	*
AI flowcharting and documentation	*	*	
Game play pacing skills	*	*	*
Ability to design controls	*	*	
Ability to design interfaces	*	*	
Ability to manage Video CG Production	*		
Ability to manage Sound/ Music Production	*		
Ability to work around technical restrictions	*		
Ability to tune product for final	*		
Ability to manage motion-capture production	(Sometimes)		
Ability to travel	(Sometimes)		

The best format for your demo is a web site or CD containing completed 3D level designs for *Quake, Half Life*, and so on. Design map layouts and script AI behaviors. Build and modify characters, create and modify triggers, and so on. Demonstrate ability to do level layouts using 3D Studio Max or Maya.

Your samples should show an understanding of game play and strong design principals. You'll want to include a text file with your levels to give instructions on how to load the levels, and provide a brief summary of your design thought process for each level.

Include in your demo samples of design documents, grid paper designs, game pitches, and game systems (as in resource economies, combat models, and so on). If your target company uses a licensed technology like Unreal, you should

FROM THE EXPERT

"Demo turn off? Big ideas done poorly."

- Murray Taylor, Studio Head/Worldwide Art Director, Infogrames

use the same technology to create levels in your demo. Post your work on the Web. Write articles. Get visible! Show your work and generate interest.

Game Programmer Demos

To get a game programming job, a great way to stand out is to present a portfolio of code samples and games you have developed. If you're just starting out, create a game of your own or clone an existing game, yet add an original idea. Create your own software tools for game development. In short, design an application that showcases your coding ability and strengths.

Code Games!

Your demo need not be too complex; rather, you want to demonstrate your grasp of current game programming techniques and technologies. Do this by creating a few small, self-contained games. The more robust and complete the game (multiple levels, beginning and ending sequences, and so on) or tools, the more attention you will get. Your aim is to demonstrate that you understand how a video game works and how it is designed. You'll want to include a text file that gives any instructions on how to load the game, and provide a brief summary of your design thought process or what you learned technically.

Create Tools

Example tools that you can create for working on a game include image loaders for bitmap or GIF files, audio loaders for WAV files and MP3s, tile map editors, preview utilities for audio and image files, or wrapper classes that will make it easier to use a popular API like DirectX.

For each game or tool you have coded, show screenshots. Consider creating small AVIs that quickly walk through a level of your game or demonstrate functionality. This way, when someone hops onto your web site, she can get a quick feel for your abilities without having to take time downloading and then running your game or tool.

Show Samples of Code

TIP

Start a freeware project or join an existing team working on one.

On your web site, make available an accurate sample of your production code, with a large enough scope to demonstrate some interaction between different sections of the code. Obviously, this is a representation of your work, so the code should be clean and well documented. Technical hiring managers want to see how you organize code and go about solving problems. This is a great way to show off your coding prowess.

Another way to generate assets for your programmer demo is to join an Open Source project. Head over to SourceForge at www.sourceforge.net. SourceForge is a repository of applications currently in development. All the source code that is being used is available for free. You can learn from looking at other people's code as well as modifying it to your purposes. One of the cool things about the Open Source movement is that you get to learn from others and extend their work in your own way.

Obtaining and Demonstrating Console Experience

Yes, it is tough to obtain console experience without having access to a development station. However, the Net has tons of technical information available on almost any game platform. Research and obtain the specific information you need so you can familiarize yourself with a console and some of the issues around it. If your target game company creates console games and you don't have this experience yet, get creative. Figure out what you can code that might assist your target game company more efficiently create games. I promise that you will be considered first for a job if you can provide your potential new boss with a solution to a problem he faces.

Recently, Sony released a Linux-based PS2 developers kit, which costs about $200. Bite the bullet and go out and purchase this kit. Train yourself, then go cut code!

For a sample of a game programmer demo, check out William Wetherill's site at `http://cdray.com/neophyle/`.

Game Artist Demos

Although some game careers don't necessarily require a demo, an Artist simply will not get a job without one!

The best format for your demo is a web site or CD containing samples of your work.

To Get Attention, Artists Must Present a Mind-Blowing Demo Reel!

Artist demos usually include clips from games previously worked on. However, if you're trying to break into the industry, you won't have professional game clips, so you will need to be creative in putting together your demo. Game companies receive literally hundreds of demo reels each month from aspiring Artists who want in the industry. Yet, from that massive pile, very few make the cut. Unfortunately, in most cases, it's the submitted material, not the individual's skills, that gets in the way of scoring the job. So, how do you stand out from the crowd and make that elusive cut?

Don't try to be a jack-of-all-trades. That is, define your 2D, 3D, or fine art skills and briefly discuss them. Are you an Animator? A Texture Artist? A Model Builder (high resolution, low resolution)? Are you good at color composition? Lighting? Spend your time refining the few elements you are exceptional at, rather than trying to be good at every aspect of art. For example, when viewing a Texture Artist's demo reel, Art Director Andrew Paquette wants to see the original texture maps and the geometry it is mapped to. He doesn't care as much what it looks like in the game engine because the maps are what he is looking at. For Artists who do lighting and rendering, all he needs to see are examples from game graphics.

Understand that, although special effects are cool to the average Joe on the street, a game industry Art Director will not be impressed by them. If you have

FROM THE EXPERT

"If you're not a strong animator, don't put animation in your reel. If you're not a great modeler but you can animate, use someone else's models. Highlight and emphasize your strengths."

- Paul Steed, Modeler for *Quake Game Series* and Author of *Modeling a Character in 3DS Max* and *Animating Real-Time Game Characters*

an effect in a scene, it should be shown to demonstrate how the effect enhances your scene, it should not be the scene itself. If you do show special effects, make sure you have worked with, and can clearly control, the effect. Default settings in most applications are weak and it's very obvious to industry professionals when they haven't been changed. Post your work on the Web. Write articles. Get visible! Show your work and generate interest. Don't forget to include a text file that provides a brief summary of your work.

Here is a list of suggestions for designing your demo:

1. Generate a series of concept drawings, color comps, and construction lay-outs based upon an original game concept or take an existing game, book, comic, or film franchise and visualize elements from it, as if you were preparing initial images for a game project. Include conceptual images of characters, objects, environments, and possible story/game scenes.

2. Based upon these concepts, and using one of the noted 3D software pack-ages (preferably one that a prospective employer is using in production or one that you can be most efficient with), generate several models. Choose examples from each asset type that you have conceived—characters, objects, creatures, vehicles, and structures.

3. Now that you have several models, it would be a good exercise to create and apply appropriate textures to fully realize your aesthetic vision. Using Photoshop, and possibly DeepPaint3D or another UV mapper, apply these textures to your models.

4. Taking your textured models, set them up for animating, if necessary, in your 3D software package. If you are not a proficient Animator, apply mo-cap or pre-animated files to your armature. If you are an Animator, create several short move animations of 30 to 60 frames, including a walk/run cycle, several periodic personality idles that reveal your ability to "act" through your character model, and a couple of dynamic action moves to stress test your model.

5. Finally, either using a standard 3D software package or a commercially available Level/World Editor, create an acceptable example showing your abilities at building an exciting, compelling environment. Keep it limited in scope so that you can use your limited resources of time and materials to make the most professional quality portfolio piece of a world.

The results of these exercises should yield quite a portfolio of game art assets that, if consistently polished to a higher production value through honest self-critiques and re-edits, and using successful marketed products as the paradigm, will no doubt fuel a much more appropriate demo presentation to prospective employers.

Concentrate on those exercises which will represent your best work towards your targeted career goal, whether as a concept Artist, Modeler, Texturer, Level Builder, Animator, or Interface Designer, and you are assured of building the best quality, focused demo presentation for your purposes.

PUTTING IT ALL TOGETHER

After you have your demo's assets organized and refined, put them on a web site, CD, or videotape. You never should be caught with an outdated résumé or web site, even if you're not actively job hunting. You will need your web site for networking.

Never make apologies for your demo. If you feel the need to apologize for the lack of quality or the lack of substance, you are not ready to send it out. Keep your demo up-to-date. Keep it fresh and exciting.

AUTHOR NOTE

"Using abstract or cartoon characters in your demo instead of realistic human or other carbon life forms is an immediate warning to an Art Director. If you can't really build characters, don't claim you can!"

- Marc

AUTHOR NOTE

"Whenever you gain employment, be sure to request that your business cards contain your personal web site address. Most companies don't object to this practice. Advertise your web site address on any and all correspondence. You want people to be able to locate you easily, even if it has been three years since you met."

- Marc

CHAPTER 10

Your Résumé, Pitch, and References

Understand that job hunting is similar to selling and marketing anything. And, in this instance, you're the product being sold!

Salespeople use marketing materials to help them make the sale. You are selling you, and your marketing materials are your demo, résumé, and a one-minute active job-hunt pitch. This pitch is similar to your one-minute networking pitch, but now your focus is job hunting itself and utilizing the wealth of contacts you have been developing with your networking pitch. After you get a job, you will be reworking your job hunt pitch back to a new networking pitch. When you're not job hunting, you're networking! The cycle never stops and when you get it in motion, maintaining your network is easy and fun.

A great résumé gains interest and helps get the interview, and the interview gets the job. Bad résumé? No interview. No job. Please, spend the time and effort to make your résumé great. If you've read the book to this point, you've learned what it takes for a killer demo; now it's time to put together the optimal résumé.

WRITING YOUR RÉSUMÉ

When putting together your résumé, it's important to keep a few thoughts in mind. First, we live in a world where, generally speaking and sadly enough, people avoid reading. (Unless, of course, it's a Harry Potter book.) Moreover, with game companies, communication is often via email and quite succinct in style. To be an effective tool, your résumé should be to the point as well.

As discussed earlier, though it may still sound strange, do not assume that the person who initially reads your résumé at that game company knows anything about the game industry. You must create a résumé that is simple to read, and you must use words that are easy to understand. Be careful to use correct game industry jargon and technical terminology.

You also want your résumé to stand out from the pack of other candidates applying for the same job. Consider your audience carefully when constructing your résumé. Everything about your résumé should be designed to satisfy what you think your audience wants. Put yourself in the shoes of the hiring managers. What would they want to see in a résumé? What qualities are they looking for? What experience do you have that fits their needs?

There are several résumé styles from which to choose, but a very targeted résumé is favored. What does that mean? It means take the time to tailor your résumé for each specific job to which you apply. This does not mean you have to write a new résumé each and every time you approach a company. If your résumé is in chronological format, it will be easy to alter and customize. For example, if you are applying for a job that requires Visual C++ experience and you have Assembly, DirectX, and Visual C++ experience, then, by all means, move the Visual C++ to the top of the list! Targeted résumés "sell" you more effectively because they deliberately position you for a specific job!

Present Your Skills in a Way to Capture the Attention of the Reader

Résumés should be designed for easy "scanability." That is, with one swoop of the eye, and in less than one minute, potential employers can scan your résumé and learn who you are, your major skill sets, and if they wish to interview and investigate you further as a candidate for the job.

Forget the One-Page Résumé Rule

Although this was the advice given in the 70s to the traditional business community, it does not apply to technology companies or creative people. Space out your résumé. Make it comfortable to look at and read. Put yourself in the reader's shoes or eyeglasses, as it were. Aren't you more likely to scan a two-page résumé that is nicely laid out and comfortable to look at, versus a one-page résumé that is written like a novel in tiny font typeset? Crammed documents make the reader feel tense. And you don't want the reader's first experience of you to be a tense one, right? Be clear. Be snappy. And be succinct in your résumé presentation. You're looking for the reader to feel comfortable and relaxed when scanning your résumé—think carefully about layout.

Instead of an Objective Statement Use a Bulleted Summary of Skills, Accomplishments, or Benefits

If you use a chronologically organized format that highlights your skills correctly, there is really no need for a summary statement. It should be obvious to the reader what you do. Just under your name, simply state your career objective: Game Designer, Game Animator, Producer, Game Tools & Technology Developer, and so on. If you are responding to a specific job posting you have seen, by all means, use the exact title of the job your interested in. Lift it right off the job ad copy.

Many game companies utilize some sort of computerized résumé tracking system that searches by keywords. This way, when a new job opens, they can easily access their own internal resources before deciding if they should advertise or assign a recruiter to the task of locating the talent sought. A Game Programmer clearly did not develop these systems. Sadly, most of these tracking system programs are not even written in C. They do not incorporate state of the art technology, and most utilize rudimentary text recognition systems. Keep this in mind when creating your résumé. Fancy fonts, odd text sizes, and graphics, although fun to incorporate in a résumé, can mess with the text recognition system. Don't risk missing a job opening due to a weak text scanning system that has coded and classified you incorrectly. Your résumé will never get flagged and pulled for review when matched against job requirements. To avoid this mess, use a Skill Summary section and use industry standard game jargon and correct technical terminology (see the upcoming résumé examples).

> **AUTHOR NOTE**
>
> "Generally speaking, I do not recommend including an Objective Statement. Most are self serving and a waste of space. Sell what you can do for a company, not what a company can do for you!"
>
> - Marc

Your Selling Points

Summarize your top two to five selling points directly under your name. In short, within the first few lines of your résumé, the reader should be able to learn the following:

- Your name

- Your function

- Your accomplishments

Here's an example of a bulleted summary of skills and selling points:

Marc Mencher
Executive Producer

www.YourName.com

- 32 published titles on XBox, PS2, PSX, Dreamcast, GBA, and PC

- Negotiation Skills, Collaboration, Project Management, and Budgeting

- External and Internal Team Management

Marc Mencher
Game Programmer

www.YourName.com

- 3D Graphics, Engines, Special Effects, Memory Management, Mathematics, and Physics

- Extensive C, C++, Windows, Linux, DirectX, OpenGL, and GNU Compiler

- PlayStation 2, XBox, GameCube

Marc Mencher
Art Director

www.YourName.com

- Experience Designing, Creating, Managing, and Delivering Low/High Poly Art Assets

- Lighting, Texturing, Modeling, Character Animation, Cinematics, and Pipelines

- PlayStation 2 (PS2), PlayStation (PSX), PC, and XBox

- Proven Record Delivering on Time and Within Budget

- Traditional Arts Background, Commercial Artist, Drawing and Storytelling Skills

- Expertise with Most Major CG Animation Software Tools like Alias (Studio, Power Animator, StudioPaint), Maya, CDRS, N-World, Mirai, 3D Studio Max, Renderman, Illustrator, Photoshop, and many other 2D/3D packages

Marc Mencher
Mission Builder / Level Designer

www.YourName.com

- Level Layouts, Models, Placeholder Assets, and Scripting Game Play Events (UnrealEd and Microsoft 3DX)

- Responsible for 10 Worlds Created as Low-Poly City Settings

- Develop Camera Angles, Pads, Paths, Power-Ups, Objects, and Lighting Using 3D Studio Max

- Item and Entity Placement, Mission Geometry, Applying Textures, Testing, and Revision

- C++, Lightwave 3D, Photoshop, Illustrator, MS Word/Excel/ Powerpoint/ Access, FileMaker Pro

Non-Industry Experience

If you're applying for a game industry job and have work experience that is not relevant to game development, summarize it and place it at the end of your résumé. If your work accomplishments can be highlighted in a way to demonstrate benefit to game development, include it. If not, keep it off the résumé. The hiring manager only cares about your experience as it relates to the relevant game development project.

WHAT NOT TO INCLUDE

Avoid providing data like marital status, health, religious orientation, and hobbies. If it has no bearing on game development, leave it out. You never know what may be perceived as negative when the hiring manager first reviews your résumé. Don't give reasons for rejection. The only exception to this rule is if your miscellaneous or personal information pertains to a game job. If so, include it. For example, one of your hobbies is flying airplanes. You even have a pilot's license. Normally, this information would be left off a résumé. However, because this industry creates flight simulation games, pilot experience can get you bonus points over the competition, especially when applying for a flight simulation art job. That you tutored Physics or Math in high school or college is also an attractive thing to list for a Programmer. It communicates team lead ability, mentoring ability, and the perception that you're good at physics and math problems.

That you were on a semi-professional sports team would also be bonus points when approaching a game development studio specializing in sports games. For a Producer (or any career), the ability to speak a foreign language is useful, especially if you did some sort of work abroad. This could make your skills more attractive to a development studio working on a Japanese conversion. Think very carefully about what personal or miscellaneous experience you reveal. If it relates to some genre of game development, tell about it. Otherwise, don't include it.

Use a Clean Font such as Arial or Times New Roman

Use regular 12-point type except when trying to draw attention, at which time you can use larger type, bold, or italics—but use these with discretion. Microsoft Word or Adobe Acrobat PDF files are most acceptable, because you'll be submitting your résumé electronically.

No Fancy Shmancy

Gimmicky résumés or résumés printed on colored paper are certainly more fun from a creative standpoint, but HR usually makes a copy for the hiring managers and the original goes into HR's files. That is, most often, the actual version of the résumé that the hiring manager will see is a photocopy. Fancy résumés on colored paper will not photocopy well, neither will the cleverly formatted résumé, which is sideways or made like a booklet.

If you are sending your résumé electronically, most likely the electronic version of the résumé will be distributed. Make sure the top portion of your document clearly and concisely summarizes who and what you are.

Be Bold with Discretion

Be very careful about what you highlight and bullet within your résumé. You are selling yourself, not the companies for whom you worked. Bold *your* title, not the company name. Also, bold and italicize any and all game titles you have worked on. Next, bold special skill sets and nothing else. Keep in mind that the reader's eye jumps to bolded text. If someone is just scanning your résumé, think carefully about what sells you and what you want the scan read to say about you. Use bold and italics sparingly.

Tell the Whole Truth—Nothing but the Truth?

Everyone has made mistakes in their professional lives; it's part of the human experience. Don't lie, but tell the truth about yourself in a positive way that positions you in the best light.

Presenting your work history, for example, using years, instead of years and months, is positioning in a positive way. Suppose you start working at Hot Smokin' Games and four months later, the company loses its publishing deal and is going to need to cut staff. You're low person on the totem pole so your job is eliminated. Bummer. Job-hunting again. The employment dates at Hot Smokin' Games were actually January 1, 2002 through April 27, 2002. Next, due to bad karma you racked up in a past lifetime, it takes you another four months to get a new job. This makes your résumé look horrible. Eight months and you have produced no game products. You can't expect the résumé reader to know the history of your last employer. Certainly, the poor business decisions the "suits" made should not negatively reflect on you. You had no involvement in those decisions, nevertheless, your résumé makes an impression and a four-month stint at a company initially can make it seem like you are a problem employee, or just not very good at your chosen profession. Stating your employment history vaguely (2002), on the other hand, can soften that first negative impression. Take credit for the work you did accomplish. Just because a publisher canceled the project does not negate the work you did.

Briefly explain your job movement, especially if you have a short tenure at a job. It is acceptable to state that you seek employment due to downsizing or company financial instability. During your face-to-face interview you will have to explain this further but at least, in a verbal conversation you will be able to easily address and remove any concerns. This is something very difficult to do in written form. In short, you did not lie, but you did position a potential negative in the most positive way you could.

Don't forget to put your web site address on your résumé. Remember that the goal of your résumé is to pique interest in an employer and generate interviews for yourself. The résumé is for nothing else. You want to make sure that your résumé has the least number of rejection points awarded when it is first read or, more realistically speaking, it is scanned. You want to make the cut so you get a face-to-face interview or at least a telephone screen. This is when you "sell" yourself and deal with any misperceptions or already upfront impressions formed from your résumé.

Take a look at the following résumé:

Marc Mencher
Game Programmer

www.YourName.com

- 3D Graphics, AI, Engines, Special Effects, Memory Management, Mathematics, and Physics

- Extensive C, C++, Windows, Linux, DirectX, OpenGL, and GNU Compiler

- PlayStation 2, XBox, GameCube

Game Programmer, Smoking Games January 1, 2002 – April 27, 2002

Member of the development team that was creating *Tribe of One*; project was cancelled.

After reading this, are you not left feeling: "What's wrong with this person? Had a game job for only 4 months? Couldn't have accomplished very much or must not be good. Reject. I have 78 more résumés to look at." This is a good example of a negative impression.

Now try this one:

Marc Mencher
Game Programmer

www.YourName.com

- 3D Graphics, AI, Engines, Special Effects, Memory Management, Mathematics, and Physics

- Extensive C, C++, Windows, Linux, DirectX, OpenGL, and GNU Compiler

- PlayStation 2, XBox, GameCube

Game Programmer, Smoking Games 2002

Unfortunately the financial instability of my current employer forces me to seek employment.

Led a team of three Programmers in the development of *Tribe of One*, a 3D Canyon Racing game similar to Pod Racing. Responsible for OpenGL engine, terrain, renderer, collision, physics, culling, Quad Tree, integration, and game AI. Also was responsible for the overall code design, program flow, and game loop. Unfortunately before this game was complete, the publisher canceled the project.

See what a difference a change in wording can make? This résumé takes credit for work accomplished. The reader may have some questions, but you are not a reject here.

If you have been in the industry for some time, your work history may reflect the volatility of the games market as it has grown from the garage to monolith-sized corporations. Still, having a string of failed start-ups on your résumé can leave the reader with a negative impression. As discussed earlier, HR probably knows little history of the industry. So, address any issues up front. Don't allow someone's lack of industry history, or natural emotional response to a résumé, get in your way of getting a job. A brief explanation of your movement, as in the preceding example, will keep your résumé in the active pile.

Accomplishments: What You Can Do for a Company Gets Attention

When writing your résumé, state your accomplishments. Don't write your job description. Most people generally understand what a Tools Programmer does. Tell them what they don't know, tell them what you accomplished in *your role* as a Tools Programmer. This is what sells *you*. Include the size of the team you managed, your budget responsibility, and so on. This is what they don't know. If you created something new and radical, talk about it. If your contribution somehow can be linked to the amazing sales figures the game generated, this is even better! The one thing to repeat in a résumé is your job function. Having the words "Game Designer" all over your résumé sure as heck should leave the impression that you are a Game Designer. Otherwise, pepper your résumé with a variety of action words, particularly when stating accomplishments.

USE ACTION WORDS

Here is a brief list of useful action words:

Achieved	Established	Organized
Advised	Evaluated	Participated
Analyzed	Expanded	Performed
Assumed	Experimented	Planned
Built	Facilitated	Produced
Compiled	Generated	Recommended
Conceived	Headed	Researched
Conducted	Helped	Responsible
Consulted	Implemented	Revised
Contributed	Improved	Rewrote
Coordinated	Initiated	Scheduled
Created	Innovated	Simplified
Delivered	Installed	Solved
Demonstrated	Integrated	Studied
Designed	Invented	Supervised
Developed	Investigated	Trained
Directed	Led	Transformed
Discovered	Managed	Utilized
Engineered	Negotiate	

Open each and every accomplishment statement in your résumé with an action word. Explain what you learned technically as a result of working on the project. Be sure to provide an explanation of what the application does and how it works. Here are some examples:

- Created art assets in the game, including building and texturing characters and numerous high-resolution models for the PS2 version. Edited character models and textures.

- Implemented sound subsystem and video subsystem utilizing DirectMedia.

- Developed proprietary UI library based on DirectDraw.

- Led the "feature team" during implementation.

- Responsible for budgets, schedules, setting art look, creating art pipeline, supervising creation of all art assets for *Force*, a real-time strategy game for XBox.

The following are examples related to specific games:

- Designed and developed *Tank Battle*, a 3D first/third person tank fighting game similar to *Battle Zone*. Developed on top of a Game Cad Engine, the game's notable features include intelligent enemy tank AI, tactical enemy engagement, 3D collision, turret tracking, and multiple camera views. This gave me some Java 3D experience as well as perfected my 3D matrix/vector math operations. I modeled and custom textured the tanks and virtual world in Multi-Gen Creator.

- Designed and developed *Deep Space*, an *Asteroids* clone done in DirectX8. This game featured 10 levels of difficulty, power-ups, shields, motion physics, precise 2D collision, and original animation; and showcases my C/C++ OOP, artwork, animation, graphics, game logic, and design skills.

- To teach myself the Massive Multiplayer Gaming concept, I designed and developed *SphereWorld*, for which I created a 3D renderer from scratch, incorporated primitive 3D objects into it, and established a client/server model using Win32/MFC sockets to connect multiple instances of the program into it.

SAMPLE RÉSUMÉS

In the preceding sections, we've covered how to put together a good résumé. On the next several pages, we show you examples of résumés that will get you noticed.

Marc Mencher
Level Designer

- PS2 and PC Games

- 3D Studio Max, PhotoShop, UnrealED, Qeradiant, Eden, BSP, Paintshop Pro

SPACE GAMES 1999 to Present

Lead World Builder (2000 to Present)

Member of the team that designed and developed *Nukem*, an action game for PS2. Managed the world builders on the team, set up their tasks, and reviewed their work on a regular basis. Specifically responsible for:

- All enemy, object, and power-up placements in the game as per design specifications.

- Creation of all documents, maps, and layouts for all levels of the game in conjunction with the Lead Game Designer.

- Made 2 of the 12 levels for the game.

- Optimized all levels of the game to increase overall performance.

- Worked closely with the Engineers to come up with new effects and debug the engine used for the title.

- Worked closely with the engine group on the development of various plug-ins for 3D Studio Max.

- Trained level designers in how to use the company's customized Max plug-ins.

- Created generic objects and furniture used in all of the levels of the game.

- Assisted in the screening of potential world builders for the company.

Level Builder (1999 to 2000)

Member of the team that designed and developed *Wild*. Specifically responsible for:

- Creating and populating large areas of terrain in the Serious Sam engine.

- Worked with artists to build the list of art assets needed for the game world.

- Worked with Programmers to tweak game specific scripts and tools.

Level Designer, Cave Games (1997 to 1998)

Member of the team that designed and developed *Awake* (PC title):

- Created documentation and detailed maps for five levels in document form based on what was needed to accommodate the story line of the game.

- Developed a large variety of puzzles, environments, and innovative areas.

- Worked closely with the Programmers on development, design, and debugging of a custom built editor.

- Responsible for placing of all agents, objects, and other content in the levels created.

Contract Level Designer, Cyber Studios (1995 to 1997)
Contract designer working on *E*, a PC title:

- Created and maintained design document for the game.

- Responsible for creating 8 of the 12 levels in the game and all content in those levels.

- Scripted and modified in the Unreal engine as needed in various levels I had created.

- Responsible for maintaining the folders and files for the game and making sure unused or out-dated files were properly archived.

- Assisted other Designers as needed in tuning and balancing.

Shake Rattle & Roll, Quake (PC title):

- Created five single player levels for this title as well as four multiplayer levels.

- Assisted other Level Designers in cleaning and optimizing their levels.

- Assisted in creating background story and roughing out the sequencing of the levels.

- Responsible for all enemy, object, and power-up placement in levels I had created.

Please review my demo: at www.GameRecruiter.com.

Marc Mencher
QA Manager/Designer

- Create Game Content, Single and Multiplayer Missions, Script Art

- Special Effects (Glow, Transparency, Shadows, and so on)

- QA Test Plans, Bug Tracking Systems, Database Tools, Managed Test Teams

- FileMaker Pro, Access, Excel, VSS, VB, C, C++, Python

EMPLOYMENT

QA Manager & Designer, Games, Games, Game, Inc.   1997 to Present

Performed as both a QA Manager and Designer. Developed QA bug tracking databases, prepared test plans, and managed the test team of eight. Worked with development and publishers including Microsoft, EA, and Activision for the following games:

- *Commander*. Balanced all the weapons, shields, and power systems for every ship in the game. Positioned every ship component with a custom 3D placement tool. Created and placed all the damage icons for every ship and object in the game. Wrote internal test-plans and managed the internal test team while working with Activision's test team using a shared QA database.

- *Alliance*. Edited more than 500 images of planets and ships using Photoshop and edited scripts to add them to the game. Used a custom 3D tool to check and adjust texture maps and to assign weapon and collision hardpoints. Made missions for both single and multiplayer.

- *Elder*. Created a model attribute database. Used Photoshop to create and edit art files and made the scripts that loaded the art into the game. Worked with five different custom tools to create animations, edit unit attributes, and design missions.

- *Collector Series*. Tested the windows implementation as well as tested all the missions with the new texture mapped models.

QA Manager, HoloByte Games   1992 to 1997

Created test plans and assigned QA leads. Developed the company bug-tracking database. Assisted development teams in Maryland, Texas, and England. Worked with project managers and marketing to develop schedules and marketing strategy. Major projects included: *Generations, Master of II, G-29, Hornet, Helix, Top Gun, Trek AFU, Tetris,* and *Falcon Gold*. Additional projects included: *Gathering, Falcon 4.0, Prix II, Legion, Soldiers*–(SNES), *Top Gun*–(SNES), and *Tetris* (Game Boy).

Mission Builder & QA Engineer, Dynamix   1990 to 1992

Mission builder for A-10. aviation history research for *Baron, A-10,* and *Pacific*. Tested many products including *Baron, A-10, Dragon, Willy,* and *Stellar 15*. Developed test plans and trained testers.

EDUCATION

BS in Technology, University of X, 1989.

Programming in C, Community College, Oakland, California, 1995.

Programming in C for Engineers, Community College, Salem, Oregon, 1990.

Please View My Demo At www.GameRecruiter.com.

Marc Mencher
Technical Director

- Artificial Intelligence, Algorithms, Client-Server Applications, and Game Engines

- 3D Graphics, Editors, Compilers, 3D Sound, 3D Sprite System, and Real-Time View-Dependant LOD

- C/C++, Assembly (6502, 65816, Z80, 68000, 8086), BASIC, and C

- PS2, PSX, Win95/98/NT, UNIX, Saturn, 32X, Game Boy, Game Gear, SNES, NES

- 18 Years of Programming Experience with Emphasis Managing Projects on Tight Schedules

EXPERIENCE

Technical Director, Electronic Arts   **2000 to Present**
Worked on the following titles: *Knockout* (PS2), *Bond 007* (PS2), *Hockey, Game Gear* and *Kings* (PSX):

- Responsible for evaluating technical aspects of product scripts/designs. Facilitate communications between internal and external groups; problem solver.

- Explore and evaluate new and upcoming technologies; report findings to appropriate group leaders.

- Become extremely knowledgeable on all new platforms; educate and aid developers in these areas.

- Evaluate hardware needs to internal divisions and recommend appropriate upgrades.

- Firefight projects, when needed.

Technical Director, Hot Smokin' Games   **1998 to 2000**
Worked on the following titles: *Logan5*, an action game for PSX, and *Tsunami*, an action game for PC (Win95/98):

- Overall technical-management of all ongoing projects and technical assessment of all incoming proposals.

- Coordination of engineering resources to make sure technical issues are addressed and software standards are met.

- Worked with project teams to develop high-level architecture, technical specifications, and designs.

- R&D of new technology, feasibility assessment, and presentation of that technology to engineering teams.

- Technical recruiting, interviewing, and hiring of new engineers.

- Ensured that all Engineers had best tools, software, and hardware available.

- Communication of technical issues with Producers, Designers, Artists, and Audio Personnel to achieve project goals.

- Estimated, created, and troubleshot all project schedules.

- Continued improving/excelling technical and coding skills, performed other Software Engineering tasks as required.

- Acted as mentor for less experienced software engineers.

Lead Engineer, Got Game Entertainment   1996 to 1998

Managed all aspects of game-development team: four Programmers, six Artists, two Audio Developers, and two Writers. This also involved meeting with publishers and clients, planning and assessment of project deadlines, source-code maintenance, and inspection. Other duties included: project planning, requirements analysis, specification, and documentation.

Led a team in the design and development of *Watchmaker*, PC adventure game for Win95. Project involved OO-design and integration of all aspects of high-
performance 3D-graphics technology, including the following areas of development:

- OO integration of 3D-graphics engine employing multi-pass techniques and real-time dynamic lighting model.

- Rapid-App development techniques for quick testing and deployment of implementations.

- Tool creation for game-asset management, modification, importing (Alias-OBJ/Direct-3D/DXF, Soundforge).

- Extensive sound engineering using 3DSound, DirectSound, MODs, and Redbook audio.

Please view my demo at www.GameRecruiter.com.

Marc Mencher
Senior Game Artist

- Texturing, Character Creation, Lighting, and Storyboarding

- 3D Studio Max, Lightwave, PhotoShop, Fractal Painter, Deluxe Paint

- Sony PlayStation (PS2 & PSX), Win95/98, Nintendo64, and Sega Genesis

EXPERIENCE

Senior Artist, Crystal Games   1998 to Present
Lead a team of six Artists in the design and development of the following games:

- *Dash Racing* (XBox). Current Project. Worked with the Art Director and Designers on the initial visualization of the game. Responsible for the title screen. Responsible for the snow level.

- *Racing Cart* (PS2). Designed, built, and textured the Caribbean track. Responsible for the game opening fly-through of Main St. Responsible for win sequence fly-through of Main St. at night with fireworks. Assisted with the initial character creation.

- *Jexx 2* and *Jexx 3* (PSX, Nintendo64). Worked with a designer on the creation of the space level, pirate and undersea level. Created all the world mesh and level textures. Responsible for lighting. Story boarding and creating all the mesh and textures for the real-time fly-through. Responsible for the camera fly-through in the intro and the hub.

Game Artist, Itsy Bitsy Games   1997
Sought employment due to company's weak financial status.

Member of the team that designed and developed *Galactic* (PC/Win95). Responsible for creating four classes of alien space ships. Created 38 space ships. Worked with Art Director on overseeing the full motion videos (FMVs).

Artist, Head Games   1994 to 1996
Member of the team that designed and developed *Dreams* (PSX). Worked closely with Producer creating game plot. Created all the concept art. Worked closely with the Art Director overseeing the animation. Digitally painted FMV backdrops.

Member of the team that designed and developed *ManX* (Sega Genesis). Animated "The Beast." Created some of the background texture art.

MISCELLANEOUS

Fine Art Skill. Painted with oils, acrylics, and pastels for various projects.

EDUCATION:

BFA in Illustration, minor in Fine Art, Art Center College of Design, 1994.

Visit my online demo at www.GameRecruiter.com.

Marc Mencher

Executive Producer
- More Than 10 Titles Brought to Market (Action, Adventure, Sports, RPGs)

- Extensive PC and Console Experience (PS2, PSX, Win95, Game Boy, SNES)

- Track Record Producing Award-Winning Products on Time and Under Budget

- In-House and External Development Studios

- Negotiation of Contracts, Complete Business Model Preparation, Profit and Loss (P&L) Responsibilities

EXPERIENCE

Executive Producer, Got Game Entertainment   1999 to Present
Responsible for timely submission of milestone deliverables. Compile, adjust, and track schedules; lead company/client production and team meetings; and track production assets (design, source art, tools, and so on). Regularly consult and work with Producers to evaluate production risks and anticipate potential problems. Provide direction for new projects. Consult with console manufacturers regarding updates, training seminars, and submission processes.

Products brought to market: PC adventure game *Watchmaker*, PC adventure game *Tony Tough and The Night of the Roasted Months*, and an action shooter *Tsunami 2265* (PC and PS2).

Senior Producer, Hot Smokin' Games   1995 to 1998
Duties: Product development; management of producers; recommendation of new and acquired product; developed game designs/treatments to spec; selection of exterior development teams.

Productions: *Sanity* (Win95); *Werewolf* (Win95), *Pro Hunter* (PSX), *Pro Hunter 2* (PS2).

Producer / Associate Producer, GameTek   1992 to 1995
Productions: *Super Fighter II Turbo* (DOS); *Cyber Punk Adventure* (DOS); *Bureau* (DOS); *Dreams* (SNES, Genesis, Game Boy); *Pinball Fantasies* (SNES, Genesis); *Tarzan* (SNES, Game Boy, Game Gear)

ACCOMPLISHMENTS
- CGW Adventure Game of the Year (*Sanitarium*)

- Editor's Choice award in all major PC gaming periodicals (*Sanitarium*)

- RPG of the Year (*Werewolf, Mage*)

References/Writing Samples at www.GameRecruiter.com.

Marc Mencher
Director of Marketing

- Launched more than 10 Games (Children's, Action, Sports) on PC, PS2, XBox, Game Boy

- Developed and Executed Marketing Plans, Licensing, and Property Management

- Web Site Design/Development, Online Marketing Experience

EXPERIENCE:

Director of Product Marketing, Infogrames   1999 to Present
- Manage a team of three Product Managers, setting strategy for the North American territory of this top-ten video game company.

- Negotiate licensing details, propose product designs, manage product marketing, and recruit and train staff.

- Personally manage some products during busy crunch times.

Product Marketing Manager, The 3DO Company   1993 to 1999
- Started the product marketing department and shipped nine entertainment titles for the 3DO-console platform and two PC titles.

- Managed 14 properties for 5 platforms: PC, Macintosh, M2, 3DO, and Internet.

- Assisted with designing games and negotiating game development licensing agreements.

IDG Publishing

Contributing Editor, *NeXTWORLD* Magazine   1990 to 1993
Authored and edited several columns in technology and industry news, wrote technical feature stories and product reviews; made presentations at conferences and industry events.

Bay Area NeXT Group (BANG)

CD-ROM Product Manager   January 1990 to October 1993
- Marketing and operations for the premier user group on the NeXT platform; designed original products.

- Developed and executed marketing plans to support our products; edited and published a quarterly newsletter; facilitated meetings.

- Created, produced, marketed, and shipped the first third-party CD-ROM title on the NEXTSTEP platform.

BMUG, Marketing Specialist   June 1989 to June 1990

- Designed and redesigned key business systems.

- Attracted new guests speakers, negotiated and managed software publishing arrangements for CD-ROM products, programmed and hosted weekly meetings.

Portfolio available at www.GameRecruiter.com.

Products Developed:

Sex, Lies & CD-ROM

Compilation CD-ROM featuring utilities, entertainment, productivity and development tools

Bay Area NeXT Group, 1993

Nominated for *NeXTWORLD* Magazine 1993 Best of Breed Award: Best Content/Title

Products Managed:

*Pen Pen Trilcelon for Dreamcas*t, Infogrames

Bugs Bunny Lost in Time for PlayStation, Infogrames

Bugs Bunny Lost in Time for PC, Infogrames

Ballistic for PlayStation, Infogrames

Ballistic for Game Boy & Game Boy Color, Infogrames

V-Rally Edition 99 for Nintendo 64, Infogrames

V-Rally Edition 99 for Game Boy Color, Infogrames

Army Men, Studio 3DO

Killing Time, Studio 3DO

3DO Games: Decathlon, Studio 3DO

SnowJob, Studio 3DO

3DO Game Guru, Studio 3DO

Captain Quazar, Studio 3DO

BattleSport, Studio 3DO (Received 5 Stars, *Next Generation* Magazine

Phoenix 3, Studio 3DO

Star Fighter, Studio 3DO

BladeForce, Studio 3DO (Received 5 Stars, *Next Generation* Magazine

Zhadnost: The People's Party, Studio 3DO

Club 3DO: Station Invasion, Studio 3DO

Education:

BA Marketing, U.C. Santa Cruz, 1985

Developer University, NeXT Computer Inc., 1991

Developer University, The 3DO Company, 1994

Foreign Languages:

French, Mandarin Chinese

References:

Available upon request

Portfolio available at www.GameRecruiter.com

Marc Mencher
Online Game Programmer

- Multiplayer Network Servers, Clients, Applications, and Virtual Worlds

- Synchronization, Collisions, Player Validation, Protocols, Latency, Integration, and Gaming Lobbies

- Windows 95/NT (DirectX, SDK, MFC, DirectPlay, ATL, STL, SDK, MFC), UNIX

- C/C++, HTML, Perl, Lex, Yacc, Visual Basic, TCP/IP

GAME INDUSTRY EXPERIENCE

Online Game Engineer, Electronic Arts   1999 to Present
- Responsible for the design and development of Windows clients for a multiplayer match-up system. The match-up clients were written in C++ as ActiveX controls using Microsoft's Active Template Library (ATL) and the Standard Template Library (STL).

- I am also part of the Game Technology group. My responsibilities include working with the studios and Network Experience Group to design and build a web-based, ActiveX, multiplayer match-up system. I also took the lead in the automated "quickmatch" system, writing the client-side core.

Game Programmer, Crystal Dynamics   **1998 to 1999**

Left due to company layoff. While there I was responsible for the networking code, both server and client, for an online flight sim called *Kill*. Responsible for reworking the server, removing many bugs and memory leaks in the process. I divorced the game protocol from its dependencies on Microsoft's DirectPlay. I extended the game protocol as necessary to implement new features, such as a handshaking procedure for client-server and client-client synchronization and support for object collisions, score propagation, and player groupings. I also tuned the existing protocol to reduce network usage and mitigate latency issues for smoother game play. I also deal with issues regarding the game's integration with TEN, such as persistent scores and player validation.

Game Programmer, WorldPlay Entertainment   **1996 to 1998**

- While at WorldPlay, I was the Lead for a group of three programmers on a gaming lobby project, called *Xpress*. As part of the project, I worked with my manager, Producers, and the product department to write the product specifications. I worked with the systems group to define messaging protocols suitable for a massively multiplayer environment. I provided technical guidance and expertise on the Microsoft Windows SDK and MFC. I designed and wrote the entire interface for the project.

- My other projects included writing the camera positioning code for a 3D virtual world, called *CyberParc*, and retrofitting the existing code to use a new 3D graphics engine. I was also tasked with implementing several user manipulate-able objects within the *CyberParc* environment. I implemented the chat interface used in *Xpress*, *CyberParc*, and all of WorldPlay's internal games.

Quality Assurance Engineer, FTC Software   **1994 to 1996**

At FTC, I wrote and executed test plans for FTC Software's TCP/IP network servers, clients, and applications. I developed applications for testing individual DLLs; maintained the TCP/IP network for the testing lab; and administered the HTML, LPD, NFS printing, and DHCP servers for the office. I ensured that management was kept up-to-date on the state of the product. I helped to coordinate between the development, documentation, and QA departments. I assisted in releasing a Windows-based TCP/IP kernel and client product. I was also part of the team that shipped an NFS server product for Windows 3.1 and successfully brought FTC's NT NFS server product to Beta. Performed White and Black Box testing on DLLs using C, C++, and Visual Basic. I built scripting tools in C and C++. I also completed testing on a VbX interface to an SQL database.

Check out my online demo at www.GameRecruiter.com.

Marc Mencher
Game Programmer

- Simulation, Game Logic, Artificial Intelligence, Tools Development, and Scripting
- Multiplayer Architecture, Content Creation, User Interface, and Data Structure Design
- C/C++, Direct X, MFC, STL, Extensive Knowledge of Trees and Link Lists!

EXPERIENCE

Game Programmer, Softworks   Jan 2001 to Present
Seeking new employment due to company financial issues.

Member of the development team for the *Scrolls 3*, a first-person adventure/RPG coded in C++ for Win 9x/2k and XBox.

- `Synchronized the magic system to fit with the character's movements and actions.
- Implemented both game play and visual aspects of spells.
- Assisted in AI development, used line of sight to test projectiles.

Game Engineer, Storm Entertainment   1997 to 2001
Member of the team that developed *First Resistance*, a third-person 3D action/adventure game coded in C++ for Win 95/98.

- Created a complex in-game chat system, using MFC, allowing the user to use text or sound, along with a utility to generate actor-ready recording scripts.
- Designed a hierarchical tree tracking system to record the player's progress.
- Designed and implemented a script system for ease of puzzle programming.

Member of the team that developed *Force*, a 3D multiplayer real-time strategy game of high-tech armored warfare coded in C++ for Win 95/98.

- Created a framework for separate tactical-level and vehicle-level behavioral AI capable of:

    Operating in a client-server mode.

    Operating from pre-scripted behaviors.

    Performing limited situational analysis and issuing additional orders to subordinates.

- Designed and implemented game database architecture, incorporating code from other project groups.
- Worked closely with Producer/Designer and Lead Programmer to define game play mechanics.
- Modified an existing level utility and streamlined the process of manipulating large quantities of vehicle performance data.

Game Programmer, Orbital Games　　　**1994 to 1997**

Lead Engineer for *Wing Air*, a multiplayer World War II fighter/simulator written in C++ for Windows 95/NT.

– Multiplayer real-time game model with both strategic and tactical modes.

– Capability to hot-swap between tactically engaged aircraft.

– Point-based scoring system allowing strategically uninvolved players to participate in tactical encounters.

Member of the development team for *Forced Alliance*, a 3D space combat game.

– Designed and created the role-playing and supply-management systems of the game.

– Implemented a multi-tiered story flow engine.

Script Implementer, Electronic Arts　　　**1992 to 1994**

Member of the team that developed *Bard's Tale IV*, an RPG for PC/DOS.

– Designed game play elements and puzzles to be used in the game.

– Wrote the main portion of the dialog and edited any additional dialog or back-story submitted by other contracted writers.

– Designed and implemented a multi-threaded story line using a custom scripting language.

– Worked closely with Lead Programmer to flush out game concepts and tune all game play parameters.

Check out my code at www.GameRecruiter.com.

Marc Mencher

Senior Game Engineer

– Engine and Tools Development, Collision, Compression, 3D Graphics, and Pipeline

– Special Effects, AI, Animation, PS2 VU Coding, OpenGL, Physics, and Math

– Extensive C, C++, Windows, Linux, DirectX, OpenGL, and GNU Compiler

Senior Game Programmer, Luca Games　　　**1999 to Present**

Currently leading a team of seven in the design and development of an unannounced PS2 game. Specifically responsible for integrating in-game development tools, FSM based script compiler and engine, physics and collision engine, extensive math library, and cloth, rope, and vegetation simulator.

Designed and developed an OpenGL based *Collision Engine*, which allows real-time performance of systems with many hundreds of physically simulated interacting bodies.

Led a team of five in the design and development of *Bombad Racing* (PS2), architected and programmed:

Special effects, AI programming—including reasoning, combat, and pathfinding—physics, optimization work, and VU work.

Lead Engineer, Kids Games Interactive   1996 to November 1999

Systems analysis, engine, tools, and core technology development. Designed and implemented core production technologies and software architectures used to create a large number of shipped software titles. Some of the relevant technologies produced include:

— Designed and helped implement a complete asset life cycle management system, which once deployed, significantly reduced production costs.

— Cross-platform run-time animation and game engines used to ship many titles.

— Image processing tools, including integration with U.S. Animation digital ink and paint systems.

— A 3D animation pipeline.

— Managed the creation of libraries and designed algorithms for rasterization of vector based graphics files.

— Foreign language localization tools.

v Other tools and libraries as necessary.

Game Programmer, Sanctuary Games   1993 to 1996

Sanctuary Games was acquired by Kids Games Interactive at the end of 1996. Member of the software technologies development group. Worked on several relevant technologies including:

— Adventure game engine used to create *Master Lu* and *Orion*.

— Blue screen capture and processing tools.

— Video compression, including image processing based on intra-frame temporal coherence.

— Animation engine and tools.

— Production tools and pipeline.

Check out my demo at www.GameRecruiter.com.

Independent Work   1996 to 1999

In my spare time, I independently undertook many projects on Windows, Mac, and PlayStation Yaroze:

— *Fizzim*. Graphical FSM layout and automatic code generation tool.

— *Grammarian*. Graphical parser generation tool, which output scripts.

— *Mesh Viewer*. Import and real-time display of many 3D graphic formats.

— *AM Loft Mac*. Macintosh port of a lofting and skinning tool.

— *PSX Graphics Pipe*. An OpenGL, like high-performance 3D graphics pipe for PlayStation.

— *Math libraries*. A large collection of optimized vector, quaternion, and matrix math routines.

— *LParser Mac*. Macintosh port and real-time conversion of Laurens Lapre's L-System software.

Marc Mencher
Director of Art

- Primary Production Tools: 3Studio Max R2, Character Studio R2, PhotoShop 4.0, Debabelizer 4.5

- Motion-Capture Technologies, Fractal Painter 5.0, Animator Pro, and so on; R&D toolsets

- Alias|Wavefront MAYA PowerAnimator 8.5, SoftImage 3.7, Composer, Avid Media Illusions

- Studiopaint 3d; Lightwave 5.5, Parallax Matador and Advance, Disceet Logik's Flint, and

- Taarna 3D packages, Alias Studiopaint, and Wavefront, on the SGIs; Fractal Painter on Macs and PCs; and Autodesk , AutoCAD 12, DPaint Animator, Time Arts Lumena, and so on

- Mac: Adobe, Swivel3D/Renderman, Macromind Director, Pixelpaint, Freehand, Stratavision 3d, Adobe Illustrator, and Infini-D

EMPLOYMENT

Art Director/Lead Artist, Lipse Entertainment   1999 to Present

Responsible for Art Department organizational structure and management. Representative for the art staff within all management team meetings/discussions, hiring/interview process, training and evaluation process, and coordination of all in-house and external art resources. Total number of employees: 32.

- Work with the VPs of Engineering and Development, along with Programmers and Artists.

- Manage the streamlining and automating of the art production process for all products.

- Training and mentoring (goal setting) for the art staff.

- Coordination of art resources for implementation of content with Designers and Programmers, including resultant revisions of the Genesis environment to support these project-specific content needs.

- Art design and definition of the production value targeted, along with actual hands-on content creation for direct use in the game.

- Art services for both in-house and Microsoft needs for the definition and promotion of *Dragon*.

- Setting up and directing several motion-capture sessions with professional martial artists into Character Studio and 3DStudio MAX; the polishing of these captured animations along with generating new, hand animations to fill out the characterizations; the design, modeling, and texturing of all characters and environments, utilizing MAX, PhotoShop, Debabelizer, SurfaceSuite Pro, and the in-house Genesis editor.

- Explore the latest research and development (R&D) technologies for content creation, including Alias|Wavefront MAYA, Lightwave, and SoftImage.

Products: *Dragon; Genesis 3D Engine; Hollywood 3D Web tool.*

Art Director/Animator, Electronic Arts   1996 to 1999

Supervised and created computer graphics content for game development on the SGI, PC, and Mac platforms, supervising up to 30 Animators per project. Coordinated with both in-house staff and outside production contractors. Responsibilities included full knowledge of the various software packages, platforms, and techniques utilized to generate the content; training and direction of art staff; direct coordination with programming and game design staff in the development of the production, acting as the communication "hub" between the various groups; scheduling and management of all related art development tasks, in cooperation with other the team Leads in Programming and Game Design.

— Maintained a strong command of the latest tools and technologies, in order to ensure the highest quality production values, while keeping control on the most cost-effective uses of these methods in the development of the games.

— Trained and developed the art staff to strengthen the teams' overall skill set and productivity; and assisted them to coordinate these techniques with the Programmers and Game Designers.

— Responsible for the supervision of pre-production concept design, storyboards, layout, modeling, texturing, and animation, as well as generating final elements as a "working" supervisor.

— Developed a character animation setup in Maya, wherein an articulated creature is controlled by groups of slider interfaces (through Midi devices), for facial and body animations including full lip-synch.

Products: *No Remorse* (PC/PlayStation) – Game of the Year; *No Regret, Commander: Prophecy, Privateer 3.*

Art Lead, Whiz Bang Interactive Studios   1993 to 1995

Supervised and created computer graphics content for game, multimedia, film, and video product development, with up to 14 Animators and/or Illustrators coordinated per product, total of 28 artists on 2 projects. Developed these products using a combination of Silicon Graphics workstations, PowerMacs, and Pentium platforms; ranged from high-end PC and Mac platforms to cartridge and CD-ROM based systems, such as 3DO and SONY PSX, along with film and video formats.

— Coordination with other production staff members, including Producers, Directors, Game Designers, CG personnel, and Programmers; Marketing and Sales; as well as administrative management and outside investors.

— Responsible for coordinating a consistent, high-quality graphic presentation of the product during the pre-production stage of development and prototype design, through to the post-production packaging and promotional images.

Products: *Bluestar, Beyond the Wall, Wings Europe.*

Animator/Illustrator, Spectrum Games   1990 to 1993

Animator and Illustrator on 17 projects during my tenure with the company.

Products: *Civilization* (Game of the Year); *Darklands, Gunship200, Covert Actions, F15 Eagle, Knights, NFL Coaches' Club, Pirates! Gold, Lightspeed/Hyperspeed, Nighthawk.*

EDUCATION:

BS in Art, Art College, 1990

Check out my demo at www.GameRecruiter.com.

SECURING SOLID REFERENCES BEFORE YOU NEED THEM

You were so "on" during the interview. Everything just clicked. Great demo. Great résumé. Great interview. You've got this job sewn up, no doubt. Everything looks great; they just need to check references.

Huh? Didn't they see your résumé? They know you can do this job! Hmmm. Who should you give as a reference? Maybe the Technology Director you reported to would say good things about your work? Or would he? Then again, you did have a disagreement before you left. Maybe he's not a good idea. Surely, there are plenty of other people you could give as references, if only you knew where to find them…

As many job candidates have learned, the better the job, the higher the salary, the more stringent the interview process. A great résumé and a winning interview personality won't always make the final cut. Virtually all of the big game companies require a reference check before extending formal job offers. Your reference check can make or break the deal.

Determined job seekers spend most of their time creating the perfect résumé and demo reel, lovingly editing and tweaking each aspect of their presentation. But few people realize the importance of maintaining solid references. When your potential employer or your recruiter calls for references, you should be able to immediately provide a list of at least three people, including current contact information, whom you know will give positive feedback. This stage of the interviewing process should not find you scrambling for names, email addresses, and phone numbers, giving you no chance to talk to your references before your potential employer makes contact.

You don't want to risk a situation where your potential employer hears:

"Company policy prohibits us from saying anything. We can only verify title and dates of employment."

"What was it Thumper's mom said? If you can't say anything nice…."

Be well aware that your references won't be dropping you a line to let you know that they were less than complimentary. With changing company policies, employee turnover, and HR departments doing the legal cha-cha to avoid company liability, securing your references is definitely a plan-ahead task.

Don't Burn Bridges

It may sound obvious, but don't burn any bridges. When you're at your breaking point and ready to walk out the door, we've all said things we've later come to regret. Sure, your current boss may be the biggest dunderhead you've ever had the misfortune to work with, but ripping him a new one on your way out the door won't do you any favors when you need a supervisor's reference. In fact, it might poison any other potential company references.

People don't always get along. That's just life. But before you exit your current job, just suck it up and take a moment to end your relationship on a handshake and a positive professional note. If you've done good work, begrudging professional admiration can overcome personal distaste.

Stay in Touch

If you're leaving your current place of employment or, perhaps, just graduating from school, odds are others will leave as well. Make sure you know how to contact your references in the future. Handing over a list of references with outdated contact information can be just as bad as an unfavorable reference. Don't make your potential employer jump through hoops to speak to your references. It can make you look like you're hiding something. If there is any tracking down to be done, you need to do it. You can save yourself some time and frustration if you stay in touch with your references. You don't need to keep them on your daily "joke" email list, just let them know you may be using them in the future as a reference and would like to stay in touch. When you move or change jobs, be sure to let all of your references know your new contact information and they will probably reciprocate.

The Reference Checklist

You've probably looked at dozens of sample résumés as you prepare your own. Maybe you even bought a book on how to write a winning résumé. No less effort should be exerted for your references. The following is a reference checklist to keep along with your "how to write a résumé" resources.

Make a List of Potential References

For this list, consider those people who witnessed your work most closely related to the kind of job you are seeking. Also, be sure to keep in mind various kinds of references. Don't just limit your potential references to bosses; also consider colleagues, classmates, and clients.

Contact Your References

When you start the interviewing process, be sure to reconnect with your references. Take a moment to refresh their memories as to what you did for them and the results that you achieved. Let them know you may be using them as references in the very near future and would like to know what they saw as your strengths and weaknesses. Don't let some criticism dissuade you from using a reference. Rather, take this opportunity to update them on what you're doing now and how you've turned those weaknesses into strengths. If your references see that you're aware of your weaknesses and that you've worked on them, this could translate into a positive reference with regard to your character and professional determination. Also, make it clear that their reference is vital to you getting the job. Generally speaking, people like to help and they also like to feel important. Let your references know the kinds of qualities your potential employer is looking for and what they may ask about.

Know the Ending

Trial lawyers—make that, good trial lawyers—never ask a witness a question the answer to which they do not know. Know what your references will say about you *before* your potential employer makes contact. Go ahead and ask your potential reference what she will say about you. Whether positive or negative, you need to know the answer.

Follow Up

When you do move to a new job, make sure you let your references know what you're doing and how to reach you. And be sure to let them know that you would be happy to return the reference favor should they ever need it.

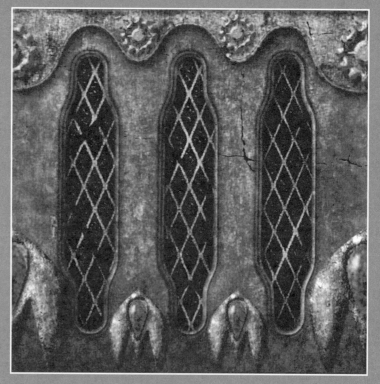

Part IV

Getting the Career You Want

Images courtesy
of Kim Oravecz

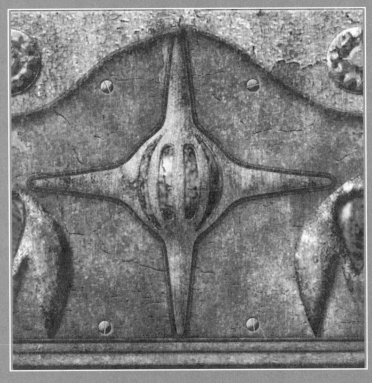

CHAPTER 11

Deploying Your Resume and Scoring an Interview

At this stage, you have developed a network, and now it is time to utilize that network to begin your formal job hunt. Your demo is ready, your résumé polished, and your references are in order. You are ready to respond quickly to a potential employer's requests after your resume has been submitted.

Responding to Classified Ads and Online Job Boards or Postings

Submitting your resume via a job ad or posting is not encouraged. Rather, classified ads and job postings should be used as a way of identifying a possible job to pursue. Not only do they inform you of a potential opportunity today, but they can provide you with juicy leads for the near future. If a company has advertised the need for a new Art Director, Lead Game Designer, Executive Producer, Producer, or Creative Director, you can bet these new people will want to hire their own staff. This is a clue for a job you could position yourself to interview for before HR even knows of the open spot. Several weeks after seeing a manager type spot advertised, call the company and find out who they hired for the job. Or pay attention to the announcements you read in the trade publications on people moving to new jobs. Send that person an email congratulating him on his new position and ask if he will need to round out his team with someone with your skill set.

Job ads should be used as a tool to focus your job hunting efforts. The odds of winning the lottery are about on par with the odds of getting even just an interview when utilizing a standard résumé submitted along with thousands of other lazy job hunters.

That harsh bit of advice notwithstanding, job ads are a fact of the job-search life and cannot be ignored. And, like the lottery, people actually do win on occasion.

Where to Find Game Industry Job Ads

The local newspaper's classified section may actually have a game job advertised, particularly if you pick a paper in an area of the country that has a larger game community, like San Jose, Los Angeles, Chicago, Austin, or Seattle. You'll see game jobs listed, for example, in the *San Jose Mercury News* and the *Austin Chronicle*. There are also a host of online job boards for people with some game industry experience. A simple search for "game jobs" on Google, Yahoo!, or other search engines should bring up a wealth of sites featuring game job ads. As this is a techno-savvy market, game companies rely heavily on advertising open jobs directly on the company web site. Useful online trade magazines like *GIGnews.com* and *Gamasutra* also feature job postings. Ads are also found in print trade publications such as *Game Developer* magazine.

Use the information learned from these job postings and then go directly to the web site of the advertising company, network with the community you have created from your prior company research, or check industry publications. Is this company actually a viable employer for you? Does it fit your job criteria? Does it make games or have projects you can get excited about? Better yet, if you could create your own job within this company, what position would it be? Educate yourself on this company. If it turns out not to be a viable option for you, input the data you have uncovered into your database. This information may become very useful in the future.

Based on your research, if the company seems like an approachable target, you must formulate your employment approach. What you could accomplish as a member of this company's team is a very effective job hunting theme to build upon. Formulate accomplishments that might be of interest to this company. Focus the way you will approach and sell yourself.

If you are compelled to answer that job ad, at least try to do it in a way that tips the odds in your favor:

- If submitting to an ad, posting, or even an open job listed on the game company's web site, be sure to mention how you were tipped off to the job so HR can gauge the effectiveness of their efforts.

- Customize your résumé and email cover by utilizing as many of the buzz-words from the job posting as possible.

- Utilize news articles, PR releases, and any other information you can uncover to help target your approach.

- Don't ever lie about your experience, but skew it the best you can toward the company's needs.

- When responding to job postings, avoid boring introduction emails. Refer to a job order number if it is given. Go the extra mile and make your intro-duction interesting. Potentially thousands of people may respond to that job ad. Just imagine how many cover emails start off with "To Whom It May Concern." Try something with a bit more zest. Be different. Try to stand out from the crowd even in your introduction emails.

I'm the Producer You Seek!

www.YourName.com

- Seven Games Brought to Market (PC, PS2, and XBox)

- Managed a budget of $7 Million and a Staff of 30

- Internal and External Team Management

My experience exactly mirrors your needs!   I caught your job post on *GIGnews.com*. Please consider me for your open Producer position.

Snail mail and fax are available but not typically used when job-hunting in the game industry. Not having email access casts immediate doubt on whether you have the actual ability to function in the 21st century, let alone participate in the development of a complex and advanced state of the art game development project. When submitting a résumé via fax or snail mail, you convey antiquated competence. Hotmail and services like it are free. Get an email address and a web site for displaying your demo.

Submitting your résumé via a next day delivery service can be utilized if you're trying for attention, but is probably a better technique only if used on a specific hiring manager. They don't often get next day mail so it has a better impact when used appropriately. Human Resources, on the other hand, gets résumés submitted this way all the time. Just like "To Whom It May Concern" letters, they tend to get ignored.

Don't Lose Control of Who Has Your Resume

I would be very cautious about sending my résumé blindly to a job ad not knowing who is receiving it. This is not a job hunting game we are playing here. If a company is serious about hiring, what reason could it have to hide its company name? Therefore, it is a safe assumption that if the job ad does not identify the company who is hiring, a third party, like a recruiting firm, placed the job ad. Some third-party employment services don't operate in a professional manner. After they get a copy of your résumé without talking to you or asking permission, they will blast it out to the world. Mass mailing produces horrible results! The employment service will not have any better response than you would.

I am not saying all third-party employment services operate this way. What I am saying is just like hiring a doctor or lawyer, you must interview and consider carefully who you trust to team with you on your job search. A partner who does not share information and just blasts your résumé out does not have your career and specific job search in mind. Avoid these firms!

Luckily, there are some awesome recruiters focused in the games market. If you think you have enough experience to be represented by one, take the time to research and interview a few firms before selecting one to team with. For more pointers on working with recruiters, check out Chapter 14, "Working with Recruiters." If you absolutely must respond to an ad that does not reveal the company, at least take some precautions. Briefly describe how you fit for the job, but only provide your name and contact telephone number or email address. Let whoever is behind the curtain reveal himself to you. Then, you can make a logical decision with full information if you wish to release your résumé and information.

CREATIVE AND WACKY WAYS TO GET ATTENTION

Hiring managers talk to dozens of qualified applicants for one position. To be successful in this market, you must discern ways to get noticed and be remembered. More importantly, you must figure out a way to demonstrate your creativity in an industry where creativity is paramount!

Don't lose sight of the fact that you walk a narrow line between standing out and being offensive or an annoyance. Luckily, this is an industry that, due to its creative nature, allows some latitude to operate within.

Here are some attention getting techniques:

- Start a newsletter and distribute it to the 100 most influential people in the game industry. You do not need to go crazy—a half page well-laid out article will work. Feature programming tips and techniques if you are a software engineer. How about 3D Studio Max short cuts for creating animations for the Artists? If you are a Game Designer, outline the successful elements that make a hit game. Marketing gurus can demonstrate your stuff with an article on clever PR techniques. Producers might try writing articles about keeping the creative vision during the development process or noting tips for maintaining development schedules. How about ideas on managing outside third-party developers?

- Attach a yellow post-it note to the face of your resume simply stating, "I am the Game Designer you seek! I can prove it! Call me at (800) 779-3334."

- Send a humorous card with your resume inside it.

- After an interview, send a telegram stating, "I want the job!!"

- A Marketing person might redesign the packaging of one of the products the company you are approaching already has on the market. Or, get on the company web page and design a box for an upcoming title.

- A Programmer could consider an AVI or a brief snapshot or video of some of the scenes programmed for products already developed. No experience in the industry? Then get to work! Create a simple game and submit the game for review. How about creating a technical quiz that covers hot technical areas like 3D Graphics, Game AI/Logic, Win95, PSX, or N64 development? Answer the questions to the quiz and submit this to the VP of Engineering along with your resume. Or, once a day for three days, email the VP of Engineering some sort of compelling technical roadblock issue with the solution to the problem. On the fourth day, admit you're the culprit in an email with your résumé and request for interview. (Don't forget to send Human Resources a copy.) During the interview, consider bringing "props" such as sample code.

- Along with the résumé, a Producer might send a page of rave reviews on the games already released to market. Or, try using endorsements from other employees, industry leaders, or clients. Here is a sample of what one Executive Producer, Sanjay Balakrishnan, sends out with his résumé (note that the names of the persons quoted, along with their titles and company affiliation, have been removed here for confidentiality):

> **Excellent Problem Solver,** "Sanjay is very creative and always looking for a way to solve any problem that arises, whether in a client negotiation, management situation or simple resource efficiency. He is very good at responding to short notice tasks and rallying his team to complete them on time. He takes tasks seriously and owns them completely. Once a goal is identified, he has excellent focus and drive achieving it."
> - <Name, title, company>
>
> **Dynamic Motivational Leadership.** "Sanjay has brought professional managerial techniques to the Simulations Division, a group that was in trouble before his arrival. The change has been dramatic in terms of morale and the quality of employees that have been attracted to the

group. Sanjay's communication skills are excellent and his treatment of people, while firm, is even handed and fair." - *<Name, title, company>*

Proven Entrepreneurial Drive. "Mr. Balakrishnan deserves a large part of the credit for seeing Hesware, in only its second year, grow to $13 million annual sales and secure $4.5 million in venture funding, with Microsoft Corp. as a principal investor. He has strength of character, is entrepreneurial, creative, and works hard." - *<Name, title, company>*

Software Pioneer and Innovator. "Sanjay Balakrishnan, founder of Hesware, could be called the Wernher von Braun of educational software for home computers. The firm has managed to achieve lift-off into what is essentially the first mass market for 'edutainment' software." - *Infoworld Magazine*, 1984

Focus on Quality, "Balakrishnan is a serious, experienced software industry professional who cares deeply about the quality of products and marketing." - *<Name, title, company>*

Targeted Job Hunt Campaign

Go to the targeted list you created when you started the networking phase of your job hunt. If you successfully spent the time networking, you already have your target list of companies to approach and specific names of people you uncovered during your research and networking efforts. Focus on your top ten companies. Create a cover email that is specifically targeted to each of your targets.

Follow Up by Telephone, not Just Email

The most important step in a targeted campaign is to follow up by telephone. If you did not get a response to your cover email, call and request an interview.

Sure, leave a voice mail message—once. If there is still no response a few days later, call again; but don't leave voice mail, just keep calling until your target answers the telephone. Directly ask your target for an interview or obtain an active job lead from her at another game company. Minimally, if you obtain no information or an interview request from your target, you have permission to email her from time to time.

Stay in touch. This is not a wasted activity. Yes, you are "forcing" a relationship that is very one-sided; some people just take a little more coaxing before they feel comfortable sharing data, and when they finally do, they could be very useful. Code these targets in your database as a "Keep In Touch" and schedule yourself every three months or so to connect either by leaving a brief voice mail message saying hello, by email, or even by mailing a card. Always remind your target who you are, updating her on your job hunt or a current development project, if you're employed. It's a good idea to maintain your network for future opportunities.

AUTHOR NOTE

"Don't rely on email only when following up. Personal contact is the most effective way to network and to job hunt."

- Marc

Although your target may be saying "no" today, or ignoring you altogether, tomorrow always brings another day and another opportunity to use your target for obtaining job leads and networking.

One very helpful technique to ease fears is to prepare yourself ahead of time. Create a telephone script similar to your one-minute pitch used during your networking phase. Before ever calling anyone, plan out the purpose for the connection and work out how you might accomplish it. After the conversation, rate yourself on how well you performed. Did you obtain your goal? If not, what happened during the telephone conversation that prevented it? Alter your approach for the next target. Self-evaluation is important. Keep calling people and keep honing your skill on the telephone. Practice makes perfect!

Reaching your target person on the telephone can be a challenge, especially if he has a secretary blocking the way. One function of a secretary is to screen calls. Don't ever let a secretary know you're a job hunter, revealing this will get your call transferred to HR. Usually, an authoritative voice, in a businesslike manner, gets your call past the secretary. If you're pressed for a reason for your call, tell the assistant, "We set an appointment to speak today," "She is expecting my call," or "I told him I would call today at 11:45 a.m." You did tell your target in your cover email that you would follow up on a certain day and time, so you're not lying here, just don't reveal the entire purpose of the call. After you have reached your target on the telephone, make sure you're effective. You have only limited time to sell yourself, so be careful what you say.

CREATING YOUR COVER EMAIL AND ONE-MINUTE PITCH

Traditionally, a cover letter is utilized to sell your skills to a specific individual in a company. The same holds true for a cover email or the pitch you use when introducing yourself on the telephone. Emails addressed to Dear Recruiter, Dear Human Resources, and To Whom it May Concern are perceived as junk mail. Do the proper research and networking and get the actual names: the name of the Producer working on the game you have interest in, the name of the Technical Manager, the name of the VP of Human Resources, the name of any hiring manager in your area of interest. Don't send correspondence to a general email box and hope it gets routed. That is giving over your control of your job search to someone else. Cover emails must be addressed to a specific individual. At a minimum, most people at least "scan" any correspondence that is specifically addressed to their individual email and address and written to their attention.

The Email Structure

Your cover email introduces who you are and why you are connecting. It should not be boring! It should contain a summary of skills or accomplishments. Do your best to anticipate what the hiring manager needs. Highlight your skills and accomplishments to communicate that you can do the job. In short, what you can do for the company is the theme of the cover email. The last paragraph of your cover email should end with a proactive statement like,

"I will call you on Monday, January 15 at 1:00 p.m. to discuss this further." This you will actually do.

Following is a sample of generating a targeted cover email. First, let's review the history of Hot Smokin' Games:

In 1998, a newly formed development company headed by former Activision veterans announced that it would publish new games. Activision made an equity investment in the company. The first two games developed were action combat sequels. The President, Amy Leader, served as a director of production at Activision before founding Hot Smokin' Games, Inc. She was the director for one of the best-selling real-time strategy games, and the producer of a blockbuster combat-simulation hit. Currently, the company is working on the next version of an action combat game.

Based on what you know of Hot Smokin' Games, here's an email approach you might try:

Hi Amy,

I am a Game Programmer who loves 3D strategy, combat, and action games. This is why I want to join your development team!

Working for Hot Smokin' Games has been my career goal. I have designed and developed a combat simulation game. Like you, I share a love for this genre. I have the following qualifications:

- 3D game programming experience with exposure to current 3D rendering techniques.

- More than 900 hours of hands-on C/C++ in addition to low-level Assembly experience.

- Trained to perform in a team with strict schedules and milestone delivery.

Take a look at my online portfolio where you will find my résumé and sample code: www.YourName.com.

If I don't know hear from you beforehand, I will connect with you via telephone on Thursday, April 22, 2004 at 1:30 p.m.

Best Regards,

Marc Mencher, Game Programmer Gone Wild!

Schedule in your database or calendar to make that call on the day and time you specified. It does not matter if you get voice mail and can only leave a message; it is your responsibility to be professional and prompt. When leaving a voice-mail message, indicate when you will try to connect again. Give your target a good five business days to return the call. You never know when someone did not respond due to a business trip or just bad timing in his or her world. Be professional and pleasant, but persistent. Get voice mail a second time? Leave another nice and upbeat sounding message and schedule another time when you will return the call. Yes, you're being a bit pushy here. Ever hear the old adage, "the squeaky wheel gets the grease?" This is your job search and you must keep its momentum moving forward. Don't let the momentum of your job search be controlled by others. You have the control. Take it.

Obviously, you don't want to cross the line and be perceived as annoying, but there is nothing wrong with being aggressive. If you're going to work on a multimillion-dollar project, you better believe the hiring manager would be more interested in a person who is persistent than one who is not. Your repeated efforts communicate that you're really enthusiastic about developing games.

Do not leave a third voice mail message, but keep calling your target several times a day for a few days. Most people answer their phones, so keep calling until they pick up. If, after a few days, you can't reach your target and they have not responded in any way, you can feel good that you have done just about all you can to work this lead. Don't make the mistake of discarding this contact, and don't harbor negative feelings about his non-response either. It had nothing to do with you personally—that person has never even met you. Instead, keep this contact in your database, but code it now to receive your quarterly or yearly accomplishment email. Move on to another target person within the same company. Eventually, you will find someone who is willing to assist you.

Three months from now, one of your cold contacts could get promoted or a new job and may need to hire a protégé. Your contact could get a telephone call from a friend working at another studio looking to fill an open spot. "Hey! I remember that persistent Animator or 3D Programmer who tried connecting with me some time ago. What was the name, Marc Mencher? I will contact him first." Networking works in wondrous ways and is the key to a successful and profitable career.

AUTHOR NOTE

"I can't tell you how many people I have cold contacted and they don't respond. But I know this is not a personal rejection of Marc Mencher. I have no idea what is going on the other end of the Internet or telephone. The only thing I do know is that I tried to connect with someone and they were not available this time. I don't create a story in my head about why my target contact didn't respond, and neither should you. This only leads to a negative emotional reaction. Job hunting is emotional enough, so don't add to the mix. Stay focused on the positive and the momentum you are generating with the other people on your list. You better bet I still keep in contact with people who don't respond. Many of them actually call me when they are ready to job hunt. The same will happen for you."

- Marc

CHAPTER 12

Interviewing

With layoffs in the news almost daily, your job search campaign is more vital than ever. There are still plenty of jobs out there, but the competition may be a bit stiffer. With that in mind, it is more important than ever to present yourself in the most attractive light. You can set yourself apart from the other qualified candidates by shining in the interview.

The job interview is the most important aspect of your search for a new career opportunity. The way you interview will determine whether or not you get a job offer. From the moment you walk in, the employer will begin evaluating you on a variety of levels including your appearance, your personality, and the way you express yourself. If you are prepared, you'll project a positive, professional image that will give you a big advantage over the competition.

Interviewing is not difficult, rather, it is a skill to be developed. If you can't role play and practice with some friends, go ahead and get some real world experience. That may mean interviewing for a job or two that you really have no interest in. You can't get a job without doing a face-to-face interview, and if reading about techniques for developing face-to-face interview skills doesn't help, and role playing with friends doesn't get "real" enough for you, put yourself through a few "real world" practice interviews.

A face-to-face interview is not the time to be regurgitating your résumé verbally. The résumé's function is to get you an interview and nothing more. The face-to-face interview is your personal one-actor stage performance. You have already set the theme of your play based on the upfront research you did, targeted cover email, and customized résumé. Your costume, the way you dress, is carefully considered. Sure, the game biz is a bit casual when it comes to what to wear at an interview, so use this to your advantage by looking more professional. Sometimes a suit is required and sometimes not, but shorts and a t-shirt are *never* acceptable for an interview. Although many companies are very casual where people do tend to wear shorts and t-shirts, this is only acceptable for *current* employees. During an interview, your goal is to come across as confident, professional, and most importantly, successful. This is how you set yourself up for getting the offer and salary negotiations. How will you ever establish your level of professionalism dressing in a t-shirt? Even highly creative people must project a professional look.

The duration of an interview is usually just a few hours, so it is impossible for anyone to really get to know you. Did you know the decision to hire is actually made in the first few minutes of your interview? The rest of the time is spent justifying this impression and the decision to hire or not.

In your own life on a daily basis, you make judgments and decisions based on limited information—so does the hiring manager talking to you.

INTERVIEWING TIPS

Interviewing is simple in that you practice the technique of projecting the appropriate impression. The following sections include tips for making that great first impression.

Smile. Be Enthusiastic. And Get There Early.

The outcome of many interviews is decided during the first 10 seconds of the introduction. Greet the employer with a firm handshake, eye contact, and a smile. Project an enthusiastic, professional image right from the start. Characteristics that contribute to a professional image are proper interview attire, self-confidence, maturity, a sense of humor, warmth, promptness, and concise answers to questions. Arriving early makes a good impression. It shows appreciation for the employer's time and allows you enough time to complete the required paperwork.

Bring an Extra Copy of Your Résumé and Any Interview Props You Can Use

If they don't have a copy in front of them, don't let the flow of the interview be interrupted. Have one ready to whip on their desk. Also, props like information you compiled on the game company, code or art samples, samples of a game design, or video game marketing plan can be useful tools used during interview.

Complete the Application in Detail. Be Truthful.

Employers look at the way an application is filled out as well as the information on it. Think of it as your first assignment, an example of how you would perform on the job. Read the directions before writing. Fill in the form neatly and completely. Don't write "see résumé." Never misrepresent your education or work experience. Present only the facts. Always write the word "open" in the space for salary desired.

Dress Professionally

Although the game industry is notoriously casual, the interview is not the time to trot out your favorite game t-shirt that, dude, you got at E3. Pressed khakis and a button down (tucked in) should be suitable for the more entry-level positions.

Take an Active Part and Set the Tone in the Interview

One way to start is by asking the employer to describe the job. Listen carefully and mentally note each duty. This tells you how to respond. Zero in on your experience and training that relate to the position and explain how past experience and qualifications will help you do the job. The best interviewees set the tone of the interview. Take control and sell yourself! This requires you to prepare yourself ahead of time for the interview.

Interact and React. And Don't Smoke.

A major factor in many hiring decisions is how well the employer gets along with you. To develop a good rapport, speak clearly, listen closely, and show interest. When the employer says something that requires an answer, comment, smile, or nod. React! Body language is important. Sit up straight in your chair, lean forward slightly, and maintain eye contact. Even if the employer lights up, you do not!

Ask Meaningful Questions About the Position

Many employers evaluate applicants by the questions they ask. Employers like specific questions about the nature of the job, the company's plans and goals, and the abilities considered most important for the position. Note: Find suggested questions to ask in the upcoming section, "Suggested Interview Questions."

Answer Questions by Speaking in Terms of the Position. Emphasize What You Can Do for the Company.

Some employers ask very broad questions like, "Tell me about yourself." Rather than talking about your childhood, family, or personal ambitions, mention specific accomplishments that show your abilities and determination to succeed in this job. Your answers should tell the employer why you would be an asset to the company, not why you need a job. Sell yourself! Twist everything you do and say into a reason for them to hire you. Emphasize accomplishments and be ready to give examples or proof of what you say.

If You Want the Job, Close the Interview by Asking for It!

Many employers feel that a desire for the position is just as important as the ability to do the job. A very effective interviewing technique is simply to ask for the job. One way to do this is to ask the employer: "Do you think I can do the job?" If the answer is "Yes," say, "Great! When can I start?"

Just because you want to dress clowns for a living doesn't mean you can dress like one for an interview.

No smoking allowed.

STRIKE THREE—YOU'RE OUT

You can do lots of things to make a good impression, but there are lots of things you can do to make a bad impression. The following are ways to strike out in an interview:

- Inability to take criticism.
- Lack of interest, passivity.
- Over-emphasis on salary.
- Condemnation of past employer.
- Lateness.
- Lack of preparedness.
- Avoiding eye contact.
- Lack of tack, manners, or maturity.
- Narrow interests.
- Indecisiveness or failure to articulate clearly.
- Overbearing or over aggressive. Nobody likes a "know it all."

Discuss Salary *After* the Employer Mentions a Figure

Because you've written "open" in the space for salary desired, the employer may ask how much money you're looking for. Respond by saying: "I'm very interested in the position and I'd like to earn as much money as I'm qualified to earn. How much would you offer someone with my qualifications?" If the employer makes a firm offer and you want the job, accept it on the spot. If you're doubtful or undecided, ask for a day to think it over. Never refuse an offer of employment until you've had time to think about it.

Say "Thank You" in Person and in Writing

Before leaving the interview, thank the employer for taking the time to talk to you about the position. Follow up with a personal "thank you" email or card to the employer, stating once again why you'd be an asset to the company and expressing your interest in the position. Get names, collect business cards, or get the correct spelling and title of all individuals you meet with. Spelling mistakes are death.

SUGGESTED INTERVIEW QUESTIONS

In the previous section, I mentioned that interacting with a potential employer during an interview is important to a successful meeting. Questions are a great way of being interactive. So in the following sections, I've included lists of actual questions you can ask potential employers, as well as questions potential employers may be asking you. Be sure that when you're doing the asking that you ask questions at the appropriate time, and prepare yourself ahead of time to make sure you have answers to the questions you may be asked.

Questions to Ask *During* an Interview

The following are questions that are appropriate for you to ask during the interview:

- Tell me more about my day-to-day responsibilities. Note: Listen for items that are emphasized or repeated by the employer; these are their hot buttons. You will want to tailor the discussion of your skills relating to these particular areas.

- How soon are you looking to fill this position?

- What is the potential of this position?

- How do my skills compare to other candidates you have interviewed?

QUESTIONS TO ASK *AT THE END* OF AN INTERVIEW

The following are questions that are appropriate for you to ask at the end of the interview:

- What is your time frame for this decision? When should I expect to hear from you?

- How did I do?

- I have really enjoyed meeting with you and your team and I am very interested in the opportunity. I feel my skill and experience would be a good match for this position. What is the next step in your interview process?

- Before I leave, is there anything else you need to know concerning my ability to do this job?

- Do you have any concerns?

TOUGH INTERVIEW QUESTIONS YOU MAY FACE

Many potential employers like to throw out questions not specifically related to the position. As you read through the list below, think about how you might answer them:

- How would you describe yourself?

- What do you think of your last boss?

- I see you have moved around a bit. Why is this?

- Where do you see yourself in five years?

- Tell me something about yourself.

- Have you ever failed?

- What are your strong points? Your weak points?

- Why did you leave your last job?

- How much money do you want? I need an exact figure.
- What is the most difficult thing you have ever done?
- Which qualifications do you feel make you a better candidate for this job than anyone else?
- What do you feel would be your main contribution to this company?
- But you have already done this work. What makes you think you would be interested in staying with us?
- Are there any questions that you have before I let you go?
- What are your future goals?

NOT ONLY IS THE COMPANY INTERVIEWING YOU, YOU'RE INTERVIEWING THE COMPANY

AUTHOR NOTE

"Gaming news web sites are a great resource for this type of information. You can search the archives for the name of a company to find out articles about layoffs, defections of prominent people, and canceled games."

- Marc

It's important to look at a company for any obvious flaws that would affect you as an employee. High turnover is a good indicator that something may not be quite right. Although it's not unusual for a game development company to have a yearly turnover rate of 25 percent or more, you might not want to work for that company. In a one year period, a quarter of the population quit or was fired. On the other hand, a company with a low turnover, say less than 8 percent, is a good indication that the staff is content with the management.

TURNING INTERVIEWS INTO OFFERS

You're the one job hunting, so you're the one in the driver's seat. It's up to you keep the job search moving forward and without losing control. Turning the interview into a job offer is also your responsibility.

During the First Interview

During the first interview, focus on building a relationship with the people who are involved in the hiring decision, but particularly with the person you identify as the final decision-maker. The goal of your first interview is to probe and obtain company information like what problems does the hiring manager or development team have to deal with? During an interview, you're trying to stand out as the obvious candidate to hire. You must develop strategies to prove that you are the best candidate for the job. You must address the hiring manager's needs, come up with solutions, and show more interest and competence than your competition. Believe it or not, most jobs are created specifically for the person who is hired to fill the job. Why not influence the hiring manager to structure the job for you? In fact, during the second and third interviews, you should help define the job and, of course, highlight yourself for it!

During the first interview, be sure to take good notes. This will be vital to your follow-up. Jot down your experience with each person you meet. Was this person friendly or formal? Why might this person wish to hire you? Make sure each person sees the benefit of having you on the team. Issues about how you may fit for the job come up with everyone. Listen carefully so you can verbally combat these concerns both during the interview and in the follow-up contact. If you think the company has any concerns about hiring you, address them up-front.

Following Up After the Interview

Following up after an interview is the most important step in the job search process. This is *not* about simply contacting the hiring manager to request a hiring decision status. If this is the approach you take, as many job seekers do, then you have lost control.

Keep in mind that you don't go to an interview with the goal of walking away with a job offer. Yes, on occasion, some people do get hired on the first interview, but this is not the norm. Most people average at least three interviews at a company before a hire decision is made. Therefore, during your first interview, you must uncover ways to maintain the company's interest in interviewing you a second time and eventually hiring you.

CLEVER WAYS TO FOLLOW UP AND MAINTAIN INTEREST

The decision to hire is something akin to the decision between buying a cheap or an expensive car. You must help the hiring manager make this purchase decision. Do the features and benefits you bring to the table justify the dollars?

- Create a proposal about solving an issue.
- Create level designs, art assets, or simple development tools, especially if they help solve an immediate problem.
- Have an influential game industry person email or telephone on your behalf.
- Submit references and then follow up to schedule another interview.

When you follow up on your interview, do so with each person who interviewed you. To help you do this, refer to the notes taken during your first interview. Remember when you jotted down whether this person was person friendly or formal? Now, follow up with a similar tone. Although you must not spam the same generic thank you email to each person you met, you also don't need to create 12 individual emails. Rather, you left the interview knowing who the few decision-makers might be, so follow up with them. If those were four people, you will need four personalized thank-you emails.

It's your job to push forward to the next step. In your follow-up email, state what you expect the next steps to be. Push for another meeting. Devise a compelling reason for a second interview. Present a proposal for solving some of the issues uncovered during the first interview.

WRAP-UP

During the interview process, your goal is to co-create a job that works for both you and the hiring manager. Position yourself with your résumé, position yourself with your body language and appearance, and position yourself versus the competition. In short, place yourself in the position of creating a job description for yourself, which includes a list of your responsibilities.

CHAPTER 13

Salary Negotiation

The unique aspect about negotiating compensation with a game company is that the employment package often contains a royalty percentage based upon the successful sale of the game in the market. The amount of this royalty is based upon individual and group participation. The game industry rewards for the level of your creativity and your willingness to take risks. Although your counterparts in the traditional business world may earn a higher base salary, they probably don't have the same opportunities to "hit the mother load." Ask the ID software folks if they think the game industry underpays. The *Quake II* team shared millions of dollars.

AUTHOR NOTE

"I negotiate bonus, stock, vacation time, sign-on bonuses, relocation, visas, green cards, office space, severance pay, and timing of the first performance or salary review. I negotiate for secretarial support, extra insurance, guaranteed paid attendance to industry conferences, and education reimbursement."

- Marc

When thinking of negotiating, most assume a win/lose scenario. But the pros don't look at negotiation this way. They know that a successful negotiation is one in which both sides feel like winners. Keep in mind that when you sit down to bargain, you don't have to win on every issue. Score major victories, but concede on small points. Ask yourself, "What can I give up that will please the other person without compromising what I want?" This is called coming from a win/win perspective when negotiating. There is a wealth of books written on the art of salary negotiation; take the time to study the subject. You should be prepared when the time comes.

Though everything is negotiable, and compensation is not limited to just a base salary, understand that most *entry-level* positions have set salaries that are subject to very little, if any, negotiation. However, you won't be entry-level for long!

IMPROVING YOUR NEGOTIATING SKILLS

The best person to negotiate salary is you. The negotiation is ultimately about the work you are willing to perform in return for compensation. Understandably, this is a difficult issue to negotiate through a third party. However, you may choose to allow a third party, such as a recruiter, to negotiate on your behalf. If you do use a recruiter, get the best representation available. Your negotiator must have game industry knowledge and preferably first-hand experience specifically with your work functions. If the recruiting firm you choose is staffed with amateurs who only know some industry buzzwords, never played a game themselves, let alone have hands-on experience in the development of a game, don't expect professional, effective representation. For more information on recruiters, and whether you should be using them, be sure to read the next chapter in this book.

When negotiating compensation, you want to avoid being aggressive or confrontational. You also want to avoid the perception that you are only interested in money or benefits, not the job itself. Always come from a space that you're "psyched" about the job and can't wait to get started after you work out a few details. Simply talk first about the job itself, and then explain why it is you want something. You will avoid being perceived as selfish if you speak in a collaborative way.

Also, make sure you are negotiating your salary with the right person. You're negotiating with the wrong person if your compensation requirements are almost the same as the person you're talking to. If you discover this is the case, move the negotiation on to this person's supervisor who should be at the correct level to negotiate with you.

Don't make the mistake of paying too much attention to the hiring manager who says the job is only paying $60,000 when you know you must earn at least $70,000 to stay afloat. Always postpone salary negotiations until the end of the interview process. If you interview well, you can position yourself for a job that has not yet been completely defined. Remember that in the interview process your goal is to co-create a job that works for both you and the hiring manager. During this customization, make sure the job is appropriate for your salary requirements.

Preparing for Negotiation

The best way to prepare for negotiating compensation is to get clear on your goals and gather all the facts for each company.

When negotiating compensation, don't foolishly focus solely on the base salary. The game industry is an amalgam of small start-ups, established third-party developers, and corporate giants. Issues such as the availability of publicly traded stock, IPO status, royalty percentages, and bonus programs play a significant factor in your compensation package, so pay attention to these numbers and your options.

Determine the market rate salary range for your type of position. Decide *before* each interview the salary you want versus what you need to live on, as well as what you will be willing to compromise based on the specifics of each of your target game companies. The degree to which a compensation package is negotiable depends on the position, the manager, the game company, and your perceived value. Again, be realistic—entry-level salaries are less negotiable than salaries for mid-level or executive positions.

THE DREADED SALARY QUESTION

Here's how to address salary questions during the interview:

- "What are your salary requirements?"

  Summarize the requirements of the position as you understand them and then ask the interviewer for the normal salary range in the company for that type of position.

- "How much did you earn on your last job?"

  Tell the interviewer that you would prefer learning more about the current position before you discuss compensation, and that you are confident you will be able to reach a mutual agreement about salary at that time.

- "The salary range for this position is $28,000 to $32,000—will this work for you?"

  Tell the interviewer that it does come near what you were expecting, and then offer a range that places the top of the employer's range into the bottom of your range. For example, "I was thinking in terms of $32,000 to $36,000." Be sure, however, that the range you were thinking about is consistent with what you learned about the market rate for that position.

Avoid answering the question, "What are you currently earning?" until the end of the interview. To do this, simply request delaying salary conversations until you understand more about the job. Let the interviewer know that you are very interested in working for his company and that you are willing to make an investment, so salary won't be a problem. If you feel forced to answer this question, don't answer with a specific number; rather, provide the hiring manager with a salary range. For example, "My skills in the market go for about $78,000 to $92,000. Let's focus on defining the specifics of the job. I know we will work out a win/win on salary."

Whenever possible, try to highlight the common goals and points of agreement between you. After all, this isn't war; it's a negotiation. For the most part, you both have similar goals. It's your ideas on how to achieve these goals that differ.

When responding, use phrases that show you agree with the other person's position such as, "I agree with that," or, "That's a great point." If you make the other person feel like a winner, both sides will be.

Understand Your Skills and Their Worth

Enter into compensation negotiation with a firm understanding of your skills and what they are worth. Be prepared to defend or present justification. If you've ever seen a debate, you know the most prepared person usually wins. How did you arrive at your compensation expectations? Share this data with your new employer. Here are a few things you can do to research and prepare:

- Find printed evidence to back up your oral arguments. Collect surveys and articles. Bring these to your interview and use them.

- Highlight or underline key facts to make them leap off the page.

- Factor the entire compensation package including, for example, tuition benefits, investment options, health plan, and any perks, along with salary into your negotiation discussion.

- For a more realistic picture, compute the total dollar worth of these benefits and add this figure to the salary. If it is important to you, you may decide to negotiate benefits rather than an actual dollar amount increase.

Sometimes, the trade-off of a slightly lower base for a chance to join a start-up company and obtain founder's stock is sensible. Or, if you're making a transition into the industry from another discipline, initially, you may have to prove yourself in the market before commanding the salary you actually deserve. This is fine. Remember: this industry rewards risk taking. Another reason for accepting a lower base salary is that the position you are considering may place you in the industry spotlight, thus making you very visible and positioning you for other opportunities. Perks like car allowance, airline or fitness club memberships, first class travel, and special development equipment can also offset base salary. Your creativity is the limit here—just get clear with yourself and your goal.

When negotiating, reach for your goal, but be prepared to accept any offer between a minimum and maximum range. All companies operate within some sort of compensation structure. You can't guess this structure, but you can assume that that the first offer extended will be mid-range on their scale. Don't leave money on the table! Generally, there is $5,000 more available, so try for $5,000 more. Make a counter offer. You might not get it, but ask. However, don't get greedy and max yourself out compared to what others reasonably earn.

EVALUATING EXTENDED JOB OFFERS

Congratulations on hard work well done! You have what it takes and they offered you the job. Should you accept it on the spot? Was it the salary you were hoping for, and if not, are you comfortable negotiating a better salary and benefits package? Is this the right move for you long term? Basically, it comes down to assessing the job offer! The first question most people ask me is "Should I accept the job on the spot if they offer it to me?" Of course, there are exceptions to the rule, but generally giving yourself a few days to analyze the salary, company, and how it works with your plan is advisable. Most companies are happy to give you the time, as bad hiring is a costly mistake. They would rather you spend the time up front than on the first week of the job.

Salary, Benefits, and Perks—The Meat and Potatoes

Luckily at GameRecruiter.com, we have a financial planner help us assess the offers that are made to our candidates on behalf of our client-companies! In lieu of having me as a Career Coach with a financial whiz at my beck and call, I suggest the following. On a sheet of paper or spreadsheet, make a list of your current salary and all the benefits and perks you are currently receiving. If you do not have anything to list on this side, chances are you should jump over the desk and kiss the person who just gave you a chance in our industry!

Start with your current salary at top on the left and the offer on the right. Salary can be defined simply as the amount of money given to you every other week for the job functions you perform. But is it really? For some of us, it is part of our self-esteem; for others, it is a means to an end. Regardless, you must make sure that the salary offered to you is reasonable for the position, and that when you factor in possible cost of living differences, if relocation is necessary, are you being paid enough to maintain or exceed your current lifestyle? Remember, your $80,000 in Eugene, Oregon afforded you two acres of land and a *huge* savings account but in San Francisco, you bought yourself a studio apartment with enough left over to eat some Top Ramen.

Benefits or perks often can make up between an additional 25 to 50 percent of your current salary, and most people often overlook a chance to increase their employment package by paying attention to these benefits. No two game companies have the same benefits program. For example, Microsoft is plagued with the reputation for not paying the highest salaries in the game industry. But is this really true? Their game division offers employees a very robust benefits program. This is a perfect example of the need to review and understand a specific employee benefits program. The average Microsoft employee receives an additional 35 percent in her compensation package. It can be confusing, but it is important to understand these benefits.

A few years ago, I negotiated for a Senior Programmer not only a killer job but equity ownership in the game company. I was dancing around my office! I helped him fulfill his dreams and also set him up for long-term growth! I was amazed to discover he and his wife were not as excited as I was. Turned out, they were hooked on the lower-than-expected base salary, and because they lacked the knowledge to understand the stock award, did not realize the significance of the employment offer.

Benefits also come in the form of the following:

- Health insurance

- Retirement plans 401(k)

227

- Bonuses and raise reviews

- Stock options

- Employee stock purchase plan

- Royalties and bonuses

- Miscellaneous

Health Insurance

Most game companies provide a choice to employees of either a Preferred Provider Option (PPO) plan or a Health Maintenance Organization (HMO) plan. When choosing, consider that, although more expensive, PPOs give you the choice of doctors and care. Although more cost effective, most HMOs require doctor referrals for specific care thereby allowing your primary physician to make those choices for you. Human Resources will help you determine the type of plan best for you. Dental, vision, disability, and life insurance are also sometimes included. Dependants can usually be covered, although the company may charge you a fee to help cover their insurance premiums. Some companies will provide benefits for domestic partners, if you are unmarried but have a long-term partner.

Remember that the higher up the ladder you go, the richer your benefits package should get. Although at entry level you may receive a life insurance benefit of one or two times your salary, a VP at the same company may be negotiating a million dollar policy that also accumulates cash value at retirement.

Retirement Plans, 401(k)

Some game companies offer a company-sponsored retirement account. The company withdraws the amount of money you specify from each of your paychecks, pre-tax, and deposits it in the account for you. Monies then accumulate interest and dividends without any tax due until you withdraw from the account at retirement. Most company 401(k)s allow you to invest in different mutual funds, bonds, or savings accounts. You should evaluate all of the options, and based on your risk/reward profile, invest accordingly. Some companies match your contribution up to a specific percentage of your salary. If your employer offers that benefit, remember that your automatic return on that contribution is 100 percent return on your money in addition to whatever the money earns in interest or dividends. It's frequently a good idea to diversify your retirement account into different investments. Keep in mind that there are significant IRS penalties to cashing out a 401(k) or any other tax-exempt retirement savings plan before you reach the age of retirement.

Bonuses and Raise Reviews

Most game companies do a performance review at specific times of the year, either based on your length of employment or on a calendar date. For both bonuses and raise reviews, see if you can get a written document stating what your job performance goals are and what your bonus or raise structure would be if you met those goals. If your company does annual reviews and you are accepting a lower salary, sometimes asking for quarterly or semi-annual reviews can help increase your salary quicker. If your written goals are very specific, and you accomplish them, you'll be able to argue convincingly that you deserve that raise and/or bonus.

Stock Options

Employees benefit when the company gives you the choice (or "option") of buying company stock at a set price. If the company is publicly traded on the stock market, the option price is usually whatever the stock market price is on the day you start work. If the company stock goes up, you can sell your shares at a profit. If it goes down, obviously, it's of no value to you at all. The incentive is for the employees to work hard for the company to increase the company's profits and stock price and therefore their own profits from stock options.

If the company is privately held, the price is based on whatever the company owners or investors have set. Privately held stock can't be sold on the open market; your employee contract may have specific circumstances in which it can be sold back to the company or transferred. If the company is already public, you'll probably get fewer options, but they'll actually be worth something. If the company is privately held, the options should be greater, because there's a significant chance that they'll never have actual cash value.

Stock options, whether for public or private stock, usually have a *vesting* schedule, such as four or five years. This is the schedule for how soon you can buy those stock shares from the company. The incentive, of course, is for you to stay with the company so that more of your stock options will vest!

Employee Stock Purchase Plans

These plans allow you to buy company stock at a set price. This price is usually based upon the stock market price of the company stock on one or sometimes two specific days every year, possibly with a discount percentage (such as 10 percent off) as well. If you choose to participate in this kind of plan, the company will do regular withdrawals from your paychecks for the stock purchases. This money is post-tax—that is, taxes have already been withheld for it from your salary. However, any profits are considered capital gains and will be taxed accordingly. So if you sell any of this stock, you'll pay capital gains tax on the difference between how much you paid for the stock and how much you sold it for. Usually there's a cap on how much stock you can purchase in the employee stock plan, based upon a percentage of your salary.

Royalties and Bonuses

These two items are performance-based incentives that can add *significant extra income* to your complete package. Royalties are generally based on either gross or net sales and you have the ability to negotiate your specific percentage. Remember that you must compare apples to apples when evaluating different offers. A higher percentage rate is not the key to more money; you must evaluate the company's accounting practices and distribution channels. Remember, a higher percentage on *nothing* is still *nothing*! Bonuses are also based upon the sales of the project or completion of milestones, and they are usually an amount that is divided between the development team for a particular project. Performance incentives are clearly spelled out in the employment offer extended by the game company.

Miscellaneous

Car allowances are another way for a game company to increase your income while creating yet another deduction for themselves. Note to self: If a "start-up" company offers you a Lamborghini as a sign on bonus, make sure it is in your name and not a corporate lease, as someone at the company does not understand how to manage his VC funding and you will probably be driving your soon-to-be severance package to work every day. Personal Assistants, on-site daycare, education assistance, corporate legal plans, cafeteria plans, and many other perks are often available in larger, more corporate-type game companies.

Other forms of compensation come in:

- Paid vacation time
- Paid holidays
- Expense accounts
- Flexible work schedule
- Relocation expenses
- Special equipment, software, or tools
- Education programs
- Termination agreement

After you have broken down the compensation package, take time to also assess the game company and the specific position offered.

Assessing the Game Company

First, you need to assess the game company:

- Where is this game company going?
- What are the short- and long-term prospects in the industry?
- Is this company gaining or losing market share?
- In your opinion, do they have a game concept or license that could hit it big and that you're excited about developing?
- Do you feel this company would be a good career move?
- What about the work environment and culture—is this in sync with you?
- Is this company going to grow or go through a transition such as a merger within the foreseeable future?

Assessing the Position

Additionally, you need to evaluate the position:

- What specific projects will I be working on?

- May I obtain or submit a job description for approval?

- What are my responsibilities?

- What are my prospects for growth, both in position and compensation?

- What is the length of my daily commute?

- How much travel will be required in this job?

- How much power will I have to influence decisions about my project?

- What new skills can I learn at this company?

- Is there the opportunity to be mentored or to become a mentor?

- How will this job affect my personal lifestyle? Will they require excessive overtime?

- What is the work environment?

- What is the job and company stability?

SALARY SURVEY

The following statistics reflect current average salaries for common game developer positions, based on level of experience and taking into consideration typical bonuses. The information is designed to give a reasonable approximation of what you can expect to make in a particular position. It is important, however, to keep in mind that salaries will vary based on a company's geographic location, bonus structure, and financial bottom line.

Methodology

The following statistics are based on job placement orders received by GameRecruiter.com. Client companies reflect a geographically and financially diverse cross-section of the game industry. The numbers also include information from online research and confidential candidate surveys.

Cost of Living

When considering salaries, it is important to keep in mind the impact of geography. The paycheck for an entry-level Artist in Marin County, California, for example, might look considerably larger than that for an Artist in a similar position in Minneapolis. However, the average cost of a 2,000 sq. ft. home in Marin County is $370,000, whereas a same size home in Minneapolis averages $178,000. In other words, your friend in Northern California may be taking home $75,000 compared with your $50,000 salary, but a proportionate chunk of that is going to significantly higher living expenses.

prepared by GAME RECRUITER

Game Developer Salary Statistics

August 2002

Intro

We've all heard it or read it somewhere: the game industry has surpassed the film industry in total sales. For the year 2000, according to the Interactive Digital Software Association (IDSA), the computer and video game software industry generated just over $6 Billion USD in total sales. In short, we're not just geeks in dark basements wearing weird clothes anymore. We're geeks in dark basements wearing weird clothes and making money doing it.

The following statistics reflect current average salaries for common game developer positions, based on level of experience, and taking into consideration typical bonuses. The information is designed to give a reasonable approximation of what you can expect to make in a particular position. It is important, however, to keep in mind that salaries will vary based on a company's geographic location, bonus structure, and financial bottom line.

Methodology

The following statistics are based on job placement orders received by GAME RECRUITER. Client companies reflect a geographically and financially diverse cross-section of the game industry. The numbers also include information from on-line research and confidential candidate surveys.

Cost of Living

When considering salaries, it is importance to keep in mind the impact of geography. The paycheck for an entry-level Artist in Marin County, California, for example, might look considerably larger than that for an Artist in a similar position in Minneapolis. However, the average average cost of a 2,000 sq. ft. home in Marin County is $370,000, while a same size home in Minneapolis averages $178,000. In other words, your friend in Northern California may be taking home $75,000 compared with your $50,000 salary, but a proportionate chunk of that is going to significantly higher living expenses.

GAME RECRUITER

Tel 866 358 GAME - Fax 866 358 4219 - Email resumes@gamerecruiter.com

All amounts are based on U.S. dollars

Programmers

Entry (Junior)	$ 40,000 - $ 70,000
Mid-Level	$ 75,000 - $100,000
Lead	$ 90,000 - $125,000

Artists

Entry	$ 25,000 - $ 35,000
Mid-Level	$ 40,000 - $ 75,000
Art Director	$ 80,000 - $110,000

Designers

Entry	$ 40,000 - $ 55,000
Mid-Level	$ 50,000 - $ 65,000
Creative Director	$ 80,000 - $110,000

Producers

Entry (Associate)	$ 40,000 - $ 70,000
Mid-Level	$ 50,000 - $ 70,000
Senior/Executive	$ 75,000 - $ 95,000

Audio

General	$ 40,000 - $ 70,000

PR/Marketing

Marketing Manager	$ 70,000 - $ 90,000

"Even as global economies rise and fall, programmers enjoy one of the most stable positions, earning from $40,000 for a Junior or Entry Level position to $125,000 for Lead Programmer. In addition to the base salary, game companies often offer bonus programs based on the sales of the games created. You can earn some serious cash for creating a hot selling game. Ask the guys who created *Doom* at id Software about their bonus or check in with the development team for Namco's *PacMan Worlds*."

- From the upcoming book *Get in the Game! Careers in the Game Industry* by Marc Mencher with Game Industry Gurus Dustin Clingman, Matt Scibilia, and many more! Available in stores Fall 2002 from New Riders Publishing.

WRAP-UP

No great revelation here, but negotiating compensation is a tough thing to do. Most people fall apart on salary negotiations. It's stressful and certainly creates anxiety. Because there is such discomfort with the confrontation and risk taking negotiating entails, most job hunters get the short end of the bargain. However, with effective negotiation, you can increase your salary, royalty, and stock options. Negotiating compensation can even get you a better position.

CHAPTER 14

Working with Recruiters

Headhunter. Executive Search Consultant. Career Agent. Demon Seed.

Along with lawyers and used car salesmen, recruiters are often the people that people just love to hate. Admittedly, there are unprofessional recruiters in almost every industry, including the game industry, just as there are certainly unprofessional Programmers, Artists, Producers, Designers, and so on. But an experienced, ethical, and competent recruiter can mean the difference between your dream job and no job at all. When you begin your job hunt, odds are you'll come into contact with a recruiter either through a posted job or referral. What, precisely, is a recruiter and should you run the other direction?

Generally speaking, a recruiter matches job candidates with open job positions. For example, if Hot Smokin' Games, Inc. is looking for a Programmer, a recruiter will help find the right person to fill that position. Hot Smokin' Games, Inc. then pays the recruiter a fee if it hires that producer. If a recruiter asks you (not the company) to pay a fee for placing you, do *not* use that recruiter.

WHY NEWBIES SHOULD *NOT* USE RECRUITERS

If you are an industry newbie or a recent graduate, you should probably wait until you have a few years of game industry experience under your belt, or at least two shipped titles, before using the services of a recruiter. Why? Without a few years of hands on game development experience, recruiting firms may only get in your way of breaking into or furthering your career.

Companies pay fees to recruiters to find specific talent that they could not otherwise locate themselves. Most recruiting contracts with game companies specify a 12-month representation period. What this means to you is that after a recruiting firm submits your résumé, that studio cannot hire you for one year without paying a recruiter's fee. Chances are, if you have very little experience, a company will not want to hire you and, for all intents and purposes, you are locked out of that company for a year. Even if a different entry-level position opens up, the company would still have to pay the recruiter's fee. Generally speaking, companies do not want to pay fees for recent grads. In short, unless you have at least two professional game titles under your belt, you will be better served by representing yourself.

Time passes quickly and if you follow the principles found in this book, you should have at least two professional titles under your belt faster than you ever dreamed possible. While you're in job strategy mode, you should take a moment to learn a bit more about recruiters so when your time comes, you'll know what to expect from your recruiter.

WHY INDUSTRY PROFESSIONALS *SHOULD* USE RECRUITERS

If you can always represent yourself, why would anyone ever use a recruiter? Particularly if you are in a high demand/low supply position? Let's say you went to the Hot Smokin' Games web site where you found series of job openings listed, as well as contact information where you can send your résumé. If you can send your résumé directly to the company, why even bother with a recruiter?

Avoid Wasting Time

By using a recruiter, you don't spend your time searching for job postings, company contact information, and application requirements. There are thousands of computer game companies just in the United States. A simple web search will turn up dozens of game companies and that's just the tip of the iceberg. Most of the companies have different application requirements. Recruiters have immediate knowledge of hundreds of job openings and they know exactly how each company wants your résumé to look.

Leap Over the HR Pile

When you send in your résumé to a company, you rely on Human Resources to route it. HR departments receive hundreds, if not thousands, of résumés for every position from secretary to CFO. Your résumé will land somewhere in that pile and hang there until the busy HR staff has the time to sort and distribute to the appropriate hiring manager.

Good recruiters, on the other hand, have long-term relationships with hiring managers and can market you directly to the appropriate manager within the company. For example, a recruiter with a long-standing relationship with the Hot Smokin' Games hiring manager could give her a call and speak directly with her about you and your qualifications. On the other hand, if you cold-called the hiring manager, chances are she would be "away from her desk" or would just ask you to send your résumé. And, to be honest, you couldn't blame her. These folks get tons of calls and inquiries and there is just so much time in a day. In short, recruiters help hiring managers cut to the chase.

Benefit from Honest Feedback and Savvy Spin Control

Recruiters get frank feedback from the company on how you performed in an interview. Armed with this candid information, an effective recruiter can clean up any "mess" made by the candidate during the interview.

For example, one recruiter represented a technically qualified candidate, but the guy suffered from a bad attitude due to past work experiences. Despite pre-interview prep with his recruiter, bad attitude reared his ugly head. Not impressed with Mr. Attitude, the hiring manager did not extend a job offer despite dead-on technical qualifications.

Immediately after learning the candidate was rejected, the recruiter contacted the hiring manager to discuss exactly what went wrong in the interview. Armed with the hiring manager's candid information, the recruiter was able to perform some savvy spin control, clean up the candidate's mess, and convince the hiring manager to give the guy a second interview. The second interview went much better. The candidate understood what went wrong, the hiring manager understood why it went wrong, and Mr. New Attitude was hired.

Reap the Rewards of Inside Information

Recruiters (at least the one's you should work with) are paid by the company, not the candidate. As a general rule, if a company can pay a recruiter's fee, they're not in it for the short-run. That is, companies who work with recruiters are typically more financially stable, so you will not find you have relocated to Austin from San Francisco just to be out of a job two weeks later. Recruiters will focus you on the stable, paying jobs, and keep you informed of unadvertised and unique opportunities.

NOTE

Generally speaking, hiring managers are reluctant to give honest feedback directly to a job candidate. However, they usually feel completely free to let loose and give the recruiter the real lowdown on what transpired.

NOTE

If you wonder why you are more qualified than your office mate but she has a much better compensation package than you do, odds are it's because she had a strong recruiter negotiate her employment package.

Enjoy a Higher Salary and Better Employment Package

A recruiter who is focused in the game industry market will know what your salary level should be, compared with others who have similar skills. If you have not done the best job in the past negotiating your base salary and benefits program, a good recruiter can help you in this area. A recruiter knows the hiring company and what can and can't be accomplished for the specific position for which you are interviewing. A recruiter knows how much stock, vacation time, and bonus percentages are typically awarded for your level. A good recruiter also knows how far to push the salary negotiations and such.

Benefit from Long-Term Career Management

"When I grow up I want to be a Vice President of Development!" Career growth does not simply happen on a wish and a prayer. After you have found a recruiter you can relate to, let him help you formulate your short- and long-term career goals. After you have outlined a plan of action, over the next several years, you and your recruiter can execute it. Keep in mind that it is no coincidence that most Manager, Director, or VP level people within your company have long-standing relationships with a recruiter and obtained their senior-level positions through this recruiter.

SO, WHY DO SOME RECRUITERS HAVE BAD REPUTATIONS?

If all of the preceding is true, and recruiters are so darn peachy keen helpful for company and candidate, why the bad reputation? Well, professional, ethical, and well-established recruiters play out the preceding scenarios. The bad reputation comes from recruiters who do things like scan job ads, match buzzwords off your résumé, and blast fax out your information—often without asking your permission—risking your confidentiality. The bad reputation also comes from upper management within the game company itself. If your boss spoke highly of a recruiter, wouldn't you think to use its services to get a new job and leave that boss? Most of the hiring that occurs is for mid-level talent. They are truly the worker bees of the industry and the hardest to recruit and retain. You can bet the same VP of Engineering who is trashing a recruiter has one in his back pocket!

Creation of a Professional and Effective Presentation Package

A good recruiter will not just take your existing résumé and blast fax it out—you can do this yourself. Rather, a good recruiter will help you work on your presentation package. Yes, a presentation package does include a résumé, but one that is laid out to correctly highlight your experience as it relates to the specific job you want. Blasting out a generic résumé will result in a high reject factor. In addition to a tailored résumé, a presentation package also includes a mini biography about who you are, along with complete references. This is an important first step. Your résumé and presentation need to open doors. If a recruiter is only interested in getting his hands on your résumé and does not spend any time working on your presentation, you have a weak and ineffective recruiter working for you. Your résumé will probably be blasted out to every game company on the planet, risking your confidentiality and getting you rejected from consideration for a job that you are totally qualified to handle.

Creation of a Job Search Strategy

After your presentation package is in order, a good recruiter will co-create with you a *job search strategy* that considers your location desires, salary requirements, and career objectives. This search strategy is particularly important because you don't want your recruiter submitting your résumé to companies where you have strong personal contacts. The search strategy will include a list of companies that you will approach and a list of companies the recruiter will approach on your behalf. The search strategy keeps both parties on the same page. You never have to ask yourself, "What is that recruiter doing for me?" It is outlined in a mutually agreed upon search strategy!

Complete Job Description and Company Education

After the search strategy is established and you indicate interest in some of the jobs the recruiter has highlighted for you, expect to see written detailed job descriptions from the recruiter. If these cannot be provided to you, your recruiter probably does not have a good relationship with the hiring companies. The recruiter should also be able to educate you about the company—the company's financial strength, how well the management team works together within the company, short-term and long-term company plans, and how well the bonus program has worked for other employees. In other words, all of the upfront information you need to make the decision as to whether you really have interest in the job or not. Then, only after you have established interest, will a good recruiter release your résumé.

Feedback and Constant Communication

A good recruiter will constantly update you on the status of your search. During an active job search phase, you can expect to hear from your recruiter on a weekly basis if not more often. If you are passively looking around (just want to hear about new things when they pop open), you can expect to hear from the recruiter every other month or so.

Preparation for an Interview

A good recruiter, having a strong relationship with the hiring client, will prepare you for interviews whether face to face or via telephone. The recruiter knows the hiring manager and what the company seeks technically, as well as interpersonally. Because you will enter the interview process with much more information and insight into the company than someone who has not used a recruiter, your chances of getting the job are much higher!

Support and Negotiation

Job-hunting can be emotional and stressful. Your recruiter is your support system, scheduling all interviews, as well as managing the process and flow of your communication with the hiring company. Your recruiter not only helps you and the hiring company establish a mutually beneficial employment relationship, he helps ensure—when choosing between several job offers—that you stay in line with the search strategy you set in motion for your short- and long-term career goals.

Relocation and Continued Communication

Finally, you can expect your recruiter to help you with the resignation process from your current job, help you and your family move (if needed), locate housing, address any visa issues, and so on. You can also expect to hear from your recruiter from time to time ensuring that you have adjusted properly to your new work situation and troubleshoot problems if any exist.

CHAPTER 15

Staying Employed

It goes without saying that you should always do your best, but there are a few other key items that will help keep you employed and/or get you employed elsewhere if you decide to leave your current position.

BE A TEAM PLAYER

No one likes a *prima donna*, particularly other Game Developers. When you join a team, remember that you're the new person. This is the time to make friends and take advantage of the time to learn from people who have been around the industry. Connect interpersonally with your team. Try to work with each member individually, even if this requires you to initially work some extra hours. No matter what career you have chosen to pursue, offer to help your teammates or ask to sit and familiarize you with the companies coding or artistic styles, culture, and so on. Learn to work effectively within whatever type of environment or culture you have joined.

Take the time to earn the respect and trust of your fellow team members. As you do this, more and more complex tasks will be assigned to you. You will earn the privilege of having creative input and be awarded the freedom to be innovative.

Weak team skills can cost the team projects. If you want to be a loner and a rebel, have fun making games alone in your bedroom.

FAQ

Do I have to work 60-80 hours a week?

Yes, if a project is in a state that needs that level of attention. Numerous things can cause a project to be pushed up. It's important to remember that this is the entertainment industry. People work hard to craft their works with precision. In order to put up with the game industry, you really have to love games.

NOTHING LASTS FOREVER, BUT YOU'LL BE READY

This is not a downer, it is a hard fact of today's economy. Advanced technology companies tend to be less stable. It is unusual for our generation to meet a person who actually had the luxury of staying with the same company for 20 or 30 years. This is why job hunting is no longer something that happens when you change jobs.

You should be virtually job hunting all the time. Do it informally on a regular basis. Don't expect your employer to tell you in advance that the company could not obtain its second round of venture funding and therefore can no longer employ you. Or that a merger means that you will be losing your job. You should always be aware of what may adversely affect your current job especially with the rate of consolidation and growth in the games market. You need to keep your finger on the market both inside and outside of your company.

> **NOTE**
>
> Statistics show that the average job hunt can take six months! Be proactive in your career planning and not reactive to whether that killer game you just helped create sells or not.

Don't depend on the business acumen and skill of the management team running the company. This is your life and your career, so take control of it! Wonder why that guy who started working as a Game Tester the same time you did is now an Executive Producer? Well, chances are he has a well thought-out career objective and job search campaign. Do you?

Plan your career moves from one job to the next. Don't have them thrust upon you. Keep focused on what marketable skills you have. Always have an up-to-date resume. Always collect copies of your hard work for demo purposes.

DAY ONE OF YOUR NEW JOB SHOULD ALSO BE DAY ONE OF YOUR NEW INFORMAL JOB SEARCH

Begin by creating a new job search folder, which you either keep at home, in your briefcase, or in an easy-to-get-to spot in your office. Don't keep this file in your company's computer system. This is the one folder you will snag the day you come to work and discover you have lost your job or that you are no longer able to gain access to your computer files and work you have done.

Don't know what marketable skills are hot to have? Go visit game company web sites and read their open job ads related to your areas of interest or current expertise. You will get a good idea of what skill sets are in demand and what skills you may have to develop. This is also a good way of helping you focus your school training. Job ads can be utilized to teach you the buzzwords of the industry and can even help tailor your resume.

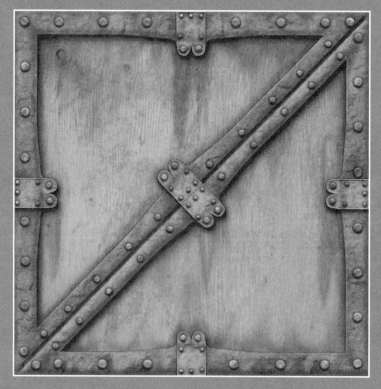

Part V

Resources

Images courtesy
of Madeleine
Wettstein

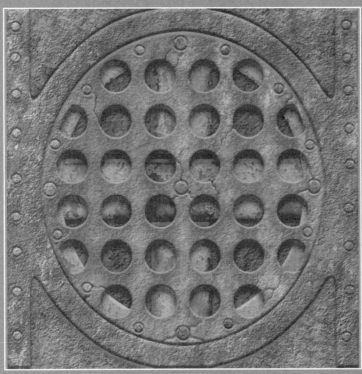

Appendix A

Resources

In this ever-innovative industry, it is important to stay current with industry trends. If you're not in a company environment where you can catch the latest buzz, you should consider joining a game industry association. Also, try to attend at least one game-related conference, and be sure to read trade publications both online and print. Involvement in national and local game development organizations and user groups, along with an up-to-date awareness of the state of the industry, are vital to landing a job.

FROM THE EXPERT

"Getting involved and building a strong network of awareness and contacts is the best way to ensure a long, varied career in building games."

- Matt Scibilia – Founder and Art Director, BigSky Interactive Inc.

NOTE

For an extended and updated list of many of these tables (new books, multimedia programs, and more), be sure to visit this book's web site: www.GameRecruiter.com/gamebook.

Associations

Name	Description	URL
Association for Computing Machinery - SIGGRAPH	ACM SIGGRAPH is dedicated to the generation and dissemination of information on computer graphics and interactive techniques. It is probably best known for the annual SIGGRAPH conference.	www.acm.org
Computer Entertainment Software Association (CESA)	A Japanese organization, CESA intends to promote computer entertainment software development in Japan.	www.cesa.or.jp
European Leisure Software Publishers Association (ELSPA)	Trade association representing the interests of European game publishers. Anti-piracy efforts are a key focus.	www.elspa.com
Interactive Digital Software Association (IDSA)	The U.S. association dedicated to serving the business and public affairs needs of companies that publish video and computer games for video game consoles, personal computers, and the Internet. The IDSA owns the Electronic Entertainment Expo trade show (E3). A leading source for consumer, economic, and other industry data, as well as information on related market trends.	www.idsa.com
International Game Developers Association (IGDA)	Independent, non-profit professional association for developers of interactive entertainment. College, university, and tech-school students of a similar level are eligible to join as student members, gaining access to all the benefits of regular membership at a 75 percent discount. Please note that proof of valid student ID is required.	www.igda.org

Name	Description	URL
IEEE Computer Society	Today boasting nearly 100,000 members, the IEEE Computer Society was originally founded in 1946 and is the largest of the 36 societies of the Institute of Electrical and Electronics Engineers (IEEE). The Computer Society's vision is to be the leading provider of technical information and services to the world's computing professionals.	www.computer.org
The Independent Games Developers Trade Association (TIGA)	A UK-based trade association representing the business and commercial interests of independent games developers— those that are not controlled by publishers and whose principal business is the development of games, across any platform.	www.tiga.org.uk

Conferences and Tradeshows

Name	Description	URL
D.I.C.E. Summit	Put on by The Academy of Interactive Arts & Sciences, the D.I.C.E. Summit is designed to foster and stimulate discussions surrounding the creative process and the future of interactive entertainment. In conjunction with the Summit, the Academy presents its annual Interactive Achievement Awards. Typically held in Las Vegas.	www.interactive.org
Electronic Entertainment Expo (E3)	Acknowledged as the must-attend, must-exhibit event for everyone who matters in interactive entertainment. Over 62,000 of the world's most influential retailers, distributors, developers, investors, and media gather for three days of intensive deal-making. There's nothing else like it in the world. Most recently held in Los Angeles.	www.e3expo.com
ECTS	European interactive entertainment conference in London. Something like the E3 of Europe.	www.ects.com

Conferences and Tradeshows continued

Name	Description	URL
GameOn	Relatively new international conference on intelligent games and simulation held in London. Sponsored by The University of Wolverhampton and The Society for Computer Simulation International - European Council. Their web site address isn't the prettiest, but the conference offers a wealth of information.	`www.scit.wlv.ac.uk/ ~cm1822/gameon.htm`
Game Developers Conference (GDC)	Traditionally held every March in San Jose, California, GDC launched a European version in 2001. GDC promises an independent and unbiased forum where game development professionals from around the world gather to share ideas and build the skills essential to creating the next generation of interactive entertainment. Companies in the industry demonstrate the future of hardware, software, and services. Industry luminaries lead lectures, tutorials, panels, and roundtables covering all aspects of game development for all platforms and all genres.	`www.gdconf.com`
International Mobile Games Convention	Brings together leaders in the field of mobile gaming to provide a comprehensive overview of the latest applications and market developments. Last held in Barcelona, Spain.	`www.ef-telecoms.co.uk`
SIGGRAPH	Annual gathering of the international computer graphics community. SIGGRAPH showcases the next generation of powerful hardware and software. Event location changes.	`www.siggraph.org`
Xtreme Games Developer miniConference (XGDC)	The conference is open to the public and targeted to all levels of Game Developer from newbie to seasoned professional. The XGDC is a technical conference lecture series, consisting of game programming tutorials and lectures. Most recently held in Santa Clara, California.	`www.xgames3d.com`

Schools and Training Programs

Name	Description	URL
Center for Digital Imaging & Sound (Vancouver, British Columbia)	CDIS offers diploma programs, certificate programs, and part-time courses in game development. In the Electronic Game Art and Design Foundation program (EGADF), students learn the process of game development by working as game Artists and Animators in the context of a development team. Focus is on the fundamentals of game design through interaction with the tools and processes used in the industry. Recently, CDIS offered $35,000 in game development scholarships for females.	www.gameschool.com
DH Institute of Media Arts (Hollywood, California)	DHIMA's stated mission is to assist the Artist and technology in becoming one—a true digital artist.	www.dhima.com
DigiPen Institute of Technology (Redmond, Washington)	DigiPen Institute of Technology is a higher education institution that offers the following degree programs: Baccalaureate Degree of Science in Real Time Interactive Simulation. (Emphasis on Computer/Video Game Programming); Associate Degree of Science in Real Time Interactive Simulation. (Emphasis on Computer/Video Game Programming); and Associate Degree of Applied Arts in 3D Computer Animation.	www.digipen.edu
Full Sail Real World Education (Winter Park, Florida)	This is a 25-year-old school focusing on training all forms of entertainment. It offers degrees in Game Design & Development, Computer Animation, Digital Media, Film/Video Production, and more. Regardless of which program you choose, one of Full Sail's fundamental goals is to encourage the union of art and technology—right and left brain—enabling artists to develop craftsmanship while the technically inclined enhance their creativity.	www.fullsail.com

AUTHOR NOTE

"I believe Full Sail has the best game development program in the United States. This is a 15-month 'Game Developer Boot Camp.' This program is not for the weak hearted. This school's motto is 'Real World Education' and just like in the industry you're on tight project deadlines and will find yourself coding games day and night! You also graduate with several games that are awesome to use in a demo! What I like best is that this is one of the only schools I could find that actually hires game industry professionals to teach students. Most other programs I have reviewed only teach theory. You will graduate with over 900 hours of hands-on C++ game coding experience. This is so much more coding experience than any Computer Science degree I know of."

- Marc

Schools and Training Programs continued

Name	Description	URL
GameInstitute. com (online)	Offers a variety of game development courses covering many of the latest technologies and techniques. Whether you are a beginner who needs some help getting started or an experienced Game Programmer looking to expand your bag of tricks, GameInstitute is confident that you will discover a number of courses that suit both your experience and interest levels.	www.gameinstitute.com
Gnomon (Hollywood, California)	School of visual effects for film, television, and games. Gnomon's curriculum and facilities have been designed to constantly evolve and change to reflect any new demands that may arise from the entertainment industry.	www.gnomon3d.com
International Centre for Digital Content (Liverpool, UK)	The Centre offers a masters/ postgraduate diploma in Digital Games. The MA Digital Games was developed after consultations with the regional games industry and recognizes the needs of the game industry. The program provides its students with practical skills and production methods to meet the needs of the industry and places an emphasis on collaborative methods and an ability to research and implement projects.	www.magames.livjm.ac.uk
NAD Centre (Montreal, Quebec, Canada)	The Design and 3D Animation for Video Games program offers 40 weeks of cutting-edge training for candidates with prior studies, work experience, or distinctive skills in visual arts (art, film, television, photography, computer graphic design, illustration) or any other related field (architecture, industrial design, and so on) who possess a keen interest in video games.	www.nad.qc.ca

Name	*Description*	*URL*
National Centre for Computer Animation at Bournemouth University (UK)	Offers both undergraduate and postgraduate courses in computer visualization and animation.	`ncca.bournemouth.ac.uk`

Print and Online Magazines and Newsletters

Name	*Description*	*URL*
Animation Magazine	Monthly print magazine with news and features about the animation industry.	`www.animation magazine.net`
Computer Graphics World	Print magazine covering innovations in visual computing.	`www.cgw.com`
Develop	European trade monthly for everyone in development—from Coders and Artists to Producers, lawyers, and musicians. Includes reviews of and opinions about the latest moves in the industry. Free to UK readers and available for a token postal charge to overseas subscribers.	`www.developmag.com`
Edge	Monthly interactive entertainment magazine devoted to covering the future of video-gaming technology.	`www.edge-online.com`
Flipcode	Gaming and multimedia news and information site with an emphasis on development.	`www.flipcode.com`
Gamasutra	Associated with *Game Developer* magazine, this e-zine features news, articles, and tutorials. Requires registration to read most of the articles.	`www.gamasutra.com`
GameDAILY Newsletter	Daily email newsletter featuring the day's top game industry headlines, including changes and movements in company management.	`www.gamedaily.com`
Game Developer	Monthly magazine providing technical and industry information to professional game Developers. Features technical solutions, new product reviews, and strategies for creating innovative, successful games.	`www.gdmag.com`

Print and online magazines and newsletters continued

Name	Description	URL
GIGnews.com	Online magazine for game industry professionals. Features news, tutorials, career advice, inside information, high profile interviews, and more.	www.gignews.com

Books

Book, Author, Publishing Info	Description
3D Game Art F/X & Design, 1st Edition (September 12, 2001), by Luke Ahearn; The Coriolis Group; ISBN: 1588801004.	Covers the technology of game elements including 2D and 3D effects. Discusses each part of computer games from an Artist's view: interfaces, menus, characters, game textures, 3D models, and games levels or worlds. It teaches all the pieces used to design a computer game. The reader will learn the specialized skills, tricks, and techniques used to create professional quality game art and be able to use those design segments when building individual games. CD-ROM is included containing a large assemblage of game development software and art elements.
Game Architecture and Design: Learn the Best Practices for Game Design and Programming, 1st Edition (November 18, 1999), by Andrew Rollings; The Coriolis Group; ISBN: 1576104257.	Addressing itself to industry Programmers and Managers, this book makes the case that Game Developers should manage software the same way the other computer companies do it—even though they may not want to hear it. The real-world perspective on the video game business includes dozens of case studies and anecdotes from the field, including behind-the-scenes details on some well-known recent titles. Besides notable successes, there are also plenty of stories of what can go wrong.

Book, Author, Publishing Info	Description
Game Design Perspectives, 1st Edition (June 2002), by Francois Dominic Laramee (Editor); Charles River Media; ISBN: 1584500905.	This unique compilation of design articles provides Designers with insight into how their colleagues approach game design, where they have stumbled, and how they have succeeded. The articles are written by a diverse group of Designers with a wide variety of gaming backgrounds. The topics covered range from proper design documentation, user interfaces, design theory, characters, and storytelling, to quality management, platform- and genre-specific design issues, relationships between Designers and the user community, and game development project management. If you are just beginning in game design, you'll find new ideas to complement and compare with your own designs. Producers and Managers will also benefit from "The User Community" and "Managing a Game Development Business" sections.
Game Design: Secrets of the Sages, by Marc A. Saltzman.	One of the first books to cover the game industry from the business side, this is a compilation of game industry insights from more than 140 industry insiders. From Sid Meier to Shigeru Miyamoto to Peter Molyneux (and that's just a few of the Ms), this is one of the first books, if not *the* first book, to cover the entire spectrum of the game industry in a well-organized, comprehensive, and easy-to-understand style. Now out of print, word is Saltzman may be publishing it online. Check www.GameRecruiter/Gamebook for updates on where you can find it.
Game Design: Theory and Practice (with CD-ROM), BK&CD-ROM Edition (February 15, 2001), by Richard Rouse; Wordware Publishing; ISBN: 1556227353.	Focuses on how you can ensure your title has the best game play possible. The author discusses in detail key game design topics including game balancing, storytelling, non-linearity, player motivations, input/output, Artificial Intelligence, level design, and play testing. This book delves into the entire breadth of interactive games, covering computer, console, and arcade titles, and spanning a variety of gaming genres including strategy, adventure, simulation, action, role-playing, sports, and war games.

Books   continued

Book, Author, Publishing Info	Description
Game Programming Gems 2, BK&CD-ROM edition (October 1, 2001), by Mark DeLoura (Editor); Charles River Media; ISBN: 1584500549.	The second volume in this successful series, contains a completely new set of more than 70 articles on diverse topics that can be used in your own game projects. Written by game programming experts, each contribution provides a hands-on solution to programming problems or a creative method for reducing programming time and redundancy. Edited by Mark DeLoura, former editor-in-chief of *Game Developer* magazine, and a group of top-notch area editors, this collection covers the major topics needed to develop a state-of-the-art game engine.
Mathematics for 3D Game Programming & Computer Graphics, (December 18, 2001), by Eric Lengyel; Charles River Media; ISBN: 1584500379.	This book illustrates the mathematical concepts that a game Developer would need to develop a professional-quality 3D engine. It starts at a fairly basic level in areas such as vector geometry and linear algebra, and then progresses to more advanced topics in 3D programming such as illumination and visibility determination.
Physics for Game Developers, 1st Edition (November 15, 2001), by David M. Bourg; O'Reilly & Associates; ISBN: 0596000065.	Aimed at the game developer or student/hobbyist interested in physics. Reviews all the math for creating realistic motion and collisions for cars, airplanes, boats, projectiles, and other objects, along with C/C++ code for Windows. Although this authoritative guide isn't for the math-averse, the author's clear presentation and obvious enthusiasm for his subject help make this book a compelling choice for anyone faced with adding realistic motion to computer games or simulations.

Other Online Resources

Name	Description	URL
3D Café	Developed to assist and inspire by offering tutorials, product reviews, focused feature articles, as well as the industry's largest database of free 3D geometry.	www.3dcafe.com

Name	*Description*	*URL*
3dRender.com	Maintained by freelance 3D artist Jeremy Birn, who also works as an author, lecturer, and consultant on computer graphics topics, the site features a wealth of links, tutorials, resources, and references.	www.3drender.com
The Animation World Network	The largest animation-related publishing group on the Internet, providing readers from more than 145 countries with a wide range of interesting, relevant, and helpful information pertaining to all aspects of animation.	www.awn.com
CFXWeb	Game programming and demo news site. It is updated quite often and features some good tutorials, links, and other related features.	www.cfxweb.net
CodeGuru	CodeGuru is about the sharing of code. Almost all of the code that you can find is presented as part of an article.	www.codeguru.com
Game AI Page	Dedicated to the topic of Artificial Intelligence (AI) in games. Includes community discussion and resources.	www.gameai.com
Game Development Search Engine	Allows specific searches for game development information on some of the major game development sites. Its stated purpose is to provide a starting point for game development research.	www.gdse.com
Mad Monkey	Focuses on the independent gaming scene and features information on projects currently in the works, programming tutorials, message forums, and much more.	www.madmonkey.net
Mr-GameMaker	Features tutorials on topics related to game development, including some hard-to-find information.	www.mr-gamemaker.co.uk/
Programmers Heaven	Features loads of links, compilers, reference materials, and resources on any type of programming, including game development.	www.Programmersheaven.com

Newsgroups (Online Bulletin Boards for Game Business Related Discussions)

Newsgroup	Description
comp.games.development.art	Creative use of visual art in games
comp.games.development.audio	Music, sound, speech production
comp.games.development.design	Designing game play and rules systems
comp.games.development.industry	Business news, project management, jobs
comp.games.development.programming.algorithms	Abstract algorithms for games
comp.games.development.programming.misc	General information on programming games

Game Publishers and Affiliate Studios

Electronic Arts (www.ea.com)	Key Franchises
Electronic Arts Redwood City, CA (Corporate Headquarters)	Bond: TWINE, Jayne's, Tiger Woods
Electronic Arts Canada Vancouver, BC	FIFA, NHL, Need for Speed
Electronic Arts Seattle, WA	Motorcity Racing
Electronic Arts Australia (on the Gold Coast)	
EA.Com San Diego, CA	
EA.Com (formerly Kesmai) Charlottesville, VA	
Maxis Walnut Creek, CA	The Sims, Sim City
Origin Systems Austin, TX	Ultima, Ultima Online
Westwood Pacific Irvine, CA	Nox, Command & Conquer
Westwood Studios Las Vegas, NV	Command & Conquer, Legends of Kyrandia
Tiburon Entertainment Maitland, FL	Madden
Dreamworks Interactive Los Angeles, CA	Medal of Honor, Jurassic Park, Tai-Fu
Bullfrog Guildford, Surrey, England	Theme Park, Dungeon Keeper, Syndicate
Square/EA (joint partnership)	
Square Japan (Corporate Headquarters)	Final Fantasy
Squaresoft Honolulu, HI	

Notable third-party developers

Irrational Games Boston, MA	*System Shock, The Lost, Freedom Force*
Stormfront Studios San Rafael, CA	*Andretti Racing, Nascar*
Rogue Entertainment Dallas, TX	*Alice*

The 3DO Company (www .3do.com*)*   *Key Franchises*

The 3DO Company Redwood City, CA[1]	*Army Men, Battle Tanx, Meridian 59*, High Heat *Crusaders of Might Magic*
Team .366 (internal develpment team responsible for High heat Baseball)	
3DO Texas Austin, TX	*Crusaders of Might & Magic*
New World Computing Agoura Hills, CA	*Might & Magic*

Sony Computer Entertainment (formerly 989 Studios) (www.989studios.com)   *Key Franchises*

Sony Computer Entertainment Japan	
Sony Computer Entertainment Europe	
Sony Computer Entertainment Foster City, CA (formerly 989 Studios)	*Blasto*
Sony Computer Entertainment Santa Monica, CA (formerly 989 Studios)	
Sony Computer Entertainment (formerly Eidetic Studios) Bend, OR (acquired 3/2000)	*Syphon Filter*
Sony Computer Entertainment San Diego, CA (formerly 989 Studios)	*Twisted Metal, Extreme Sports*
Redzone Interactive San Diego, CA	*NFL Gameday, Gamebreaker*
Verant/Sony Online San Diego, CA	*Everquest, Star Wars MMP*

Notable first-party developers

Naughty Dog Santa Monica, CA	*Crash Bandicoot*
Incognito Studios Salt Lake City, Utah	*Twisted Metal Black*
Insomniac Studios Los Angeles, CA	*Spyro the Dragon*
Solworks Carlsbad, CA	*NHL Faceoff*

[1]*Cyclone Studios, San Mateo, CA, was acquired by 3DO around March 1998; studio was shut down and the employees moved in-house to 3DO in Redwood City in Dec. 1998.*

Killer Game San Diego, CA	*NCAA Final Four*
Suckerpunch Productions	*Un-named original title, Rocket*
Pandemic Studios	*C-Force, Dark Reign & Battlezone*

Game Publishers and Affiliate Studios   continued

Activision (www.activision.com)	*Key Franchises*
Activision Santa Monica, CA	
Raven Software Madison, WI	*Soldier of Fortune,* *Hexen*
Neversoft L.A.	*Tony Hawk, Spiderman*
Elsinore Studios Miami, FL	*Cabela's Big Game* *Hunter*

Notable third-party developers	
Pandemic Studios Santa Monica, CA	*Dark Reign, Battlezone*
Savage Entertainment Culver City, CA	*Heavy Gear*
Hypnos Entertainment Soquel, CA (Bay area)	*Jack Nicklaus Golf*
EXAKT Games Los Angeles	*Street Lethal*
Luxoflux Santa Monica, CA	*Vigilante 8, Star* *Wars: Demolition*
Nihilistic Novato, CA	*Vampire*
Paradox Moorpark, CA	*X-men, Wu-Tang*
Grey Matter Santa Monica, CA	*Castle Wolfenstien*

Havas Interactive (www.havas.com)	*Key Franchises*
Havas Interactive, Inc. Torrance, CA (Corporate Headquarters)	
Havas Interactive UK	
Havas Interactive Ireland Dublin, Ireland	

Havas Interactive Europe
    (aka Coktel)
    France	

Havas Interactive Deutchland German	
Havas Interactive Espana Madrid, Spain	
Sierra Studios (aka Sierra Online)[2] Bellevue, WA (Corporate Headquarters)	

[2]*Quick History lesson: Sierra Online, which owns the studios listed under it above, was first acquired by Cendant Software (around 1996), whose parent company is CUC International, prior to their acquisition by Havas Interactive (around 1999), whose parent company is Vivendi.*

Dynamix Studios Eugene, Oregon	Tribes
Blizzard Entertainment Irvine, CA	Warcraft, Starcraft
Blizzard North San Mateo, CA	Diablo
Knowledge Adventure Glendale, CA	JumpStart
Davidson & Associates Torrance, CA	Math Blaster, English Blaster
Impressions Software Cambridge, MA	Pharoah, Zeus, Lord of the Realms
Papyrus Design Group Watertown, MA	Nascar Racing
Flipside.com Berkeley, CA (develops front-end web/game site)	
Won.net -Bellevue, WA (develops server side technology for Sierra and Flipside.com)	
Berkeley Systems Berkeley, CA	You don't know jack

Notable third-party developers

Relic Entertainment Vancouver, BC	Homeworld
Valve Entertainment Kirkland, WA	Half-Life
Barking Dog Vancouver, BC	Homeworld Cataclysm
Gearbox Dallas, TX	Half-Life - Dreamcast

Midway Home Entertainment
(www.midway.com)

Key Franchises

Midway Home Entertainment San Diego, CA	Hydro Thunder, Ready 2 Rumble
Midway (aka Williams Entertainment) Chicago, IL	NBA Jam, Blitz, Cruisin USA
Midway West (formerly Atari/ Time Warner Interactive)[3]	Gauntlet Legends, SF Rush

[3] Atari was first sold to Time Warner Interactive and later sold to Midway.

Game Publishers and Affiliate Studios   continued

Notable third-party developers

Avalanche Software Salt Lake City, UT	*Ultimate MK3, Rampage, Off Road Challenge*
Point of View Tustin, CA and Austin, TX	*Blitz, Ready 2 Rumble, Sports Car GT*
Digital Eclipse Emeryville, CA	*Midway's Arcade Hits, Dragon's Lair*

SEGA (www.sega.com)   *Key Franchises*

Sega of America San Francisco, CA	
Sega.Com (formerly Segasoft) San Francisco, CA	
Sega of Japan	*Sonic, Daytona, Virtua Fighter*
Visual Concepts San Rafael, CA (acquired by SEGA around March 1999)	*NFL 2K, NFL 2Kl, NBA 2K, NBA 2Kl*

Notable third-party developers

Tremor Entertainment Burbank, CA	*SegaSwirl, Railroad Tycoon Dreamcast*
BlackBox Vancouver, BC	*NHL 2K*

Infogrames (www.us.infogrames.com)   *Key Franchises*

Infogrames North America (formerly Accolade) San Jose, CA	*Slave Zero, Jack Nicklaus Golf*
Infogrames Los Angeles, CA	
Infogrames Lyon, France	
Paradigm Entertainment	*Spy Hunter, Looney Tunes Duck Dodgers*
GT Interactive (purchased by Infogrames around July 2000)	
GT Interactive Offices in San Francisco, Europe, and New York (Corporate Headquarters)	
Singletrac Studios Salt Lake City, UT	*Twisted Metal, Jet Moto, Rogue Trip*
Humongous Entertainment/ Cavedog Entertainment Bothell, WA (Cavedog was an internal studio working on RTS games Total Annihilation.)	*Freddie Fish, Putt Putt, Backyard Sports*

Notable third-party developers

Apogee/3D Realms Garland, TX	*Duke Nukem*
N-Space Orlando, FL	*Duke Nukem PSX*
Epic Megagames Raleigh, NC	*Unreal, Unreal Tournament*
Legend Entertainment Chantilly, VA	*Wheel of Time*
Oddworld Inhabitants San Luis Obispo, CA	*Abe's Oddysey, Munch's Oddysey*
Reflections	*Driver*
Pitbull Syndicate Europe	*Test Drive, Demolition Racer*
Appeal	*Outcast*
DarkWorks	*Alone In The Dark*
Eden Studios	*V-Rally*
Particle Systems	*Independence War*
Beyond Games	*Motor Mayhem*
Shiny Entertainment Laguna Beach, CA	*Sacrifice, Messiah, MDK, Earthworm Jim*

Konami Computer Entertainment
(www.konami.com)

	Key Franchises
Konami Computer Entertainment Redwood City, CA	*ESPN Basketball, ESPN Baseball, Frogger, Bottom of the 9th*
Konami Honolulu, HI	*ESPN Sports*
Konami Japan	*Metal Gear Solid, Castle Wolfenstien*
Konami Uxbridge, Middlesex, England	

Acclaim Studios (www.acclaim.com)

	Key Franchises
Acclaim Glen Cove, NY	
Acclaim Studios (formerly Iguana) Austin, TX	*Turok, Quarterback Club*
Acclaim Studios (formerly Iguana West) Salt Lake City, UT	*ECW: Anarchy Rulz*

Notable third-party developers

Osiris Studios Santa Cruz, CA	*HBO Boxing*

Game Publishers and Affiliate Studios   continued

Interplay/Titus (www.interplay.com)	*Key Franchises*
Interplay Irvine, CA	*Baldur's Gate, Fallout*
Black Isle Studios Internal studio	
17 degrees East Internal studio	
Flat Cat Internal studio	
VR Sports Internal studio	
Tantrum Internal studio	
Digital Mayhem Internal studio	*Run Like Hell*
Interplay UK	
ENGAGE Games Online Irvine, CA	
Titus France	
Bluesky Games San Diego, CA	*Superman*

Notable third-party developers

Planet Moon Sausalito, CA	*Giants*
Player 1 Santa Monica, CA	*Dead in the Water,* *Robotron 64*
Press Start Sunnyvale, CA	*Knockout Kings,* *Andretti Racing*
Confounding Factor Bristol, UK	*Galleon*
Bioware Edmonton, Canada	*Baldur's Gate*

Nintendo (www.nintendo.com)	*Key Franchises*
Nintendo North America Washington	
Nintendo Japan	*Pokemon, Mario, Zelda, Donkey Kong*

Notable first-party developers

Rare Manor Park, UK	*Perfect Dark, Banjo* *Tooie, Banjo Kazooie, Goldeneye 007,* *Conker's Pocket Tales*

Notable third-party developers

Retro Studios Austin, TX	
Left Field Productions Westlake, CA	*Excite Bike, Kobe Bryant*
Acclaim Studios (formerly Iguana Entertainment) Austin, TX	*Turok, Quarterback Club*
Acclaim Studios Salt Lake City, UT	*ECW: Anarchy Rulz*
Angel Studios Carlsbad, CA	*Smugglers Run, Midtown Madness*
Factor 5 San Rafael, CA	*Star Wars: Battle for Naboo, Indiana Jones and the Infernal Machine*

Microsoft (www.microsoft.com) *Key Franchises*

Microsoft Redmond, WA (Corporate Headquarters)	*MS Flight Simulator*
Access Software Salt Lake City, UT	*Links*
Bungie (had studios in San Jose & Chicago)	*Oni, Halo, Myth, Marathon*

Notable third-party developers

Ensemble Studios Dallas, TX	*Age of Empires*
Digital Anvil Austin, TX	*Freelancer, Loose Cannon*
Rainbow Studios Phoenix, AZ	*Motocross Madness*
Gas Powered Games Kirkland, WA	*Dungeon Siege*
Turbine Entertainment Westwood, MA	*Asheron's Call*
VR-I Boulder, CO	*Microsoft Fighter Ace*

THQ (www.thq.com) *Key Franchises*

THQ Calabassas, CA (Corporate Headquarters)	*Rugrats, WWF, MTV Sports*
Pacific Coast Power & Light (PCP&L) Santa Clara, CA	*Championship Motocross, WWF*
Heavy Iron Studios Culver City, CA	*Evil Dead, Scooby Doo*
Volition Champaign, IL	*Summoner*
Genetic Anomalies Lexington, MA	*Star Trek Conquest, WWF Online*

Game Publishers and Affiliate Studios   continued

Mattel (www.mattel.com)	*Key Franchises*
Mattel Interactive El Segundo, CA	*Hot Wheels, Matchbox,* *Barbie*
Mindscape Novato, CA	
Red Orb Entertainment Internal studio	
SSI (Strategic Simulations Inc.) - Internal studio	*Panzer General,* *Harpoon*

PF Magic
   Internal studio
   (Used to be in San Francisco)
	Dogz, Catz, Petz

Broderbund Novato, CA	*Mavis Beacon,* Print Shop
The Learning Company Fremont, CA	*Carmen Sandiego,* *Reader Rabbit*
Banner Blue	

Notable third-party developers	
Ultimation Petaluma, CA	*Silent Hunter*

Eidos (www.eidos.com)	*Key Franchises*
Eidos San Francisco, CA	
Crystal Dynamics Menlo Park, CA	*Gex, Soulreaver*

Notable third-party developers	
Ion Storm Austin, TX	*Diakatana, Deus Ex*
Kronos Entertainment Pasadena, CA	*Fear Effect, Cardinal* *Syn*
Core Entertainment Europe	*Tomb Raider*
Cinematix Studios Tempe, AZ	*Revenant*

LucasArts (www.lucas.com)	*Key Franchises*
LucasArts San Rafael, CA	*Star Wars, Monkey* *Island*[4]
Industrial Light & Magic San Rafael, CA	

[4]*Note: Verant is doing Massively Multiplayer Online Game based on Star Wars universe.*

Notable third-party developers

Pandemic Studios	*Star Wars* licensed title
Luxoflux	*Star Wars Demolition*

Hasbro (www.hasbro.com)   *Key Franchises*

Hasbro Interactive Beverly, MA (Corporate Headquarters)	*Centipede, Scrabble*
Hasbro Interactive Alameda, CA (formerly Spectrum Holobyte)	*Falcon 4.0, Star Trek*
Games.Com Alameda, CA	
Hasbro Interactive Hunt Valley, MD (formerly Microprose)	*X-Com Alliance*

Take 2 Interactive   *Key Franchises*

Take 2 Interactive New York, NY	*Austin Powers*
Rockstar Games New York, NY	*Grand Theft Auto, Moho, Smugglers Run*
TalonSoft Baltimore, MD (acquired early 1999)	*Dogs of War, Rising Sun, Battle of Britain*
Mission Studios Shaumburg, IL	*JetFighter*
Tarantula Studios	
Alternative Reality Technologies	

Notable third-party developers

DMA Design Edinborough, UK	*Grand Theft Auto, Wild Metal*
Angel Studios Carlsbad, CA	*Smugglers Run*

Gathering of Developers (acquired by Take2 Interactive)

The companies below have publishing ties with Gathering of Developers and Take2 Interactive:

3Drealms Dallas, TX	*Duke Nukem*
Delphine Software Paris, France	*Moto Racer, Fade to Black*
Edge of Reality Dallas, TX	*Tony Hawk, Monster Truck Madness*
Epic Megagames Raleigh, NC	*Unreal, Unreal Tournament*

Game Publishers and Affiliate Studios continued

Gathering of Developers (acquired by Take2 Interactive)

Human Head Studios Madison, WI	*Rune, Blair Witch 2*
Phantagram Ltd. Seoul, Korea	*Revenent, Kingdom Under Fire*
Pop Top St. Louis, MO	*Railroad Tycoon*
Remedy Entertainment Helsinki, Finland	*Max Payne, Death Rally*
Ritual Entertainment Dallas, TX	*Heavy Metal FAKK2, Sin*
Terminal Reality Lewisville, TX	*4x4 EVO, Nocturne*
Third Law Interactive Dallas, TX	*KISS Psycho Circus*
Triumph Studios Amsterdam, Holland	*Age of Wonders*
Wolfpack Austin, TX	*Shadowbane*

Fox Interactive
(www.foxinteractive.com)

	Key Franchises
Fox Interactive Los Angeles, CA (Corporate Headquarters)	*Alien vs. Predator, Croc, Die Hard,* *Buffy the Vampire Slayer, X-Files,* *Planet of the Apes, World's Scariest* *Police Chases*
Fox Family Worldwide Los Angeles, CA	
Fox Sports Interactive Los Angeles, CA	
Page 44 (formerly Fox Interactive) San Francisco, CA	

Notable third-party developers

Radical Entertainment Vancouver, BC	*NHL Championship, M1V* *Sports, Jackie Chan Stuntmaster*
Monolith Kirkland, WA	*NOLF, Aliens vs.* *Predator*
The Collective Laguna Beach, CA	*Buffy the Vampire* *Slayer*

Capcom

	Key Franchises
Capcom Co. Ltd. Osaka and Tokyo, Japan	*Street Fighter, Resident Evil,* *MegaMan, Powerstone*
Capcom Digital Studios Sunnyvale, CA	
Capcom London, England	
Capcom Honk Kong, China	

Namco	*Key Franchises*
Namco Ltd. Tokyo, Japan	*Galaxian, Pacman,* *Ridge Racer*
Namco Hometek, Inc. San Jose, CA	*Pacman 3D*
Namco Europe Ltd. London, England	

UbiSoft	*Key Franchises*
UbiSoft Wimbledon, UK	*Rayman, Evolution2*
UbiSoft, USA San Francisco, CA	
RedStonn Entertainment Morrisville, NC	*Rainbow Six, Rogue* *Spear*
UbiSoft New York, NY	
UbiSoft Montreal, Canada	
UbiSoft Dusseldorf, Germany	
UbiSoft Milan, Italy	
UbiSoft Barcelona, Spain	
UbiSoft Brussels, Belgium	
UbiSoft Netherlands	
UbiSoft Denmark	
UbiSoft Bucharest, Romania	
UbiSoft Casablanca, Morocco	
UbiSoft Shanghai & Beijing, China	
UbiSoft Tokyo, Japan	
UbiSoft Sydney, Australia	

Index

SYMBOLS

A

Lead Animators, 98-99

Lead Artists, 96-98

Lead Concept/Storyboard
Artists, 100

Lead Game Designers, 47-49

Lead Level Designers, 46

Lead Programmers, 69-71

Lead Testers, 34-35

leads. *See* contacts (for job leads)

Level Designers, 44-46

list of accomplishments (in
resume writing) example, 176

sample resume, 182-183

licensed games, 12

LightWave, 18-19

Linux, 80

list of accomplishments (in
resume writing), 175-176,
180-181

long-term career management,
advantages of recruiters, 238

low-level programming
languages, 17

M

Macintosh, 80

magazines (resources for further
information), 253-254

maintenance of project tracking
worksheet, 129

management

developing skills in, 120

selling concepts to, responsibilities of Producers, 131-134

management strategies, for
Producers, 140

managers/supervisors. *See*
supervisors/managers

marketing

for Artist jobs, 116-117

collaboration with,
responsibilities of
Producers, 140

role of, 14

Marketing Directors, sample
resume, 189-191

massively multiplayer online
games (MMOGs), 82

mathematics, educational
background needed for
Programmers, 88-89

Maya, 18-19

Metroworks Codewarrior, 76

Microsoft, history of game
industry, 7

Microsoft Excel, 15

skills needed for Game
Designers, 52

skills needed for testing
games, 39

Microsoft Project, 15

skills needed for Game
Designers, 52

Microsoft Visual Studio, 76

Microsoft Word, 15

skills needed for Game
Designers, 52

Microsoft XBox, 82

Microvision, history of game
industry, 5

milestone descriptions,
responsibilities of Producers,
136-138

Mirai, 20

mission statement, writing design
documents, 55-56

MMOGs (massively multiplayer
online games), 82

VOICES THAT MATTER

HOW TO CONTACT US

VISIT OUR WEB SITE

WWW.NEWRIDERS.COM

On our web site, you'll find information about our other books, authors, tables of contents, and book errata. You will also find information about book registration and how to purchase our books, both domestically and internationally.

EMAIL US

Contact us at: **nrfeedback@newriders.com**

- If you have comments or questions about this book
- To report errors that you have found in this book
- If you have a book proposal to submit or are interested in writing for New Riders
- If you are an expert in a computer topic or technology and are interested in being a technical editor who reviews manuscripts for technical accuracy

Contact us at: **nreducation@newriders.com**

- If you are an instructor from an educational institution who wants to preview New Riders books for classroom use. Email should include your name, title, school, department, address, phone number, office days/hours, text in use, and enrollment, along with your request for desk/examination copies and/or additional information.

Contact us at: **nrmedia@newriders.com**

- If you are a member of the media who is interested in reviewing copies of New Riders books. Send your name, mailing address, and email address, along with the name of the publication or web site you work for.

BULK PURCHASES/CORPORATE SALES

The publisher offers discounts on this book when ordered in quantity for bulk purchases and special sales. For sales within the U.S., please contact: Corporate and Government Sales (800) 382-3419 or **corpsales@pearsontechgroup.com**. Outside of the U.S., please contact: International Sales (317) 581-3793 or **international@pearsontechgroup.com**.

WRITE TO US

New Riders Publishing
201 W. 103rd St.
Indianapolis, IN 46290-1097

CALL/FAX US

Toll-free (800) 571-5840
If outside U.S. (317) 581-3500
Ask for New Riders
FAX: (317) 581-4663

WWW.NEWRIDERS.COM

Solutions from experts you know and trust.

OPERATING SYSTEMS

WEB DEVELOPMENT

PROGRAMMING

NETWORKING

CERTIFICATION

AND MORE...

Expert Access.
Free Content.

New Riders has partnered with **InformIT.com** to bring technical information to your desktop. Drawing on New Riders authors and reviewers to provide additional information on topics you're interested in, **InformIT.com** has free, in-depth information you won't find anywhere else.

- **Master the skills you need, when you need them**

- **Call on resources from some of the best minds in the industry**

- **Get answers when you need them, using InformIT's comprehensive library or live experts online**

- **Go above and beyond what you find in New Riders books, extending your knowledge**

As an **InformIT** partner, **New Riders** has shared the wisdom and knowledge of our authors with you online. Visit **InformIT.com** to see what you're missing.

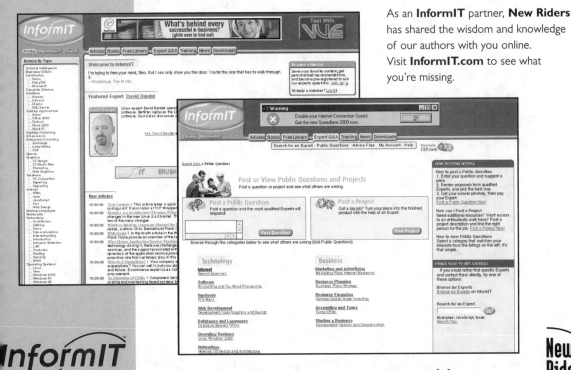

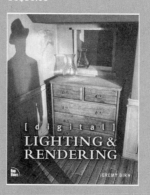

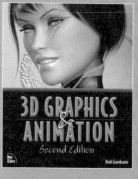

Colophon

The images from the cover were taken from the game *Tsunami* 2265; a vibrant anime-style game that hurls you into an intriguing tale, rich with dramatic twists and turns. The story is structured to create a perfect mix between hectic and destructive shoot'em up sections, and intriguing arcade phases. During the adventure phases, you control either of two main characters, Naoko Hikari and Neon Shima, leading them inside secret military bases held under tight surveillance. With the aid of their most powerful Mech, you must reveal the secret that hides behind E.L.EN.A., a mysterious source of energy and untamed power. The shoot'em up sections immerse the you in thrilling battles where speed and piloting skills are essential to survive enemy attacks. Every level entails a myriad of objectives related to the story-path, all necessary for the completion of the mission. The well-structured story reveals itself step by step with every mission. And, during gameplay, vividly animated sequences narrate the events. *Tsunami 2265* is published by Got Game Entertainment (www.gotgameentertainment.com), a publisher of games for PC and other platforms. Founded by industry veteran Howard Horowitz with over 15 years of experience, Got Game Entertainment is committed to bringing to market quality games offering exceptional entertainment.

This book was written and edited in Microsoft Word, and laid out in QuarkXPress. The fonts used for the body text are Garamond and Mono. It was printed on 50# Husky Offset Smooth paper at R.R. Donnelley & Sons in Crawfordsville, Indiana. Prepress consisted of PostScript computer-to-plate technology (filmless process). The cover was printed at Moore Langen Printing in Terre Haute, Indiana, on 12pt., coated on one side.

VIEW CART 🛒   [   ] search

▸ Registration already a member? Log in. ▸ Book Registration

Publishing
the Voices
that Matter

OUR AUTHORS

PRESS ROOM

| web development | design | photoshop | new media | 3-D | server technologie |

EDUCATORS

ABOUT US

CONTACT US

You already know that New Riders brings you the **Voices that Matter**.

But what does that mean? It means that New Riders brings you the

Voices that challenge your assumptions, take your talents to the next

level, or simply help you better understand the complex technical world

we're all navigating.

Visit **www.newriders.com** to find:

- ▸ **10% discount** and **free shipping** on all purchases
- ▸ Never before published chapters
- ▸ Sample chapters and excerpts
- ▸ Author bios and interviews
- ▸ Contests and enter-to-wins
- ▸ Up-to-date industry event information
- ▸ Book reviews
- ▸ Special offers from our friends and partners
- ▸ Info on how to join our User Group program
- ▸ Ways to have your Voice heard

New
Riders

WWW.NEWRIDERS.COM